Cramer's Choice

Cramer's Choice
*Memoir of a Baseball Card
Collector Turned Manufacturer*

MIKE CRAMER

McFarland & Company, Inc., Publishers
Jefferson, North Carolina

ISBN (print) 978-1-4766-9357-6
ISBN (ebook) 978-1-4766-5106-4

Library of Congress and British Library
cataloguing data are available

Library of Congress Control Number 2023037422

© 2023 Michael J. Cramer. All rights reserved

No part of this book may be reproduced or transmitted in any form or by any means, electronic or mechanical, including photocopying or recording, or by any information storage and retrieval system, without permission in writing from the publisher.

Front cover: (left to right) Sports cards featuring Babe Ruth, Tom Brady, Nolan Ryan, Kobe Bryant, and Willie Mays (Cramer Sports Promotions/Pacific Trading Cards)

Printed in the United States of America

*McFarland & Company, Inc., Publishers
Box 611, Jefferson, North Carolina 28640
www.mcfarlandpub.com*

To my wife of 49 years, Cheryl Cramer.
Without her, Pacific Trading Cards would never have existed.
She is the greatest person in my life.

Acknowledgments

Thank you to my mother and father, Arnold and Dorothy Cramer, who gave me life and a sense of humor—but, more importantly, never threw away my baseball cards.

Thank you to my four children, Rachael, Angela, Cory and Michael, for being there for me and for being the adults you have become. "Good job, guys!"

To my grandchildren, who were truly the reason for writing this book. None of you got to see Pacific in its glory days. My hope is that all of you will read all about it in this book. When you do, you will understand why you are able to go to college. Lilly, Ryder, Kellan, Shiloh, Taliah, Elise, Remy, Jude, Paxton, Finn, Ezra and Liv: keep your dreams alive!

To my brother Marty and sisters Kathi and Anji: thanks for always being there.

Thank you to Uncle C.J.: you changed so many people's lives for the better by letting me come to Dutch Harbor that first year in 1969.

To my brother-in-law, Kris Poulsen: you were a big influence on me at the right time. You were and always will be the greatest crab boat skipper ever.

A big thank you to Ann Hicks, Rae Randall, Kathi Estes, Mom, Marty Cramer, Felix Mendez, Victor Mendez, Chuck Bennett, Frank Torre, Steve Jackson, Allie Heber, Michelle Cramer, Bridget Jones, Tracie Lester, Chuck Jones, Rob Hicks, Art Munoz, James Cotton, Bryan Cloutier, James Bailey, Jon Merwin, Andrea Anderson, Stefania Madyzak, Maria Mendez, Bob Wilke, Keith Gentile, Bruce Chappalear, Jack Wallin, and all the people who ever worked at Pacific: thank you so much for all your help!

To Jeff Morris, for your great marketing ideas and inspirations and for helping me remember some of the stories in this book.

To Phil Roth: you were a big influence back then, and now!

To Shannon Johnson, the best customer service and quality control person ever!

To Tom Owens, a great inspiration for this book.

Acknowledgments

To Mike Kipling, Marjorie Walter, and Jim Fowler, the smartest team of lawyers ever.

To NFL quarterback Tom Brady: I have never met you, but I thank you for being so good!

A big thanks and hug to Victor Temkin: you were there when I needed you the most. Best of all, you're still there.

A special thanks to my editor, Diana Star Helmer. You kept me focused and inspired and helped make this book a reality.

Table of Contents

Acknowledgments — vii
Preface — 1
Introduction — 3

1. The Early Years — 5
2. Dutch Harbor, Alaska: King Crab Fishing — 15
3. A Family on the Edge of the World — 25
4. Sea Legs and Land Legs — 41
5. The Move to Seattle — 56
6. The Million Dollar Topps Deal: Game Changer #1 — 65
7. The DF-1 Card Wrapping Machine: Game Changer #2 — 71
8. The Kid and the Candy Store — 85
9. 1991 Pacific Plus Football Cards — 98
10. Growing by Leaps and Bounds — 106
11. Playing with the Big Boys — 125
12. Major League Baseball Players Association License: My Dream Comes True — 147
13. Turning and Burning — 154
14. What a Way to Start a Century! — 172
15. Pacific After Baseball — 191

16. Life After Pacific	211
17. The Comeback Kid	219
Epilogue	227
2000 Pacific Tom Brady Rookie Cards Checklist	231
Index	235

Preface

A baseball card starts as a blank sheet of paper. Print ink on that paper in the image of a baseball player, cut the sheet into trading card–size pieces—and that piece of paper can turn into gold....

That was my job for some 30 years: printing paper that could turn into gold. It was the ultimate prize for a baseball fan and trading card collector. I designed, printed, cut, collated, packaged, and sold trading cards for a living. I got to choose which baseball players to picture on the cards. I chose how to present their photos, the colors, the motifs, the arrangements. I made every choice. I even invented a trading card brand and gave it that name:

Cramer's Choice.

How did I get to do that, you might ask?

Here is the story of how a baseball fan, card dealer, and all-around entrepreneur (with humble beginnings) turned his baseball card-collecting passion into a dream job. Here is how I built a company that created sports trading card designs, innovations and brands still being used some 30 years after their introduction.

Introduction

Like a lot of boys born in 1950s America, my first love wasn't a girl: it was a baseball card. I had a major league crush and, like many American men, I never outgrew it. But unlike a lot of guys, I never put my hobby on hold.

Before I hit high school, I had a personal collection of more than 500,000 cards and a mail-order trading card business. I wanted to make baseball cards. But I needed more capital.

I was still in high school when I became an Alaskan king crab fisherman. The work was dangerous, demanding, and exciting enough to later inspire the long-running cable TV series *Deadliest Catch*. But the pay was tantalizing bait; in just months, a kid like me could make more money than my dad earned all year.

After 10 years of fishing, I could afford to devote myself to cards. I incorporated Pacific Trading Cards and began designing, manufacturing and distributing cards around the country and the world.

I called my company Pacific, after the ocean that led me to the riches of the Bering Sea. From 1980 to 2004, Pacific created more than 200 different successful trading card products. But Pacific wasn't like Topps and Fleer and other big-name companies. Pacific wasn't owned by a group of investors; the only owner was me. And I was, at heart, a card collector—and, most of all, a fan.

I always wanted Pacific's cards to show a fan's perspective. And I want this book to give other fans a perspective that hasn't been available anywhere else: a behind-the-scenes look at the birth of a major card company, from one kid's overgrown collection, to making prototype cards with scissors and glue, to converting old candy-wrapping machines to wrap baseball cards, to a factory employing hundreds, to using a new-fangled gadget called a computer.

I was hands-on in every facet of the company, from photographing NFL game action for cards to overseeing national publicity campaigns with partners like Advil and McDonald's of Canada.

Current card companies still emulate Pacific's design innovations, and Pacific cards remain some of the hobby's most sought-after; in 2021, one of Tom Brady's 2000 Pacific rookie cards realized an auction price of $117,000.

But I learned from fishing that tides always change. Pacific was part of the 20th-century baseball card boom, but when the bubble inevitably burst, the 21st-century baseball card industry had to reinvent itself.

I had to do the same. My continuing adventures after Pacific have incorporated friendships made and lessons learned on the high seas of crab fishing and the dangerous waters of corporate America. My new challenges have been as diverse as world travel, military history, world-class painting competition, golf, grandchildren, and cancer.

But I never forgot my first love.

When I was diagnosed with cancer in 2020, I told my kids and grandkids a few of the stories in this book. My children Rachael, Angela, Cory, and Michael, my daughter-in-law Kristine and my granddaughter Shiloh wanted to hear more about what I had done in my life. They told me I needed to write a book.

The first person I remember saying that was former major leaguer Bob Uecker: "That's a great story! You should write it down." This from a well-known story-teller! Over the years, Matt Burrows, Will Spence, and other collectors inspired me with similar thoughts.

Finally, I just did it.

I had nothing else to do; I'm just trying to get through this cancer stuff. I have to have a blood test every three months for the rest of my life. I didn't know how to write a book, but I said to myself, Just do it. Just figure it out, like you figured out how to convert a DF-Packaging machine to wax wrap baseball cards. It can't be as hard as that was.

Just figure it out.

1

The Early Years

I believe that collecting baseball cards was in my blood from the day I was born. That day was December 9, 1952, in Brewster, Washington, a small town along the Columbia River in central Washington State.

My family lived in the nearby logging town of Twisp, Washington, where my dad worked in the sawmill. I was nine years old when the sawmill closed, and my parents moved us all to San Manuel, Arizona, where Dad had found work in the copper mine.

I played my first baseball game in San Manuel that summer. They say you never forget your first love, and I've loved baseball my whole life.

On Saturday mornings, I started watching the *Major League Baseball Game of the Week* on TV, with Dizzy Dean and Pee Wee Reese announcing. My family had two old black and white TVs; one had a picture but no sound, the other had sound but no picture.

I was nine years old in 1961 when I bought my first pack of cards for a nickel, a 1960 Fleer All-Time Greats. They must have been leftover cards from the year before, but, when I opened my first pack, the very first card I saw was Babe Ruth.

He was pictured batting. I turned the card over and read his statistics. He could pitch *and* hit, and he hit home runs like no one else before him.

I thought he was the greatest player ever.

I was hooked. The basepath of my life changed when I was nine years old.

I put that card in my back pocket and must have taken it out a hundred times to look at on my walk home.

The very next day, I got out my old red wagon. Then I knocked on neighbors' doors, asking the people if they had any pop bottles I could haul away for them. I filled my little red wagon over and over, taking the empty bottles to the local grocery store and turning them in for three cents each, five cents for the big ones. In about a week, I had more than six dollars and 50 cents in my pocket.

I went back to Leo's corner store. They still had 1960 Fleer Greats.

I bought the remaining 22 packs in the display box, and the store owner let me have the box.

I ran almost a mile home and jumped on my bed to open the first pack. I found a Walter Johnson card in that pack! Johnson, one of the greatest pitchers of all time, quickly became my favorite player because he had played for Washington. (I was born in Washington, and the Senators were from my state, right?) Not right, I learned later—but by that time the Senators were irrevocably *my team*....

Sitting on that bed, opening packs, I discovered those cards had numbers. I carefully placed each card in numerical order and found that I had cards numbered one to 79.

I had my first baseball card set.

Babe Ruth, my very first baseball card. When I was a kid, I carried this card everywhere in my back pocket. As beat up as it is, I still treasure it. My hobby grew into Pacific Trading Cards (Mike Cramer Collection).

I remember sitting on my bed thinking: *I must have more cards than any kid in the world!* I made up my mind to collect baseball card sets, so I would have *all* of the cards.

I read those cards over and over, memorizing every statistic. Before long, I knew the batting average for every player in that set and how many games each pitcher had won.

I carried my Babe Ruth card with me everywhere, showing it to anyone who would look. It was my most prized possession. I still have that card, as beat up as it is. I framed it about 40 years ago, and it sits on my library shelf.

That one card reminds me of what started me on the road to collecting baseball cards, to becoming a manufacturer of trading cards.

By the time I was 11 years old, I was mowing yards for money. I went back to Leo's over and over, buying cards with every nickel I could

1. The Early Years

scrounge up. With my pockets full of change, I started buying cards not just by the pack, but by the *box*. That way, I had a better chance of getting every different card in the set.

Then, in 1963, Leo's corner store got new shipments of both Fleer and Topps cards.

I discovered more players, players that were *currently* playing baseball! My favorite Washington Senators players, Jimmy Piersall and Chuck Cottier, were in that set. I liked how my MVP card of Maury Wills stood out from all the other cards, with its bright yellow polygon proclaiming "N.L. Most Valuable Player '62." I also got a Carl Yastrzemski card which I loved, even though I couldn't say his name right. (It was the biggest name I had ever seen!)

At age 11, I had more than 10,000 cards. And those cards, my brother Marty and I shared a very small bedroom.

By this time, my parents thought there was something wrong with me. I wasn't doing as well in school as I could have, even though I spent most of my time studying. The trouble was, I was studying *baseball*.

I owned a book listing all the players that ever played in the Major Leagues. I read about each one, and I knew all the Hall of Famers by heart. I could name every player I had a card of and recite their statistics: each hitter's batting average, each pitcher's ERA.

I could tell you each man's card number, too.

I wanted cards of as many players as I could get and always tried to build complete sets. I spent hours organizing my cards by team, by card number, by different years. I even bought a baseball magazine at the local store so I could read more about the players.

In the back of my baseball magazine, I discovered an ad for a company that sold baseball cards. I mailed them 25 cents for their catalog and learned that a huge variety of cards were out there, cards that I wanted to find.

That's why I found lawns to mow and other odd jobs: to earn money to buy more cards.

My collection grew by other means, too. Friends and neighbors heard that I collected cards and gave me the cards that had accumulated at their own houses. I had shoe boxes of 1950s cards and boxes (and boxes) of Post Cereal cards, which for a time printed six cards on the back of each box. I guess it was a popular breakfast; I had thousands of those cards!

I had great help from people I knew, though most of my friends weren't into cards like I was. Collecting cards was simply in my blood. I don't know why—but I'm thankful that it was.

My dad, wanting to look out for me, kept saying, "You have to quit playing with those cards and *learn* something! You can never make a living off baseball cards."

Neither of us could know how wrong that statement would turn out to be.

* * *

In 1964, our local store got a shipment of Topps 1964 football cards. I bought some and became a Packers fan. After all, they had Jerry Kramer, who had to be related to me (though they obviously spelled his name wrong). What did I know? I was only 12 at the time!

When I learned that other kinds of cards existed, like football cards ... well, it was one more thing to collect! Cards were cards, and I liked all of them.

Football cards led me to NFL football, and I learned that I liked that, too. My favorite football cards were of the Dallas Cowboys, because of the big stars on the shoulders of their uniforms. My favorite team was Green Bay.

In 1964, I was into Little League and baseball cards (Cramer Family Archives).

I liked both football and baseball as a kid. Baseball, however, played the biggest part in my young life—and, by extension, my family's life.

In 1965, my dad took a job as a millwright for Reynolds Aluminum in Phoenix, Arizona. As my parents got ready for the upcoming move, I overheard them talking in a way that really worried me: "What are we going to do about Mike's cards? Some of the neighbors are asking if we're really going to haul all that stuff to Phoenix."

Lucky for me (and I suppose, in the long run, lucky for them) we did take all my cards to Phoenix.

On that move, we drove by Phoenix Municipal Stadium. A spring training game was in progress, and out of the car window I could see Willie Mays, number 24, and Willie McCovey, number 36, in the outfield, the first actual major league baseball players I ever laid my eyes on.

I knew their faces from the pictures on my cards. But to see them in person—in the very same sun that was shining on me—that was a big connection. I thought, *My heroes on those cards are real. My heroes are real people!*

Right after my family moved into our new home in Maryvale (all 1,007 square feet of it), my dad took me to a spring training game at Phoenix Municipal Stadium. He dropped me off at the stadium, then went to visit his parents nearby.

I got to watch the San Francisco Giants play the Chicago Cubs. My first major league game, ever! So what if it was spring training? That didn't matter to me at all.

Willie Mays, Willie McCovey, Jimmy Davenport, Ernie Banks, and Ron Santo were all out there on the field and I saw them in person, up close for the first time. You could sit anywhere at a spring training game back then, so I went down to the third base side and got myself a spot right next to the field. Jimmy Davenport was playing third base and I was mesmerized by his fielding. He could catch any ball that was hit his way and throw the runner out in one smooth, easy move.

When the seventh inning ended, I noticed that some fans were starting to go and just leaving their scorecards, programs, and pencils behind. I couldn't believe anyone would miss part of a baseball game—*and* throw away a great souvenir! Sure, most star players were out of the game by now, but Cap Peterson and Willie McCovey were still playing. I went down into the stands, scooped up a couple programs and pencils, and decided I was going to get myself an autograph!

The game ended. I went to the entrance behind the stadium where a sign said PLAYERS ONLY. There was an open door and steps going straight down a dark tunnel to a door that read PLAYERS LOCKER ROOM. I stood at the top of those steps, my program and pencil ready. Then the first player came up the steps—closer, closer....

I froze and just stared at him. I have no idea who it was.

He just walked by me. I didn't get his autograph.

I made up my mind I wouldn't miss the next player to come up those steps. I heard the door squeak and footsteps on the concrete, walking up the steps to the top—I was right in front of him, blocking him from leaving! I handed my program and pencil right to him. He took them, signed his name on the cover, handed it back, and walked off to his car.

I was shaking, I was so excited. This was easy! I had my first autograph of a real major league player! I stared down at the signature; it was Giants outfielder Cap Peterson. *I had seen him play today!*

This was easy! I couldn't wait to get *all* the Giants players' autographs!

Just then the creaky door opened.

A flood of players came running up the steps. They got to the top—and charged right by me. They hustled to their cars without stopping; not one of them signed my program.

I decided I needed a better plan.

I went down those dark steps, stood right by the locker room door, and waited for the next player to come out.

It worked! Pitchers Bob Shaw and Ron Herbel came out, and both signed my program!

I stood there for a long time after that. At last, I turned to go and was about halfway up the stairs when I heard the door open. Turning, I saw a giant man running right at me—right over the top of me—

"*Oh, shit!*" he said.

Turning back, he grabbed my arm and hoisted me to my feet. "Kid, you're not supposed to be down here!"

"Can you sign my program?" I said. Without a word, he signed the cover and headed back up the steps. Following him into the light, I read his signature: "Willie Mc."

Willie McCovey. I knew it was Willie McCovey!

That was the Greatest Day of My Life (up to that point).

My dad was there waiting for me when I came up those steps, and he saw that I had the biggest grin a kid could possibly have. I'd only gotten a few autographs, but I was as happy as a clam in a bucket of water that day.

* * *

Times were tough when we first moved to Phoenix, buying the house and the land that went with it. My dad was working a good job, but we were living paycheck to paycheck.

My brother and I came home from school for lunch one day, and there was nothing to eat but one can of creamed corn and milk. My mom thinned the creamed corn with the milk, and we had that for lunch.

I know my parents must have worried about money after the move, but those sparse days didn't last long. And I sure didn't worry: for me, Phoenix's West Osborn Road in the late '60s and early '70s was the perfect place for a kid in seventh grade, a life surrounded by baseball cards and Little League and neighborhood kids and animals.

Once we got settled in our home, I mowed neighbors' yards and found other odd jobs to make money to buy cards. And in 1966, I began to write to baseball players to get autographs.

Through one of the hobby publications, I purchased a mimeographed address list of retired baseball players. Produced and sold by a man named Jack Smalling, the list contained home addresses for hundreds of professional players, past and present. There were even instructions on how to write to players to get autographs.

1. The Early Years

I thought this was exciting. I picked out the first 10 Hall of Famers on the list and addressed 10 envelopes, one to each player. I put a folded, stamped, self-addressed envelope in each envelope (for the players to send the autographs back to me).

A stamp cost only a nickel back then. As the list suggested, I also added blank three-by-five-inch index cards, one or two baseball cards of that player, and a note saying how much I liked him and asking him to please sign my cards. I had plenty of 1960 and 1961 Fleer Greats that pictured Hall of Fame players, so I often included those.

Once I mailed those first envelopes, I went out every day to check the mailbox, waiting for my autographs to return.

After about two weeks, the first letter of response came to me in the mail. Baseball Hall of Famer Frankie Frisch had signed my baseball cards *and* my three-by-fives! He signed *Frankie Frisch, "The Old Flash."* I loved that! What a thrill to get a Hall of Famer's autograph!

Over the next week or two, I received answers to the remaining nine letters. Some players, including Max Carey and George Sisler, returned my cards and added a signed, black and white Hall of Fame postcard. Wow ... a bonus! I was hooked on autographs and wrote to many players over the next few years. At one time, I had close to 1,000 different players' autographs.

Of course, I wanted to be like my heroes. Luckily, the Phoenix area was a real playland for a sports-crazy kid like me. I signed up for Little League and got picked for a team named the Mets. We played our games right across the street from my house, at the Little League field on the grounds of the school I would attend that fall.

I was the new kid on the team, and when no other kids raised their hands to play catcher, I did. I got good at it, too. I just wanted to play, and because I was a catcher (and sometimes even a pitcher), I got to play every game.

One summer night, I was up to bat. My dad was watching the game, sitting on the trunk of our car parked in our driveway. (Our house was just across the street along the first baseline. My dad had a pretty good view of me when I was at bat, particularly when I batted left-handed.)

But that night, I was hitting right-handed.

I took a swing at a pitch and missed. I dug myself in at the plate, determined to hit the next pitch....

I did hit that next pitch, for a foul ball that went over the first base side—over the eight-foot-high chain link fence, across the street—right through my bedroom window.

I heard glass shatter and people at the game gasping, "He broke his own bedroom window!"

Heart pounding, I looked across the street. My dad was shaking his head.

When the game was over, I went home and cleaned up the glass, and Dad put a piece of plywood over the hole.

My window was repaired the next day. But there was actually a bright side.

The ball was in *my* room, so I got to keep it—and it was a brand new ball!

That summer, I rounded up friends who played baseball, and we gathered in the mornings to play at the fields across the street. I always brought the ball that had gone through my window. It was our best ball.

At that young age, I wanted to hit home runs over the outfield fence. I batted left-handed, like the great NY Giants outfielder Mel Ott, and I kicked my left leg high in the air as I swung at the pitch, like I had seen Ott do on his baseball card. That leg kick generated extra power. Mel Ott hit 511 home runs in the *majors*.

The high kick worked for me, too. I hit my share of home runs that summer. We actually wore out my new ball; the cover came off after hours and hours of use. But I took that ball home, wrapped it in black electrical tape, and we kept using it until we found a better ball.

* * *

My parents thought my card collection was big even before we moved to Phoenix. But in Phoenix, my collection ballooned to a size that made my previous stockpile look puny! More yards to mow, more brush to cut, and plenty of other work meant more money in the pocket for a motivated kid like me.

When Topps baseball cards came out in 1967, I bought my first box of 36 wax packs. I opened the first pack standing on the sidewalk right outside the store. I couldn't believe what I was seeing. These cards were beautiful! They were the most colorful baseball cards I had ever seen.

I went right back into that store and bought another box.

That year, I started running ads in the local Phoenix newspapers, offering to buy trading cards and sports memorabilia. There was plenty for me to buy. Phoenix was not the big city it is now, but it was a growing area. People were migrating there from the East Coast and Midwest, bringing their trading cards with them, then discovering that storage was an issue in their new homes.

Cards weren't worth much back then, but lots of people did save them. I was the perfect outlet for them, offering a loving home for the cards they'd accumulated. I was only 15, excited to buy and make their collections part of my own.

1. The Early Years

One thing that helped me greatly in buying collections was *The American Card Catalog*, a book that came out in 1967. Written by Jefferson Burdick, it documented and cataloged every trading card known at that time and was the standard guide for all collected cards, including their current worth.

I bought the book at a local bookstore. When buying people's collections, I could show them the current values of their cards, then make my offers. More people sold their cards to me because the values were in writing in a published book.

For example, 1933 Goudey Gum Co. baseball cards were listed with values of 20 cents each. The exception was card #106, Lajoie, one of the rarest cards in existence. Lajoie was valued at a dollar.

And yes, I still have that book.

I had amassed upward of 500,000 trading cards by age 15. My cards were all over my small bedroom, stacked in boxes to the ceiling. I did have a footpath to my bed, but boxes and boxes of cards surrounded the path!

My sister, Kathi, said years later, "They weren't only in *your* bedroom. You had them stacked down the hall and in the kitchen cupboards!" (Remember, my family of six lived in a 1,007 square foot house....) But Kathi, Anji, Marty, and I were just kids. We thought it was a big house. We didn't know any better!

My whole family knew I was obsessed with cards, but they put up with me. Sure, my folks worried sometimes, but I think they understood that, in a way, my cards were good for me. Collecting kept me busy and focused on something I was interested in.

One day, a guy called because of my ad in the newspaper. He said he had every set of Topps and Bowman baseball and football cards, 1948 to 1962, plus tons of other cards. I went to his house to look at them and knew, right then and there, I wanted to buy those cards.

"Okay," he said. "I want $125."

In 1968, you could buy a good, low-mileage used car for $125.

It was a lot of money, but I had that much in my pocket. We made the deal. Those cards were in mint condition and became the cornerstone of my personal collection.

When my dad found out I had spent that much of my hard-earned money on baseball cards, he was, well, beside himself. He kept repeating over and over, "You better learn to change the oil in our car, because you're not going to make a living selling baseball cards."

* * *

My dad bought a milking cow that summer, a black and white Holstein. Then Dad taught me how to milk the cow—by hand, of course—and let me know that the cow was my new job.

Since our tiny house was on one acre of land, we had room for a cow. We'd always raised different animals, rabbits and chickens and turkeys, to help feed the family. But this was our first cow.

I think Dad was trying to wean me off baseball cards, so he gave me something else to keep me busy. If that's what he was doing, it didn't work!

In the spring, even with chores I had to do, I could almost always find time for spring training baseball games. Phoenix Municipal Stadium was my favorite place to see a game and get players' autographs. I was not driving yet, so I had to take the bus or stick out my thumb and hitchhike; people were friendly and helpful back then. No one was really afraid to hitchhike, and drivers weren't afraid to give rides.

In 1968, I started selling my first cards. I had so many that my bedroom barely had room for me, my brother, and our old army surplus bunk beds. So I sorted out my duplicates and made various complete sets of Topps, Fleer, Bowman, and Play Ball cards. Then I mimeographed a sales sheet, listing the sets I had for sale, along with my prices.

Once in a while, I placed an ad to sell some sets in one of the hobby publications, *Ball Card Collector* or *The Trader Speaks*. When I got orders, I sent my price sheet out along with the cards. I sold many of my duplicate sets through the mail.

My dad was happy to see me sell some cards! My bedroom was still overflowing with them (yes, I was still buying—I was replacing what I sold!) But at least I was showing that I *could* sell cards.

I couldn't wait for *The Trader Speaks* to arrive in the mail each month so I could read about cards and see what other collectors were offering for sale or trade. I still have some of the early 1969 copies with my old childhood home address on them.

Amazing as it was, I had, without realizing it, started a baseball card mail-order business.

I was still just a kid in school, trying to clean out his room and make a little money. But that mail-order business was the beginning of Pacific Trading Cards, Inc.

Pacific was incorporated in 1980.

2

Dutch Harbor, Alaska
King Crab Fishing

In December of 1968, the month I turned 17, my life's basepaths were re-chalked again.

My mother's brother, Uncle C.J., came to Phoenix for Christmas. He was a pioneer king crab fisherman; he'd started fishing in 1964, the early days of king crab fishing, out of Dutch Harbor, Alaska.

His stories of crab fishing and Dutch Harbor mesmerized all of us, but especially me and my dad. There were mountains of adventures in Alaska—and money to be made! I was just a kid in my freshman year at Maryvale High School in Phoenix, but I knew I wanted to experience that adventure and have the chance to make a pile of money.

I was just old enough that my uncle made a suggestion. He said I should come to Dutch Harbor that summer and work with him on a crab boat.

I jumped at the chance!

And my dad, mom, and uncle made it happen.

Now, in the real world, things like that just don't exactly happen. How many parents would let their 17-year-old kid fly off to the Aleutian Islands for the summer to work in a dangerous—potentially deadly—job? But they let me make the choice. They must have known better than I did that this choice could change my life. And it did, for the better.

When the school year ended, I said my goodbyes to my parents, brother and sisters. I would be gone from home for a little more than three months. I could tell my dad was excited for me—and a little envious of my new adventure.

At age 17, I boarded a Western Airlines flight from Phoenix to Seattle. There, I would transfer and fly to Anchorage, Alaska. I had never been on a plane before, or traveled alone, but I was on my own now. I knew every decision I had to make would be mine and mine alone, and I knew I had to make the right choices.

In Anchorage, I spent the night in the Roosevelt Hotel; I'd catch the flight to Dutch Harbor the next day. I got to the hotel early enough to go to a movie, and that film became my first adventure in that life-changing summer. I saw *The Longest Day*, a war movie starring John Wayne. It's still my favorite movie of all time and the beginning of my life-long fascination with military history.

The next day, I boarded a Reeves Aleutian flight to Dutch Harbor. The plane was an old converted DC-3 military surplus plane, so worn out I could see light through the floor of the plane.

The weather was rough all the way to the Aleutian chain. Bouncing in my seat, I looked out the window at the green specks of land peeking between the fog and clouds. I could feel the cold wind blowing in through the floorboards below my seat.

The flight time was about three hours, but about an hour into it, the pilot came back into the cabin and told us the Dutch Harbor airport was closed due to bad weather. We would have to land at Cold Bay on Unimak Island and wait it out until Dutch Harbor opened up.

In Cold Bay, a Reeves Aleutian Airways employee pointed to a building right off the runway, an old World War II Quonset hut, saying, "That's the bunkhouse. Go there and they'll have a room for you, with dinner at 6:30."

Everyone from that plane stayed at the bunkhouse, the passengers and the pilots, too. By the next morning, the weather had cleared enough we could leave for Dutch. (Once you get up north, you quickly learn that Dutch Harbor is often called just "Dutch.") All of this was new for me and incredibly exciting. I saw a new world before me and knew that few people would ever get to experience what I was about to.

Dutch Harbor was an old World War II army base that had once housed 50,000 army personnel. Now, in 1969, most of the buildings remained, along with the bunkers and gun emplacements. But there were no phones, no restaurants, no hotels … just plenty of mud, hard work, and money to be made.

Uncle C.J. picked me up at the tiny Dutch Harbor airport and we drove straight to the docks where the crab boat was tied. We got on board, met the captain of the boat—and went right to work getting the fishing gear ready to catch crab.

My first fishing trip out of Dutch Harbor was a big learning experience. I was young, green, and full of energy, which was good, because I did not know how a crab boat functioned. And I had to learn quickly; I was one-third of a three-man crew.

The work on the boat was extremely physical. I soon realized I would have to learn to work all day and all night, hard, with little or no sleep. I had to keep up with my share of the work, and I did keep up.

2. Dutch Harbor, Alaska

With all the pushing and pulling of gear, bending and straightening and tossing crab in the tank, my muscles ached constantly. And Uncle C.J. constantly yelled instructions to me, his greenhorn, over the noisy hydraulics.

But Uncle C.J. taught me the ropes. I quickly became useful on deck. My muscles grew. I got in shape, and the aching went away. I felt a great sense of importance to be part of a boat crew, doing my job. I was young, but the seasoned fishermen taught me well. They wanted me to learn quickly to do my job right; they needed my help on deck to make the boat work efficiently.

We constantly worked on the crab pots. A crab pot is just a big trap made with a steel bar frame, measuring seven feet high by seven feet wide by three and a half feet deep, webbed with nylon mesh. Two tunnels, wide enough for a crab to get in, are angled in such a way that, once in the pot, the crab can't get back out.

But the crab don't really want to escape: there are bait jars inside the

In 1969, my Uncle C.J. invited me to fish crab out of Dutch Harbor, Alaska. Here we are together in Dutch (Cramer Family Archives).

traps, full of chopped herring that are leaking fish oil, which is why crab go in there in the first place.

We stacked pots on board when we wanted to move them to better fishing grounds. Working with the roll of the boat made the 700-pound pots seem lighter; I found I could push them into place with relative ease if I just waited for the wave. We pushed the pots up to the rail on deck, tied the first pot to the rail, then tied the next pots onto the first. Tying them up kept them from sliding across the deck with the swells when we were sailing.

When we hauled the very first pot of the season off the bottom of the Bering Sea, I was pretty excited. How many crab would be in the pot?

The pot reached the surface. Uncle C.J. yelled, "Riders!"

I could see two crab hanging onto the web mesh, clinging to the top of the pot. I soon learned "Riders!" meant crab riding up that didn't even get into the pot. Riders were a very good sign; they meant a school of crab had just moved into the area where we'd set that pot, and they were still clamoring to get in when we raised it!

I picked the two crab off the top of the pot and tossed them into the tank.

The tank I tossed the crab into was below deck in the ship's hull. A small door on the tank cover was opened, and a heavy aluminum funnel inserted into it. Crab went from the deck, down the funnel, and into the tank where they would live for a week or more with circulating water but no food. When we got back to Dutch Harbor, we'd take the crab straight to the cannery.

Every crab was sorted by hand. When we dumped the pot out onto the deck, the stack of crab might be as deep as four feet. Right away, I'd start tossing big keepers into the tank.

Keepers had to be six and a quarter inches across the shell. If they were too close to call just by looking, we had a metal measuring stick. Undersized crab were tossed back into the Bering Sea to grow bigger. If we happened to catch a female, she was thrown back right away; females are the reproduction source for the crab industry. It was illegal to keep them. But we rarely caught female crab, as they pretty much run in schools of their own on the ocean floor.

That first pot had about 60 big male keepers. Sixty keepers in a pot was a good haul! Those riders had given the right indication.

I was in for another treat. Many boat crews cook and eat a few of the first big male crab caught in a season. That first mouthful of fresh-caught king crab right out of the cold Bering Sea is a rare experience.

But after that first celebratory feast, crab were just part of the job. Once, later that season, I was tossing crab off the top of the pile when a big crab, buried halfway down, reached his big claw out of the pile—and grabbed my shinbone just below the knee!

"He's got me!" I yelped.

The guys on deck kind of froze for a second. That buried crab kept putting on the squeeze.

"Get these other crab in the tank so I can get this thing off of me!" I hollered.

But, of course, the guys couldn't toss crab any faster than they already were. It was probably just a few seconds, but it seemed to me like a lifetime till the crab that had me was uncovered. I pinched his underbelly—he let go!

Of course, that little episode was very funny to the other guys on deck!

In a few days, we filled our boat's tanks with crab and headed back to the cannery in Dutch Harbor.

At the cannery, the tanks were drained, then emptied of crab. Then I got down inside the tanks to sweep up the barnacles and other crab debris. The tanks were a huge volume of space, able to hold more than 100,000 pounds of crab, as many as 16,500 individual crab. Each tank had divider boards to keep the crab from moving too much while in the tank—if they did, they might rub against each other, which could actually kill them. The boards were removed while unloading the tank; it took two of us to place them back in their slots once the tank was clean.

I was now officially a king crab fisherman.

The crab boat fleet (all of the independent vessels out catching crab that season) caught more than eight million pounds in 1969. We caught our share of that eight million pounds with only three men on deck. (No wonder we got little to no sleep during the days of the season!)

But it was worth it. Back then, a crew share was 8 percent each. In 2022 dollars, our season's catch would have equaled $710,000. My share would have been equivalent to nearly $60,000 in 2022 dollars.

I was making serious money for a kid.

We knew that the more crab we caught, the more money we'd take home. And, in 1969, there were no quotas or limits on how much crab we could catch. There would be quotas in later years, but by that time, the price of crab had risen.

I worked the whole summer of 1969. In late August, I had three months' earnings in my pocket, and I knew my couple of checks were worth way more than what Dad made all year as a millwright.

I also knew I had to get back home to Phoenix for school. Uncle C.J. asked the captain of a processing ship, the *Theresa Lee*, if I could ride the ship down to Bellingham. It would save me having to spend some of my hard-earned money on expensive airfare. I know I felt like I was on my own, but I was young, and I did have people looking out for me.

When we got to Bellingham, I took a Greyhound bus to Seattle. I spent the early morning before my flight home visiting Sick's Stadium. Sick's was home to the new Seattle Pilots—my new favorite team. No game that morning, just me taking a look at the stadium where the Pilots played, and where my other team, the Washington Senators, used to play.

I boarded the flight to Phoenix later that day and was suddenly back home with my parents, my brother and sisters, a pile of cash, the cow—and my cards.

* * *

I put some of my fishing money in a savings account. I was frugal, very frugal (*squeaky* frugal), except when it came to cards. I wasn't afraid to spend my money on them. Early on, back in the lawn mower days, I'd wanted to make money so I could buy cards. Even at that young age, I somehow realized that if you had money, you could get what you wanted.

In my case, I wanted cards.

So, with some of my new money, I ran ads and bought more card collections. But I also got my little mail-order business going again and sold some cards. This freed up space to store the new cards I was buying. The business kind of sustained itself.

I guess I always had a drive in me to make money to get what I wanted.

Some big collections came to me that year, and I was able to buy them because I had the money to do so. One collection that later played a huge part in my life came from a call I got on one of those ads I had placed.

The lady on the phone told me she had eight-by-10-inch paper photos of old baseball players.

I had pretty much memorized my *American Card Catalog* by that time. I remembered seeing the photos she seemed to be describing.

I drove out to Sun City, Arizona, to see the lady and her baseball photos. She was right: she had old, thin-paper baseball player photos, 175 of them in beautiful condition. Each picture was an eye-catching sepia-tone photo of a Major League player. The player's name was printed on his photo as well as the date (ranging from 1909 to 1913) and the words "Sporting News Supplement."

Sure enough, they were in my book as M101–2 Sporting News Supplements.

And she had the entire set, including the team photos.

I'd brought my copy of the *Catalog* with me; the price listed was 25 cents each for the players and 75 cents each for the team photos.

She wouldn't sell for my $50 offer, so I asked how much she wanted.

2. Dutch Harbor, Alaska

She came right back with "One dollar each."

I quickly paid her. I wanted that collection.

Those photos would come into play years later, when I was making my Baseball Legends sepia set in 1980. I used these outstanding photos on many of the cards appearing in that set.

* * *

My sophomore year ended and, in the summer of 1970, I read something in *The Trader Speaks* that really got my attention. There was going to be a baseball card show in Detroit that September—a *national* baseball card show.

This would be the first card show of its kind, a gathering of collectors from all over the country. Card shows before had been smaller, regional meetings, a lot of times held at somebody's house. But a national show?

I had to go.

And I did. I called the people putting on the show, sent the money for my room at the Cadillac Hotel and, a few weeks later, flew to Detroit with a footlocker of cards.

After checking into my room, I went down to the show floor. I actually got to meet some fellow baseball collectors, people that I'd bought cards from, or sold to, or just corresponded with over the past few years. I met collectors Lloyd Thorpe and Frank Nagy, two of the Detroit collectors putting on the show. They were great guys; they looked after me.

I brought my trunk full of cards down to the show floor and opened it up for them to see. Both were astonished by the cards in that locker: complete mint-condition sets of 1930s, '40s and '50s baseball cards, including my 1952 Topps set, complete with the coveted Mickey Mantle.

Frank Nagy asked if I was selling.

I said, "No, just showing." After all, it was a baseball card *show*. (I didn't know any better; it was my first show ever!)

"Close that locker," both Frank and Lloyd told me. "Close it up, take it back to your room, and take it back home."

But just then, a *Detroit News* reporter came over and asked if he could get a photo of me with the trunk. Of course, I said yes!

Lloyd and I posed, looking into the trunk. The next day the paper came out, with the photo and a caption reading, "17-year-old collector Mike Cramer hopes to find something in the trunk at the Detroit Baseball Card Show." (This was my first exposure to the idea "Don't believe everything you read in the paper." It was my trunk, after all!)

I did take that trunk of cards back to my room and back home. But I found plenty of other excitement at that show.

First, the Detroit Tigers were in town, playing my Washington Senators. Tigers announcer Ernie Harwell had attended the card show and heard that I was a Senators fan. He got in touch with me and asked if I wanted to see a game that night.

I had never been to a real major league game, just spring training games. Of course, I said, "Sure!" and Ernie Harwell arranged for me to attend the game.

The stadium was huge and full of fans. I got to see my favorite player at that time, Frank Howard. And, of course, my Senators.

* * *

The next morning after breakfast, I grabbed my Polaroid camera and headed to the elevator to go down to the show floor. I wanted to be there for the opening of that morning's card auction. The elevator was so slow, I went looking for stairs or another elevator. I found one marked "Service." Its door opened, so I hopped on, joining the people inside.

As the elevator started moving, I noticed the men in that elevator were looking at me warily.

Then I realized: one of the men in that elevator was Elvis Presley! The breakfast waitress had said he was staying in the hotel.

I swooped up my Polaroid camera and said, "My mother really likes you! Can I take a picture?"

Elvis nodded just as the elevator got to the bottom. The door opened; Elvis fans were there to greet him. I pulled up my Polaroid and took two photos.

I had to jump back in that elevator to ride it back to the main lobby. But I was grinning my head off. My pictures had developed, and there was Elvis in my photos!

I still have those photos.

At the card auction, I was able to buy thousands of cards from the 1950s. Cards from the '50s were very common back

In 1970, when I jumped into the service elevator at the Detroit Cadillac Hotel, Elvis Presley was there first. I took this photograph with my Polaroid camera.

2. Dutch Harbor, Alaska

then, the junk cards of the day, and I was the only one buying them. I also bought, for about 10 cents each, hundreds and hundreds of 1910 T-206 cigarette baseball card commons (the non-stars). I was hooked on them.

Frank Nagy saw how excited I was to get the T-206 cards. He sat down with me and told me all about the set and how that set contained the rarest card in baseball card collecting. That card is of a player named Honus Wagner, who had his card discontinued because the cards were issued in cigarette packs, and he didn't want youngsters to smoke.

Frank told me that if I wanted him to assemble a set of these cards, and if I had the money to pay for them, he could put a set together for me. The set would contain 520 players, including the rare Southern Leaguers, but would be missing one or two very rare cards—which meant no Honus Wagner.

The cards would cost one dollar each, in excellent condition. I said yes, I would buy those cards! Frank said that when he had the cards assembled, he would send them out to me and, if I liked them, I could send him a check.

About three months later, a box arrived at my home from Frank Nagy. When I opened it, there was my nearly-complete set of 1910 T-206 Baseball Cards.

They were beautiful. I sent Frank a check and enjoyed those cards for years after. Eventually, I completed my T-206 set, including the Honus Wagner, Ed Plank, and all of the other rare cards. And, over time, I added a few hundred "back variations" (the same cards, but printed by different cigarette manufacturers whose brand logos appeared on the card backs).

That auction back in Detroit had been a great turning point in my collection. But I had a big problem after the auction ended.

I had purchased too many cards! With my trunk and all those cards, I didn't see how I could fly back home. My cards were too heavy for baggage, and I certainly didn't want to pay to ship them home.

But I had met two collectors from California, Jim McConnell and Ed Broder, who had driven out for the show. Those guys saved me and my cards by offering to give me a ride back as far as Flagstaff, Arizona. From there, I could get a Greyhound bus back home to Phoenix.

We loaded my trunk into their car trunk along with our luggage. The rest of my cards went in the back seat. There was barely enough room for *me* with all those cards! But I made myself skinny while Ed and Jim shared driving duties, 26 straight hours to Flagstaff.

And I made it home to Phoenix with all of my newfound treasures.

When I finally got home, I showed my parents the newspaper with my photo and then the two Elvis photos. It was hard for them to believe that all that could happen at a baseball card show!

My dad also saw that I brought home even more cards than I had taken with me. He just shook his head and muttered, "That kid is going to have to learn he can't make a living on baseball cards."

The Detroit card show had been a great start to the school year, and the rest of 1970 went by without a hitch. I tried out for the high school baseball team that spring as a catcher, and I was going to make the team, but my dad told me I needed to get a job. I was going to be 18, he said, and I was wasting my time playing baseball.

Looking back, he was probably right.

I worked in a bakery that summer.

But it would have been fun to play baseball.

3

A Family on the Edge of the World

The spring of 1970 was the first time I heard my parents talk about Dad and Uncle C.J. buying a crab fishing boat together.

My dad had a good job. Our family was just getting settled in and feeling comfortable for the first time that I could remember, living on Osborn Road in Phoenix. Sure, the house was small, but my sister Kathi had gotten married, which freed up some space. Still, my dad was very adventurous, and he couldn't forget what I had been able to do that summer of 1969.

When I'd gotten back home to Phoenix, my dad had wanted to hear all about my experiences in Dutch Harbor. The adventures I had as a crab fisherman were even more interesting to him than the money. I had been out on a boat in the Bering Sea. What could be better than that?

Dutch Harbor was, in 1969, the last wild frontier in America, an island in the Aleutian chain with no phones, no radio, and no television. I got to experience the dream of a lifetime: fishing crab and making money. I told Dad how fun it was, when our boat was being unloaded at the cannery, to grab my fishing pole and run over to Margaret's Bay to catch salmon.

I remember my dad as an avid outdoorsman, hunting, fishing, and trapping in the foothills of eastern Washington's Cascade Mountains. Dutch Harbor sounded to him like a perfect place for an outdoorsman, a place where he could live that adventure and even make a pile of money. He was 45 years old but just couldn't get that idea out of his head; he wanted to go to Alaska and become a crab fisherman.

So my parents sold their house. My older sister Anji, my brother Marty and I all moved with them to Dutch Harbor, Alaska. My oldest sister, Kathi, stayed behind in Phoenix with her husband and daughter. But only one year later, they joined the rest of us up north.

It's incredible how my parents' decision to sell everything and move lock, stock, and barrel changed all of our lives for the better. Very few people in the world have taken a risk of that magnitude. As their child, one thing I was learning was that once you make an important life decision, do everything possible to make it happen—and don't look back.

Almost unbelievably, I didn't want to go to Alaska at first. I had my card collection, a small mail-order business—I knew there weren't going to be any cards in Alaska that I could add to my collection. I even had a girlfriend! I had no real desire to leave Phoenix.

But in January of 1971, my brother and I were pulled out of school, and we all packed into my dad's Rambler pickup. (My sister Anji had graduated the previous spring, and she voluntarily came, too.)

We pulled a trailer loaded with all our family possessions, including three trunks of my best trading cards. I was able to store the rest of my cards in my girlfriend's parents' garage. I wasn't happy for the first couple of days, having left my friends, school, and girlfriend behind.

But I got over it pretty quickly.

We headed up the freeway to Seattle to meet the *Honey-B*, my dad and uncle's newly-purchased crab boat. We arrived a few days late because our overloaded pickup broke down in the Oregon mountains, requiring repairs. But at last, we arrived at the docks in Ballard, where Uncle C.J. and the *Honey-B* were waiting.

The *Honey-B* was a wooden boat, 76 feet long, painted white with red trim. She had a captain's stateroom, four bunks, a full galley (kitchen) and one head (bathroom). I learned later that this boat, while a good and sea-worthy boat, was extremely small for fishing in the dangerous Bering Sea. But at that time, there were only a handful of big king crab boats, 100 feet or longer. Most crab boats back then were smaller, like the *Honey-B*.

In early March of 1971, we unloaded our trailer and moved everything aboard the boat, including my trading cards trunks. We brought provisions we hoped would feed our crew for the entire season, which at the time was expected to last four months. We dropped the boat lines and pulled away from the dock.

We expected the trip from Seattle to Dutch Harbor, Alaska, to take two weeks.

We arrived in Dutch one month later.

We first went through the Ballard Locks into Puget Sound, then turned north to head through the Inside Passage.

There were seven of us on the tiny *Honey-B* (the family plus one additional crew member). It was so crowded that we took turns sleeping as bunks became available.

But everyone ate when my mother cooked.

When we stopped in Juneau, Alaska, to take on diesel fuel, we had some time to explore. So my brother and I walked into town and found

3. A Family on the Edge of the World

the famous Red Dog Saloon. The drinking age in Alaska was just 18, so I ordered my first legal beer. I drank it down while Marty watched.

In a couple hours, everyone was back on board. We dropped lines and headed up the Inside Passage again. From Sitka, we cut across the Northern Gulf of Alaska, then hugged the coast on the way to Kodiak, Alaska.

Kodiak was a beautiful, bustling fishing port, with fish canneries on every dock. The canneries processed everything, from bottom fish to salmon, crab, and shrimp. We would be in Kodiak for about four days while some work was done on the *Honey-B*. We would also take on more provisions.

Four days was a long time, so I decided to see if I could find work at one of the canneries. The first cannery I went to was the Whitney-Fidalgo, where they were processing tanner crab. When I told them I had previous work experience unloading crab boats at Dutch Harbor, I got hired on the spot.

The boats I'd unload for this job packed more than 100,000 pounds of crab in their tanks. That's about 40,000 crab—I was going to be busy.

The work was back-breaking hard. I was in the tank, tossing the crab into a basket lowered by a crane. When the basket was full, it was quickly replaced with an empty one. I did that work all day and all night, with a half-hour break for dinner, which I ate in the cannery mess hall. When I emptied the tanks in one crab boat, I got off on the dock, the boat pulled away, and just like clockwork, another boat with full tanks of crab tied up in its place. The tank hatch covers were removed, and I started unloading crab all over again.

It was going to be a nice payday.

I found out that bad weather out on the Aleutian chain was going to keep the *Honey-B* tied at the Kodiak dock for more than a week. So I just kept working. During that time, I made some good money and got some built-up energy worked off.

But at last, the weather cleared, and we loaded the *Honey-B* with our people and provisions and left Kodiak, following the Aleutian chain to Dutch Harbor.

It was still winter, and the trip to Dutch in late March was rough. Snow, wind, and the seas were pounding us. A wooden boat like the *Honey-B* creaks and shudders with every swell, so you can't sleep much, even when you have a chance to sleep. And to make matters worse, the *Honey-B* was "making ice." We had to take turns knocking chunks of ice off the boat with wooden bats, sometimes all through the night. Ice buildup on a boat is very dangerous; it can make a boat top-heavy, and top-heavy boats can easily roll over.

To make things worse, with the rolling, pitching, and pounding of the boat, everyone on board except my mother experienced their first bout of seasickness—and it was miserable. Thank God, most people can get over seasickness in short order. We did, and we got our sea legs fairly quickly.

We made it to Dutch Harbor on April 1. The *Honey-B* was covered in ice; we just couldn't keep up with the buildup.

We tied up at the Standard Oil dock, got off and walked on the dock, trying to get our land legs back and trying to believe we finally made it to Dutch.

My parents had a place lined up for us to live. It was an old World War II officer's house that was built right into the hillside: only the roof could

Mom and Dad in 1972 on the boat deck in Dutch Harbor. They had brought the Cramer family to Dutch. We were truly living on the edge of the world (Cramer Family Archives).

3. A Family on the Edge of the World 29

be seen. It had a kitchen, oil stove, bedrooms—and a place for my trunks of cards, which were the first things unloaded off the *Honey-B*.

The house was in Unalaska, across from Dutch Harbor. Unalaska had a brand new high school that had just been completed. It was April, and I needed to attend school in an attempt to complete my junior year. I did finish my junior year, taking extra courses from one of the teachers. When I wasn't in school, I worked as much as I could.

When the school year ended, I went to work full-time crab fishing. I'd learned the ropes before, but there were new twists this season. I was working with my dad. And when the *Honey-B* was in Dutch, I would go see my mother (and take my dirty clothes so she could wash them— mothers are the best!).

I made myself a fairly good bankroll that season, good enough that I decided to go back, on my own, to Phoenix and Maryvale High School. I wanted to finish my senior year so I could graduate from high school. Finishing high school was important to me. I wanted that accomplishment. I didn't want to be a dropout.

I left Dutch after the summer work was over and had my Unalaska school junior year grades transferred to Maryvale High School. I was able to board with some friends in Phoenix for about half the school year. Then I moved to a house with a room to rent to finish out my senior year. I lived on my own, paid my rent, bought my food, and made all my own decisions.

Sometimes I was discouraged and wanted to just give up school and go back fishing. But I stuck it out; I lived on Hamburger Helper and Kraft macaroni & cheese. About once a month, I hitchhiked to my grandparents' house in Apache Junction to see family and eat a real, home-cooked meal. I got good grades in school, was on the track team, and never got in trouble.

* * *

During that time in school, I got my trading cards out of my ex-girlfriend's parents' garage and put them into a storage locker. There was no time for me and my cards. I was trying to get that high school diploma on my own. Just before the school year ended, I got a letter from my dad. He wrote that when I finished school, there would be a job for me on the *Honey-B*. But I would need to get up to Dutch in time to make the start of the crab season, which was in June.

I had told some of my high school friends all about my experiences in Alaska and about the money you could make in a short time. Five of them decided to go to Dutch Harbor that summer; they all found work in the Wakefield Cannery out at Captains Bay.

I flew to Dutch Harbor knowing I was a high school graduate. I had worked hard for that diploma, and I was very proud of it.

As soon as I got to Dutch, I boarded the *Honey-B* with my dad, my uncle, and a deckhand named Harvey, and we headed out to the Bering Sea king crab grounds. We fished that 1972 season until November. (There was no quota back then, like there is nowadays.) You could fish all the time if you wanted, and other, bigger boats did go out more. But sometimes the *Honey-B* stayed at the dock because the sea was too rough for small boats.

I fished crab in the Bering Sea, 770,000 square miles of blue water that at times can be the most dangerous ocean on earth. The winds can reach 100 miles an hour and the rough seas, along with freezing temperatures, could make it almost unbearable for crab fishermen.

Crab fishing is not for the faint of heart.

When the sea was too rough for small boats, I sometimes found work unloading crab boats like *The Belair*. I met her captain, Kris Poulsen. Not a big meeting, but that man would one day marry my sister Anji and become part of our family. And he would become a big influence in my life, probably without realizing it.

That winter, my dad and uncle had a falling out and dissolved their *Honey-B* partnership. My dad went to work as the chief engineer at the Wakefield Cannery in Captains Bay. He and my mother moved out to the cannery, into an old army barracks house with five rooms. In the move, they took my three footlockers full of baseball cards.

Years later, my dad told me that he actually considered just taking those lockers to the dump. They were heavy to move and took up lots of space, and my parents had moved and stored them many times.

Something must have stopped them from tossing those trunks.

I thank God my parents kept them.

My brother and I stayed working on the *Honey-B* with my uncle. The Adak Island king crab fishing season was always really good, so my uncle decided to take the *Honey-B* out west in the Aleutian chain to fish the 1972 season.

Fishing was good at the start, but it backed off in a hurry. It took longer than expected for the fleet to catch the crab quota, and the days dragged on into weeks. During the third week out there, our food was starting to run out, and we were down to pancake flour and fish (if you could catch one).

One morning when the winds had died down, we decided to take the *Honey-B*'s skiff to the beach and see if we could get some caribou meat for dinner. Dutch Harbor was still a wild frontier back then, and fishermen often carried hunting guns.

Marty, Uncle C.J. and I got to shore and had hiked about 80 yards through high, wet ferns when Uncle C.J. whispered, "Stop."

3. A Family on the Edge of the World

He aimed his 30.06 and fired—a caribou tumbled down the hill, about 50 yards ahead of us.

Dinner would be good tonight!

And it was—until a couple hours after eating, when all of us began to regret my decision to serve pancakes with fresh caribou meat cooked medium rare.

I don't know where the nautical term "poop deck" came from, but I do know I have never eaten a pancake since!

* * *

When the crab quota was caught and the Adak king crab season ended, we headed back to Dutch Harbor. I had made a pile of money that crab season and, with really bad weather setting into the Bering Sea, I decided to go back to Phoenix for a break.

I basked in the warm weather and old friends, and I made a new friend too. In April of 1973, I went to a party at a friend's house, where a girl named Cheryl Robinson noticed me. She asked a mutual friend to arrange an introduction.

I said, "Of course!" to the meeting. And the next day, the most beautiful girl in the world with big blue eyes walked into my life. She was a senior at Maryvale, just about to graduate. We hit it off right from the start.

I told her I was a crab fisherman in Alaska and I was scheduled to go back to Dutch Harbor in a week.

We dated every day for that week, all the time I had left in Phoenix.

During that time, I realized Cheryl Robinson was perfect. She was able to introduce me to her mother that week. Her father was working, so I didn't get to meet him.

I returned to Dutch Harbor and my crab fishing job but thought about Cheryl all the time. We wrote back and forth, until one day I wrote, "I can send you the money for airfare, and you can come up to Dutch to be with me, and stay with my parents."

A couple of weeks later, she agreed, and I sent her the money.

Cheryl Robinson was coming to the Aleutian Islands to be with me! I had only known her for one week, but we both knew we had something special, and we weren't going to let it go.

In mid-June, the Reeves Aleutian Airline plane—that same DC-3 military surplus plane, but this time with Cheryl on board—landed on the Dutch Harbor tarmac.

She stepped off the plane, wearing a black flowered mini dress.

No one ever wore a mini dress in Dutch Harbor. With mud everywhere, the usual attire was jeans, coats, and rubber boots.

Cheryl looked just beautiful, and I was thrilled to see her.

I loaded her bag, and we caught a ride to my sister Anji's house for lunch, where my mother joined us. After lunch, my mom, Cheryl and I crossed the bay by skiff, from Dutch to the Unalaska side. There, we rode by Jeep to Captains Bay and the Wakefield Cannery, where Mom and Dad lived. They had a room ready for Cheryl.

That summer in Dutch was the best ever. Cheryl and I worked, played, hiked, fished, laughed and, best of all, realized we were in love. Then the 1973 king crab season started up in September, and I was out on the Bering Sea fishing most of the time.

I was only able to be with Cheryl for a few days here and there. She got a job and worked in the cannery but only lasted two days. She had tried to make the best of it, but someone put a live crab on the conveyor belt where she was working, and it scared her. So we learned that Cheryl was not cut out for cannery work. The next time I saw her, she had taken a job at Vern's Aleutian Mercantile Store, a small grocery store in Unalaska. That suited her much better.

Part way through the crab season, the *Honey-B* had engine trouble and had to be repaired, so I took a job on a different crab boat named the *Scotty*. It was a Bender boat, made in Alabama, and the captain was a friend.

We got out to the crab grounds and started hauling gear. We were catching crab—but I noticed the boat was listing. There was water on the deck, and we couldn't coil pot lines because the rope was floating in seawater. I went up to the wheelhouse to speak to the captain and told him we needed to transfer fuel to right the list.

After I talked to him, the captain did stop hauling gear and transferred just enough fuel to fix the problem—temporarily. But within an hour, the list was back: the *Scotty* was starting to lay on its starboard side again.

Eventually, we put on a load of crab and headed back to the cannery in Dutch. When we got there a day and a half later, we tied up at the cannery. And when we finished unloading the crab, I packed my sea bag and got off the boat.

I only took one trip on board the *Scotty*. But my instincts told me that once was enough and that I should get off that boat.

While I was out on the *Scotty* for those seven days, a big change happened to my parents and Cheryl, who was staying with them. Dad, who was chief engineer at the Wakefield Cannery, was hired by a crab boat to be the boat's chief engineer. For Cheryl and my mom, this meant moving out of the Wakefield Cannery housing.

In Unalaska, they were each able to rent tiny, one-bedroom apartments. "The Pink Apartments" were, as you might guess, painted pink on the outside. These apartments hadn't been lived in for several years, but Mom and Cheryl had nowhere else to go. So they got to work and cleaned the floors, scrubbed the mold off the walls and bathroom fixtures, and painted those little places.

I knew Cheryl's ancestors were Norwegian, and I could see her tough Norwegian side shining through. By the time I got back from the Bering Sea seven days later, the place was livable, even though we had to have the oil stove on high to heat the place. The walls were so thin and uninsulated that the chilling wind blew right through them.

I remember one time, in early November, it was so cold in that apartment that Cheryl and I sat fully dressed, with blankets on us and our feet in the oven, trying to stay warm. But it was our very first place to live—and my three trunks of cards had a new, dry home.

The 1973 Bering Sea season was almost finished when I got off the crab boat *Scotty*. Even so, I was hoping to get in one more trip for the season—just on a different boat. That didn't happen but, as luck would have it, I did get hired for the upcoming Kodiak crab season. My old friend Kris Poulsen—who was now my brother-in-law—was looking for a crewman to leave that very day.

I had to say my goodbyes to Cheryl all over again. She would not see me for about a month, but her job as a cashier at Vern's would keep her busy. And Cheryl had a good support network: in addition to my parents, I had several more relatives living in Dutch by this time, including my oldest sister, Kathi, her husband and her daughter.

Years later, someone asked my mother how it happened that the whole extended family sort of migrated together. My mother said that it started with my dad.

"I think my husband was the only one actually wanting adventure," she said. "I didn't question his reasons for wanting to go, and I certainly didn't look at it as uprooting the family—it was just another move. I always felt that if we were all together, I had no worries."

Dad may have started the family migration, Mom said, "but the rest of us experienced a life that we still tell stories about. Of course, I was excited to go!"

So, leaving Cheryl with my family nearby, I boarded the *Belair*, a 108-foot schooner owned by the Brown and Williams Tobacco Company. They owned three crab boats, all named after cigarette brands they made, and they also made trading cards, issued in their Wings cigarettes.

Even in Alaska, fishing crab in the Bering Sea, trading cards were part of my life.

We left the Pan Alaska dock in Unalaska for the three-and-a-half-day trip to the Kodiak Island crab grounds, carrying a full load of crab pots.

It was on the *Belair* that I really learned how to work.

The fishermen aboard the *Belair* were very serious professionals. My brother-in-law, Kris, was the best crab fisherman ever, period. I was privileged to be a part of that crew. Kris's brother, Erik, was also on board, as well as Bill Cook, the boat's chief engineer. I learned a lot from these men.

The first day on the run to Kodiak, I came up to the wheelhouse for my wheel watch to relieve Kris. He asked me why I got off the crab boat *Scotty*.

"The captain wouldn't take the time to transfer fuel, and the boat listed all the time," I said. "I just didn't feel safe."

"It was a good thing you got off," Kris said. "I heard on the radio that the *Scotty* sank this morning."

A crab boat rescued the crew, but some of those men never fished again. Bobbing up and down in a life raft, waiting to get rescued in the most treacherous sea in the world could take a toll on even the toughest king crab fishermen.

I had made another great decision in my life, and that was to get off the fishing boat *Scotty* when I did.

The second day, I was on wheel watch with chief engineer Bill Cook, the big, tall man who kept the boat's engines running. Our wheel watch was four hours long; Bill and I had time to talk. I learned from him some things that would stay with me for the rest of my life.

He told me that I was one of the few people in the world who was going to make a lot of money, and I had to learn how to take care of the money I made and not blow it. He said that, with no college education, it would be even harder to earn big money. But I had a chance, because I had chosen to fish crab, and a guy willing to work hard could make a lot of money fishing crab.

The more money you make, he said, the more true freedom you get, and the more freedom you have, the more money you will want to make, to get even more freedom. Once you make your first million, you will find that the second million comes easier, and the third easier still—and so on. Your ambition and drive will take over, he said, and drive you to the top.

That sunk into me, and I learned during that Kodiak crab season that I had ambition and drive. I could work all day and night, for days and days on end. Crab fishing was going to be very good to me, and I was still really just learning the ropes.

* * *

At the start of the Kodiak season, Kris, as captain of the *Belair*, picked a place in the waters off the southern end of Kodiak Island where he thought

3. A Family on the Edge of the World

crab would be. No one was surprised when the first pot came up full of big male keepers—Kris was that good at finding crab.

We caught more than our share of Kodiak king crab during that season, a season that lasted just seven days. Because the processing ship, the *Viceroy*, was anchored up in one of the Kodiak Island bays only an hour or so from the crab grounds, we could fill our tanks with crab and unload it every single day.

We had virtually no sleep, but what a payday! Without the *Viceroy*, we would have spent most of our time taking crab to Kodiak canneries five hours away.

With the season ending, we took our last load of crab to the cannery in Kodiak (the same cannery where I had worked unloading boats when the *Honey-B* was in Kodiak). While the *Belair* was being unloaded, I was talking to the cannery plant manager. He asked what I was going to do after the season. I told him I was going back out to Dutch. He then asked if I knew Vern Robinson.

I said, "Sure! My girlfriend works at his store."

He told me that he was looking for a place to moor the processor ship *Mokihana* and that Vern might have a dock with fresh water available. He asked me to have Vern contact him when I got back to Dutch. (There were no regular phones out to Unalaska back then.)

I flew back to Dutch the very next day. It was late October, and I hadn't seen Cheryl for 16 days.

When I got back to Dutch, I went to see Vern right away and told him about the *Mokihana*. Within a week, that ship was moored at his dock, processing Dutch Harbor season crab.

It was early November, and Cheryl and I had to decide our next move. The snow was on the ground, and the freezing winds in the Aleutians had begun. The 1973 king crab seasons were coming to an end. But I had made more money than I could have ever imagined and, with our newfound freedom, Cheryl and I could easily plan our next adventure.

I made our next adventure easy: I asked Cheryl to marry me.

She said yes!

I was 20; Cheryl was only 18. We had only known each other for that one week in Phoenix before she came up to be with me in Dutch Harbor. When she got to Dutch, I was out on a boat fishing in the Bering Sea a good deal of the time. So in the five months Cheryl had been in Dutch, we really didn't get to be together that often. But we were in love and, 49 years later, we still are. And we have had a spectacular life together.

We went and told my parents we were getting married. My dad suggested a date of November 25. That was my mother and father's 25th wedding anniversary—and that wedding date went back one or two more generations in our family. We also decided, after the wedding, that Cheryl and I would go back to Phoenix for the winter, and I could finally meet her family and her dad.

We had a very small wedding, in the tiny little church up the valley in Unalaska. Even though we may have had time to, we didn't invite any outside relatives. It was just so hard to get to Dutch in the winter. And, if you could get there, you had no place to stay: there was no hotel back then, no restaurant, no phones, and no taxi. And all of us were in small apartments with really no room for guests. It was just too primitive—the only thing there was plenty of was mud.

We had about 20 days until the wedding date and, as small as it was, plans progressed easily. Cheryl and my mother did everything.

All set for the wedding, we started to pack up our belongings so we'd be ready to leave Dutch when the wedding was over. My new job was to figure out how I could bring my three footlockers of baseball cards with us back to Phoenix. I couldn't leave Dutch without them, as there was no place for me to store them.

I had heard the processing ship *Mokihana* was nearly finished with the Dutch Harbor season crab processing. The crew was getting ready to head back to the Bellingham,

I first met Cheryl Robinson in Phoenix at the end of May 1973. We only knew each other one week before I left for Dutch Harbor. In July, she came to Dutch to be with me. On November 25, we were married in Unalaska, Alaska. In 2023, we will celebrate our golden anniversary (Cramer Family Archives).

3. A Family on the Edge of the World

Washington, cold storage docks, to unload the season's crab production. The *Mokihana* was a fairly large ship, more than 250 feet long … surely it could have room on board for my baseball card trunks!

I went to see if the captain of the *Mokihana* would consider allowing my trunks of cards to ride on the boat down to Bellingham, where I would meet the boat when it arrived and retrieve the trunks.

When I met with the captain the next day, of course he didn't know who I was, and I sensed he didn't want to mess with me. When he told me he couldn't help, I said, "I am the guy that helped get the *Mokihana* moored at Vern's dock."

He took notice then. "Just a minute," he said and left me on the bridge. I could hear him on his CB radio talking with Vern, and asking Vern if he knew Mike Cramer. I heard Vern say, "Sure! Mike contacted me about getting your boat moored at my dock."

The captain came back and said, "Mike, we can take your trunks down."

I told him I lived on the beach in Unalaska, in the Pink Apartments, #2. He said he would contact me when he had a firm departure date.

I ran all the way back from Vern's dock to the Pink Apartments to tell Cheryl.

I was thrilled. I'd found a way to get my baseball cards back to Phoenix! I worried all the time about those cards Dutch Harbor, Alaska, was not a good place for that collection of baseball cards to be.

Our wedding took place on November 25, 1973. We became Mr. and Mrs. Michael Cramer. We had about 10 guests, and Cheryl wore the same black mini dress she wore six months earlier when she arrived at the Dutch Harbor airport.

The reception at my parents' house was very small, with a homemade flat cake (made by my mother). One bottle of champagne was all we could muster up.

Not the biggest of weddings, but we were happy, and that was all that mattered.

The reception was over about 10 p.m., and Cheryl and I headed back to the Pink Apartments. We had only been there a short time on our wedding night when we heard a knock on the door.

It was a runner with a message from the *Mokihana*'s captain: the boat was to leave the dock on the tide at midnight, November 25.

That was tonight! I needed to get my trunks on board!

I said, "Cheryl, we have to do this now."

"But it's our wedding night!" she protested. I saw the look in her eyes … she wasn't going to be too fond of baseball cards in the future.

But she put on her boots that night, and we borrowed my dad's Willys Jeep, loaded up those trunks, and headed to the *Mokihana*.

The captain was waiting. He told his chief engineer to show us to the engine room, where we would stow the trunks for the ride south. At almost midnight, Cheryl and I moved the three trunks down all those narrow steps into the bowels of that ship.

The engine room was warm, a perfect place to store my trunks. When we finished loading, we thanked the captain and said we would meet them in Bellingham. As soon as we stepped off the ship, they dropped the lines and slid away from the dock.

It had been snowing, and we were all wet and sweaty from moving those trunks. It was still our wedding night, and we were both tired, but we were very happy: our mission had been accomplished. In later years, we would look back on that night and laugh, realizing we were, without a doubt, the only two humans who had ever done *that* on their wedding night.

* * *

With the cards safely on the boat, Cheryl and I finished our packing and booked our flights out of Dutch. Two days later, we said our family goodbyes and headed to the Dutch Harbor airport, hoping to get out.

In 1973, a winter flight out of Dutch could be delayed for as much as seven to 10 days (and sometimes more) due to the horrible weather in the Aleutian chain. So you just showed up at the airport and, when you saw the Reeves Aleutian plane land, you knew you had a chance to get out. I say "chance" because the weather at that time of year could change in a minute, and the plane sometimes would not be able to take off once it landed.

Luckily for the newlyweds, our plane did get out that day, and we arrived in Seattle later that night.

Having been in Dutch for six months, the first thing we wanted to do the next day was eat something besides boat or cannery food (or Hamburger Helper!). We went out for breakfast and got to drink real milk, along with a great, fresh-tasting breakfast. For lunch, we ate a salad: lettuce, tomatoes, or any fresh produce was something rarely found in Dutch Harbor. And for dinner, we had McDonald's—sounds odd now, but back then, it tasted so good!

The *Mokihana* was scheduled to arrive at the Bellingham docks seven days after leaving Dutch. Cheryl and I borrowed her brother's pickup and drove to Bellingham to get those trunks off the boat. Driving that pickup truck on the freeway was scarier than fishing crab. All the cars zoomed by so fast!

In Bellingham, we met and thanked the *Mokihana*'s captain, went down those steep steps into the bowels of the ship—and there, in the engine room, sitting where we left them, were my three trunks of baseball cards.

3. A Family on the Edge of the World

I felt it was nothing short of a miracle that we got those cards out of the Aleutian Islands, off that boat, and back to civilization.

We loaded the trunks into the pickup, took them to the Bellingham Greyhound station, and shipped them to Cheryl's parents in Phoenix. A few days later, we followed them, flying home to Phoenix, too.

When we arrived at Cheryl's parents' home, her dad introduced himself to me, then immediately took me into the living room and sat me down on his green ottoman. My hair was long—down to the middle of my back—and I felt I was getting a look that said, "What has my daughter brought home?"

He asked me what I was going to do, now that Cheryl and I were back in Phoenix.

I said, "I'm not going to do anything. I'm going to take a break for a while."

That wasn't quite what Mr. Robinson wanted to hear from his new son-in-law.

He asked, "Are you going to get a job?"

I said, "No, I already worked. I'm going to take a break for a while."

He just rolled his eyes, shook his head—and muttered.

I probably should have explained to him more about crab fishing, how it was seasonal and, for six to eight months a year, it was among the hardest, most physical, and dangerous jobs in the world. That's why crab fishing paid so well and why a fisherman could afford to take a few months off after the season, to warm up and recover.

It took Mr. Robinson about five years to finally grasp what I did.

He never really understood my trading card business, either, until he visited us one year and toured the Pacific Trading Card factory.

In Phoenix, Cheryl and I rented an apartment and moved in right away. A couple of days later, my trunks showed up at her parents' house. I went over and brought them home to the apartment. My cards were finally safe with us! These were, without question, the most-traveled collection of baseball cards in the world!

Later that evening, when Cheryl's parents came for a visit, I was still sitting on the floor, trunks open, looking at my cards.

Her dad looked at me and muttered.

* * *

That winter in Phoenix, I had plenty of time and money. So I ran ads to buy cards and visited local candy wholesalers (businesses that supplied trading cards to grocery stores back then). I was looking to buy cases or boxes of cards.

One wholesaler I visited said he had several dozen cases of cards up in the company's attic. He had no idea what was up in that attic; he let me climb up there to take a look.

I could not believe what I saw—and I wanted all of it. Most candy wholesalers had return privileges with the card manufacturers, but this company had just put years and years of unsold cases in its attic.

I found more than 60 wax-box cases of cards. This was early 1974, so "older stuff" to me was 1964 and before. The cases dated back to 1964, with Leaf *Munsters* cards. (*The Munsters* was a mid–1960s TV sitcom, which gained even greater popularity in syndication.) The attic had seven cases of *Munsters* cards, with 20 boxes per case.

There were dozens of Topps baseball wax cases as old as 1967 and 21 other cases of Topps from various years. There were several cases of Topps football and basketball cards, six cases of Topps 1968 "Man on the Moon" cards, and then a lot of non-sport cases (such as the TV shows *The Partridge Family* and *Kung Fu*).

I bought all of them. Cheryl, her parents, and I opened most of those wax packs (and a lot of the cases) and got to work making complete sets. That's what my business was: I sold sets. And later, the sets from these cases would help jump-start my mail-order card business.

Our apartment started to fill up with cards pretty quickly. But I kept buying up collections. I ended up renting mini storage units, and soon I had a couple of big storage units stuffed to the rafters with cards. I didn't have time to sell much just then, so most of the cards just got stored away.

In February of 1974, I received a letter from my dad and mom, who were now living year-round in Dutch Harbor. The tanner crab (snow crab) winter season would start up soon, and fishing boats were beginning to arrive in Dutch from Seattle to gear up. Some boats were looking for experienced crab fishermen.

It was time for me to get back to Dutch and get in on that tanner crab season.

I told Cheryl we needed to start packing our stuff. We squeezed all of our possessions into the mini storage units (that were already brimming with cards). Our lease was up, so we said goodbye to the landlord and to Cheryl's family too.

We were off to our next adventure.

4

Sea Legs and Land Legs

A few days later, I flew back to Dutch Harbor, ready to get back to fishing. My dad had taken a job as chief engineer on the 100-foot boat the *Shellfish*. He told me that the captain was looking for one more crew member (only three deckhands worked on a crab boat back then). The crew would be paid a percentage of the boat's catch; my father and I would each get 8 percent.

I went down to the *Shellfish* to meet the captain. With my fishing experience, I was hired on the spot. This made the three-man crew my dad (chief engineer), the deck boss, and me. The interesting thing was, during the two-and-a-half-month season on that boat, the captain knew my dad and I were related but never knew we were father and son.

We had a fantastic season. The pots came up so full of big male tanner (snow) crab that you could not have squeezed another crab into the pot with a crowbar.

My dad and I had some of the best times of our lives working together on that boat. It was really nice to work beside each other toward this common goal every day. With only three crewmen working the deck, my dad and I picked each other up; we shared the load. We got a better chance to observe each other out in the world than most fathers and sons ever get.

We caught and delivered more than 750,000 pounds of crab to the Pan Alaska cannery that season. There were no quotas that year, so boats were able to fish until April.

The money we made was like winning the lottery.

While we were out fishing, my mother was still living in one of the Pink Apartments and looking out for a place for Cheryl so she could join me in Dutch. Cheryl, in the meantime, had flown to Billings, Montana, to visit her sister's family. In late March, one of the Pink Apartments became available, and my mother grabbed it for Cheryl and me. Shortly after that, Cheryl flew up to Dutch to join me. We had only been apart a month, but that was a month too long. She was able to get her old job back at Vern's store, so she could keep busy while I was gone fishing.

When the 1974 tanner crab season was over in April, Cheryl and I got to spend some time together. I spent the summer rigging crab pots for boats that were preparing for the upcoming king crab season, and Cheryl continued to work at Vern's.

When the 1974 king crab season started in mid–September, I got hired on my brother-in-law Kris's brand new 114-foot crab boat, the *Bering Sea*, as an extra crewman (there were four of us on deck). That boat could hold 180,000 pounds of live crab. During that king crab season, we caught and delivered more than a million pounds of crab.

When the season was over in late November and the cold Aleutian weather settled in, Cheryl and I packed up and flew back to Phoenix. We stayed a few days with her parents, then found a condominium to buy. We paid cash, so we could move right in.

I got right back into my cards. That's what I did when the fishing season was over: I was a baseball card dealer.

I designed and printed a mail-order catalog, with all my card sets and other items available for sale. I sent the new "Cramer Sports Promotion" catalog to all the collectors on my mailing list. I'd been compiling this list for years, filing contact info from collectors who ordered from my hobby magazine ads. I also added collectors' names and addresses I'd gathered when attending shows.

Ice buildup on the crab boat *The Bering Sea* in 1974. This could be dangerous, so the crew would bust the ice off with baseball bats (Cramer Family Archives).

4. Sea Legs and Land Legs

The orders flooded in.

February in Arizona means baseball spring training, and in 1975, the Milwaukee Brewers were in spring training camp in Sun City, Arizona.

I wanted to see Hank Aaron play.

Hank Aaron was a living legend. Just one year earlier, in April 1974, Aaron had broken Babe Ruth's career home run record of 714 when he hammered his own 715th in Atlanta. And, at that moment, Aaron was closing in fast on another prodigious Ruth record: baseball's all-time RBI record of 2,213.

In 1975, Hank Aaron was the greatest player in the game, and this was my chance to see him. I went to watch spring training games and took my camera along. I shot pictures of Aaron while he was in the on-deck circle and while he was batting.

I still have the photos.

At one of the games, I had a handful of baseball cards and was getting some Brewer players' autographs. A man saw what I was doing and approached me to introduce himself. Tommy Ferguson, I learned, was the Brewers traveling secretary, a position he'd held since the Brewers began as the Seattle Pilots in 1969. And his baseball background ran even deeper. In 1948, he had the distinction of being the bat boy for the Boston Braves.

He told me that he'd noticed the new 1975 Topps cards I was getting players to sign. He wanted to know where I got them, as he hadn't seen them yet and was himself an avid baseball card collector. I told him I got a sample box from the local Topps representative, but the cards weren't out to the public yet.

He liked that and started talking about his own collection of 1940 and 1941 Play Ball baseball cards. For about a half-hour, we were just two collectors talking about our baseball card collections; we could have gone on forever.

Then I told him I was a king crab fisherman in Alaska as well as a baseball card collector and baseball fan. I told him I had come to see Hank Aaron play that day. I said I was a big fan of Aaron's and had all 21 years of his Topps cards, plus a few others.

Tommy asked, "Mike, do you want Hank to sign your cards?"

I said, "Will he do that?"

Tommy said, "I'll ask him for you. Meet me here tomorrow after the game."

Wow!

I shook Tommy's hand until it nearly came off his arm. I couldn't wait until tomorrow!

I went home and dug out all of my Hank Aaron cards. (Boy, was I glad Cheryl and I got those cards onto that boat, even if it was on our wedding night!) I had 41 different Hank Aaron cards, including all of his Topps cards (1954 to 1975, counting All-Star cards and inserts), a Johnson Cookie card, and a few other regional releases.

The next day, I met Tommy after the game in the same spot we'd met before and showed him all of my beautiful, gem-mint Hank Aaron cards. Tommy told me Hank would meet us there after the game and he would sign my cards.

I couldn't thank Tommy enough, and I couldn't believe my luck!

As promised, after the game, Hank came out and met us. I showed him his cards. He was impressed that I had every one of them.

He looked at his 1954 Topps card and said, "That's my rookie card." He had a little smile on his face.

Then he said, "You have too many cards. I'll sign some today and some tomorrow."

I was a little disappointed … but I reminded myself how amazing it was to be getting even one real autograph, in person, from a real, living legend.

I laid the 1954 Topps in front of him first, and he signed it with my blue ballpoint pen. It looked beautiful with his autograph on it. Then he went right down the line, signing cards from 1955 through 1965, talking a little bit to me about each card. He knew his cards well.

Then he stopped.

"What are you going to do with these cards?" he asked. "Sell them?"

I said, "No! I collect them."

Tommy vouched for me. "Mike is a collector."

Hank continued signing his cards.

He picked up his 1964 Topps card. Looking at the back, he said, "I had a good year in 1963."

Although Hank had said he couldn't autograph all the cards that day, he did. When he finished, I thanked him over and over. All three of us were caught up in these baseball cards when, suddenly, we realized that someone had closed the gate to the parking lot where the Brewers players parked. Hank's car was in that lot! He had autographed all of my cards, and now he was stuck in the parking lot!

I ran over to the chain link gate and saw it didn't have a lock on it. I pushed open both sides of the gate so that Hank could drive out. He nodded at me in thanks as he drove by.

And then he was gone.

I met Hank Aaron in March 1975. In May, he broke the Babe's RBI record.

When he broke his first monumental record, Ruth's home run performance, I was in Dutch. I heard nothing and knew nothing of the racist

4. Sea Legs and Land Legs

backlash that preceded—and followed—his achievement. I only saw him as the great baseball player he was.

Looking back, I can see he was more than that. Here was a man at the height of a brilliant career that, through no fault of his own, was mired in controversy. Yet he must have seen something in me he liked or he wouldn't have taken the time to sign all my cards.

He was, to me, a great man.

I thanked Tommy again. And again and again. Later that week, Tommy came to my house to see my baseball card collection. I showed him my 1952 Topps Baseball set first. He was impressed. Then I pulled out my T-206, 1910 Tobacco baseball card set with Ed Plank (but no Wagner).

Seeing those cards put a smile on his face. I said, "Someday, I am going to get a Wagner and complete that set."

* * *

Cheryl and I spent most of our days packaging and mailing out card orders. But my brain was busy in the background....

In the spring of 1975, I went to see the general manager of the Phoenix Giants AAA baseball team, Ethan Blackaby. I had a promotional idea for him.

I proposed a Phoenix Giants players team set of trading cards. The card set would be given out to the first 2500 fans on a "Trading Card Night" at Phoenix Municipal Stadium. I would take all the players' photos, get the cards printed, and find a sponsor that could print their logo on the cards.

My idea came from cards I had collected, Pacific Coast League cards that go back to the early 1900s. Remar Bread made an Oakland Oaks team set for a few years in the late 1940s and early 1950s. My idea came somewhat from these cards, except I wanted to have a sponsor pay for the card printing and, in exchange, have a card night at the ballpark. The first 2500 fans would get, along with admission to the game, a set featuring the sponsor's logo. I did see a few minor league sets being made at that time, but I'm not for certain if mine was the first card night with a sponsor; it may have been. In the years after my set came out, a lot of other teams had card nights.

When I pitched the idea, Ethan loved it and said yes immediately. He also suggested Circle K convenience stores as a sponsor. I went to see them, and they signed up for the promotion. In later years, sponsors like Circle K would also be required to pay a fee to a team's major league affiliate to license the use of team logos on the cards. But when I made this set, there was no licensing by baseball. In fact, the card team set giveaway night was a new promotional concept for minor league teams. It was the first ever card night for the Phoenix Giants.

And it would be the first ever card set for me, for Cramer Sports Promotion.

I would even get to keep 500 sets of the cards (I knew I could easily sell them through my mail-order catalog).

Now, to make it happen.

There was no book or manual on how to make baseball cards, so I just had to figure out how to make them. Sure, there were some bumps in the road, but what I remember is the thrill of making my first set of baseball cards.

On the first day of the Giants 1975 season, I was at the stadium, posing the players and taking their photos with black and white film in my 35mm camera. While I waited for the photos to come back from the lab, I wrote all the copy for the backs of the cards, using the team media guides. I had selected a simple design for both the fronts and backs of the cards.

When the photos came back from the lab, I picked the best shot of each player, had the text for the cards typeset, then had a printer make a proof set of the cards.

With my proof set in hand, I went to show Ethan Blackaby my work.

He liked the cards but said the set was missing a player: himself. Ethan Blackaby was a former major league player but had never had a card made of him before. Sure, he worked in management now, but he was still part of the team.

I agreed, and we added him to the set. And, since we had to print an extra sheet to make his card (which had plenty of room for more cards), I decided to print one more card: of myself.

I had been trying to form a sports collectors club in Arizona. I thought, if I could get my message out to 2500 baseball fans with a card of myself, I might find some collectors in the mix of fans. I called Ethan to see what he thought about my idea, and he said sure, let's do it. I had a photo of me holding cards that had been taken by, and used in, the *Arizona Republic* newspaper. I got permission from the paper to use their photo for my card.

It was finally time to place the printing order for 3000 sets of cards, my first set of cards.

When the cards were given out to fans at the Phoenix Giants' card night, they were an overwhelming success. And the card I made of myself did help start a sports collectors club in Arizona. I got a great response from it.

And that was my first stint, making cards. I liked it so much, I went on making cards for the next 30 years. I would, in fact, become a major manufacturer of baseball and other collectible cards.

And all from just doing what I loved.

4. Sea Legs and Land Legs 47

* * *

I wanted to make more cards, and I had a new idea.

The Phoenix Suns were the 1975–1976 Western Conference Champs, and basketball fever was at an all-time high in Phoenix. So I made an appointment with Tom Ambrose, the director of marketing for the Phoenix Suns basketball team. I asked him if I could make a set of Suns player cards.

We made an agreement that I could make a set for the conference champs as well as an all-new set for the 1976–1977 Suns players. For the next two seasons, my Suns cards were sold at the games.

I was as happy as a clam in a bucket of water!

* * *

That spring of 1975, I got word of a brand new crab boat being built in Seattle. The captain was looking for a deckhand with experience rigging pots. Five hundred pots had been ordered, and they needed to be rigged and made ready to fish crab. It was time for me to get back to crab fishing. Fishing paid the bills at that time, and the fishing money was helping grow the baseball card business.

Cheryl and I closed up our condo and flew to Seattle. I went to Fisherman's Terminal to meet with the captain of the new 98-foot boat, the *Judi B*. After talking for just a few minutes, the captain of the *Judi B* said I could start right then and there.

I got right to work. Because I was the only crew member with extensive experience rigging crab pots, I was made the deck boss. I gathered the crew members together and began teaching them, so we could start our rigging right away. We had plenty to do in a short window of time.

We started right in on the gear. Miles of crab pot line had to be run out and cut into 40- and 50-fathom lengths. More than 1000 buoys needed inflating and painting. All these riggings for the crab pots had to be made ready and tied onto each pot, and each pot had to be finished and stacked on the dock, waiting to be loaded on the boat. It took a solid four months to build that gear.

Cheryl and I lived in a leased hotel room the entire time I worked on the gear. On my one or two days off, we went to Seattle area candy wholesalers that sold trading cards, and I bought every case of 1975 Topps baseball minis I could get my hands on. These cards were different from the regular 1975 Topps simply in that they were smaller. Seattle was one of the few areas where mini baseball cards were issued.

At that moment, Cheryl and I didn't have time to do anything more than just buy the cards and put them in storage. They sat there for a few years and quietly gained in value … a little like a fine wine.

In August, the crab pots were finally rigged, and 120 of them were loaded on the *Judi B*. The remaining pots were hauled to Dutch for us by other crab boats headed north.

I said my goodbyes to Cheryl once again; she would join me later in Dutch. The *Judi B* left Ballard through the locks, headed northeast across the Pacific Ocean to the Gulf of Alaska, then on to the Bering Sea.

My mother was still living in Unalaska and had found a tiny little house there for Cheryl to live in. Cheryl flew up to Dutch to get that house ready while she waited for me to arrive on the boat.

It was a grueling but productive 1975 king crab season for me, but I only got to be with Cheryl a few times. Our boat caught about 800,000 pounds of king crab, and we unloaded at canneries in Akutan, Sand Point and even Kodiak, but only once in Dutch—the very last load of the season.

On our way into Dutch with that last load, the weather in the Bering Sea was miserable and slow-going. The seas were huge; we were bucking into swells up to 30 feet high. One of those big green walls of water caught us right on the wheelhouse of the boat, and a flood of sea water knocked out two of the boat's pilot house windows.

Luckily, we had three-quarter-inch plywood stored on board, cut and ready to plug a window hole just in case that happened. We turned the boat around and ran with the seas while we made temporary repairs. That sea water went down through the state rooms into the galley, and most of it ended up in the bilge. It was pumped out of the boat, but it left a crusty, salty mess behind; we cleaned up salt water for days.

When I got home, I learned that the Unalaska winter had not been fun for Cheryl. The snow had gotten up to six feet deep, and the oil tank that fueled her little house and stove had gotten low. The truck that delivered fuel couldn't get close enough to the little house to deliver it because the snow was too deep.

The oil folks told Cheryl that they could roll a 50-gallon drum of oil to the tank—if Cheryl shoveled a 50-foot path through that snow from the road to the oil tank.

So she did. They delivered the oil—then handed her a hand pump. In the cold, freezing snow, Cheryl pumped fuel into a bucket, hauled it up a ladder and dumped it in the oil tank—one bucket at a time.

When I was finally able to see her again, I heard about that. She was not happy. She was pretty tough and got it done, but it was the last season Cheryl ever went to Dutch.

We were ready for warm weather. Cheryl and I packed up our belongings and loaded them onto the *Judi B*. Cheryl would ride on the boat with us back to Seattle. This was her first time doing that.

Before embarking, we ate our Thanksgiving dinner on the boat, then

4. Sea Legs and Land Legs 49

left the dock to head south. As soon as we passed Priest Rock, Cheryl was seasick.

It was a miserable trip with rough seas, snowing, blowing, and freezing. We couldn't cut across the Gulf of Alaska; it was just too rough. So we headed up the Aleutian chain toward Kodiak Island.

The boat began to build up so much ice from the freezing sea spray, we had to go into Chignik Bay, where we got out the baseball bats and started busting ice off the boat, then shoveling off the mess. In a freezing cold storm like this, the entire top structure of the boat could be covered very quickly with six inches to a foot of ice.

Cheryl felt a little better, good enough that she even helped. But as soon as the weather cleared a bit, and we were heading across the Gulf of Alaska on the great circle for Dixon Entrance, Cheryl didn't come out of her bunk except to puke for seven days straight. I really felt bad for her, but there was nothing I could do.

When we got to Dixon Entrance and the calmer waters of the Inside Passage, she emerged from her bunk and was alive again. It's amazing how a person can recover that quickly from seasickness.

Within days, Cheryl and I were headed back to Phoenix for the offseason.

My 1975 Topps baseball mini cases stayed behind in a storage unit in Edmonds, Washington.

* * *

But make no mistake, I was back into my trading cards. Later in February, I went to see my old friend Ethan Blackaby, general manager of the Phoenix Giants. We put the wheels in motion for another Phoenix Giants ballpark card night, plus another new Phoenix Giants premium card promotion.

Coca-Cola sponsored the 1976 Phoenix Giants set, and I produced the cards in color. I took all the photos except one. I also made a black and white Coke Phoenix Giants mail-in premium set that year; it was a hit too.

During that time, I was contacted by Motorola. Motorola wanted to use baseball cards to promote their upcoming sales convention. I produced a Motorola Baseball Old Timers set. I used several photos from my M101 Sporting News Supplement baseball set—these images were striking and unique. The set turned out really nice, and Motorola was very pleased.

By summer, I was ready to head back to Seattle and the boats. Cheryl stayed home in Phoenix and sorted cards, making sets and keeping our Cramer Sports Promotion mail-order business alive.

The 1976 king crab season was, well, different for me. Cheryl was not up in Dutch, and I missed her. I hired on with a really good friend and hard worker who had a 116-foot crab boat named the *Scorpio*. We were ready for a season of hard work and plenty of it, but that all came to a halt: the crab fleet started out the season on strike, wanting a higher crab price.

The boats were tied up, eight to 10 across, at the docks and canneries in Dutch. The crews just sat it out, waiting, all caught up with work. Some days, when the weather was decent, we played softball on a rocky field in Unalaska. We had plenty of bats (in case we encountered freezing cold temperatures and ice buildup on the boats) but only one ball. No one had a baseball glove, but that didn't matter; most of us could drive nails with our bare hands.

At night, most of the crews played cards. I got an idea from watching those card games. After the season was over, I went back home and started making a set of playing cards.

Fifty-two boats in the crab fleet were pictured on the cards.

The 1976 king crab season did finally start a month late, and the boats all headed out to the crab grounds at once. It was feast or famine for the crab boats. To catch a share of the quota, it was balls to the wall. Whoever worked the hardest caught the most—and, of course, the captain had to set the pots on good fishing grounds.

After five straight days of working with little or no sleep, we had all of our pots in the water, fishing. Then we went back to the first pots we'd set and started hauling the gear.

The first pot came up absolutely chock full of big, beautiful keepers.

We were on them! We hauled steady for two days, setting back every pot. When we finished hauling the last pot in the string, the boat was filled with more than 225,000 pounds of king crab. That 84 hours, from the time of setting gear to plugging the boat with crab, was the longest stretch I ever worked without sleeping more than just a catnap.

With the boat full, we took the load to Kodiak. The cannery there would pay more per pound for the crab.

The season was going great. We had delivered about 850,000 pounds of crab. As we were unloading at the floating cannery East Point, I heard that my brother-in-law's boat, the *Bering Sea*, had a man hurt and was looking for a new crewman.

I really wanted to work on Kris's boat again. It was the top boat in the fleet. I ran to the UniSea cannery through the snow, where the *Bering Sea* was tied up. I went on board and went to see Kris right away.

It had already been a long season, and we had both worked long hours with little sleep.

The first thing he said was "You look like shit."

"You too," I said right back.

He talked to his brother, Erik, for a moment, then turned back to me and said, "Let's go get your gear." I went back and got my sea bag off the *Scorpio*, and I said goodbye to Jim Trueman, a great friend.

Soon, I was on the *Bering Sea*, the best boat in the fleet, standing on the deck, heading out of Dutch to crab fishing grounds that we knew were ready and rich.

We put in a couple more boat loads of crab, but then, as fate would have it—I got hurt.

I was coiling line, the hydraulic lever was reversed—and my left hand was smashed in the power block. By the time I got to the Anchorage hospital four days later, gangrene had set in on my torn-open middle finger. I spent seven days in the hospital while the doctors stabilized my hand.

I was feeling OK and able to call Cheryl several times. But my season was over, and she wanted me to come home. I wanted to go home too. After five days in that hospital, I was tired of the bland food they served and wanted something good to eat.

I still had one good hand and could feed myself. So I asked the nurse for a phone book. She brought me one, and a large pepperoni pizza was delivered to my hospital bedside about 40 minutes later.

The nurse was not too happy about that … but it was the best pizza ever!

After seven days and one operation, I was stable enough to fly home to Cheryl in late November.

It was great to be home.

I used the word fate earlier, because that injury steered my life on a different path. At home, I was able to concentrate more on our mail-order card business and really jump up sales a few notches. Cheryl and I spent the winter, spring, and summer sorting cards, making sets and shipping orders. Collectors were buying cards, and we had plenty of good stuff to sell.

Our mailing list was growing, and we had nearly 20,000 collectors from all over the United States and Canada buying cards from us. And I saw more opportunities: I started to buy vending card cases from Topps. (Vending cases were cards packed in bulk and unsorted, 12,000 cards to a case.)

Topps had vending cases of baseball, football, hockey and basketball cards. I bought several hundred cases at a time, filling up all my mini storage space. Because my hand wasn't quite healed yet, Cheryl and her parents often unloaded the cases from the delivery truck.

That spring, I again visited my old friend, Phoenix Giants general manager Ethan Blackaby. He said that Trading Card Night at the ballpark was so successful, five other Pacific Coast League teams wanted to have one like it. So, in 1977, I produced and printed card sets for each of those five PCL teams.

I took all the photos. Cheryl and I drove down to Tucson so I could shoot the Toros' player photos. Cheryl sat on a bench, waiting patiently for me to take all the player photos. When I was taking catcher Rick Stelmaszek's photo, I noticed Cheryl there in the background. I turned the camera a bit so she was more plainly in view, then shot the photo.

She ended up being pictured on Rick's card (in the background).

Cheryl has one of those Rick Stelmaszek cards, and he autographed it for her.

* * *

Our card business was really beginning to take off. The more time I had to spend on it, the bigger it grew.

I hired more than 25 people to laboriously sort the 12,000 bulk cards from a vending case box into sellable sets. And I was getting new ideas....

I made a deal with a company that made plastic photo sheets. I wanted them to make plastic sheets for me that would hold baseball cards. The measurements worked out perfectly: one 8½-by-11-inch plastic sheet could hold nine baseball cards. So we made plastic sheets with nine small pockets. After collectors filled those pockets with cards they wanted to protect, they could store the sheets in a three-ring binder.

I took 1000 nine-pocket plastic sheets to a card show in Anaheim, California. Those sheets were a hit; I sold all of them in the first hour.

And suddenly, we were in the plastic sheet business.

Over the next 10 years, we sold more than 10 million of those sheets before other companies started making them. By then, it didn't matter to me. We were on to bigger and better things.

While we were at the California show with our very first plastic sheets, I got wind of a toy wholesaler who had some old baseball cards in his warehouse. We went to visit that company right after the show, to see what might be there. I talked to the owner, who said, "Yes, I have cards. But I only sell by the box. How many do you want?" I said, "How many boxes and cases do you have?" He said, "More than you want!"

Then he took me into his warehouse. He had 10 pallets of various trading cards. Some pallets were stacked high with cases of cards; some pallets had unopened vending cases on them.

Two pallets had 1964 Topps Baseball All-Stars cards, about 60 cases in all. I knew that set: they were postcard-size cards of 60 different players, including Mickey Mantle, Hank Aaron, and Sandy Koufax. There were approximately 6,000 cards in each case.

On other pallets were cases of Topps vending baseball and boxes of 500-count vending baseball, dating back to 1959. A few pallets had

4. Sea Legs and Land Legs

non-sport vending cases and boxes, dating back to 1959: "Beatles," *Man from U.N.C.L.E.*, "Fabian," "Nutty Awards," "Combat," and on and on.

I said, "I want all of it."

The owner just asked, "How are you going to pay?"

We came back later in the day and loaded our pickup truck and a 20-foot U-Haul trailer full of cases of cards. I then had the remaining cases shipped over to our mini storage units in Phoenix.

It was one of the best deals I made in the card business. The old Pacific Trading Cards catalogs listed the sets from that buy for years to come—and we sold those cards for years to come.

When the truck showed up at the mini storage with the cards, Cheryl's father, Frank, came to help me unload the cases. He just shook his head. He couldn't understand why I needed so many cards and thought I was wasting my money. But he was a great help unloading; he was a great guy.

In March of 1977, I held the second-ever Arizona Sports Collectors Show. This show took place during spring training in Scottsdale, at the Chicago Cubs Scottsdale Stadium. It was more than just a local show this time. I sold 30 or so dealer tables, and some card dealers came all the way from California for the show.

It turned out to be a decent show, with free autograph guests. Charlie Grimm and Ernie Banks signed for hours for free. In those early days of hobby shows, we never thought of charging collectors a fee to get a player's autograph. Why would we? Players always signed for free back then.

That show had the largest attendance of any card show ever held up to

Topps baseball vending cases, 12,000 cards per case. In 1976, we ordered hundreds of them to make complete sets of 660 cards to sell in our mail order catalog (Cramer Family Archives).

1977. Our secret? The 5000-plus fans who came to watch the baseball game could only exit the stadium by passing through a hall—and that hall just happened to be where the card show was being held!

When the game ended, 5000-plus baseball fans flooded into the hall all at once. Dealers were so busy, they didn't know whether to fish or cut bait.

For about 10 minutes, we heard all the standard comments from baseball fans:

"Oh, I had those, but my mother threw my cards away when I went to college."

"What's that card worth? I have one."

"I had cards! I put them in my bicycle spokes to make noise."

When the rush was over and the crowd had left the hall, Goodie Goldfaden, a dealer from California, yelled out, "My God! What a crowd! Did anybody sell anything?"

The dealers did make some sales but, mainly, we exposed 5000 fans to the hobby of collecting sports memorabilia. Cheryl and I were prepared and managed to hand out more than 500 of our catalogs, and that paid off in future orders for our trading card business.

* * *

That year, 1977, Topps released a set of Baseball Cloth Stickers. The cards were released regionally, and Arizona was one of the places they were sold.

I went to every candy wholesaler in the Phoenix area and bought every case I could get my hands on (which was most of them). We made sets and put them in our catalog. I listed them with a time-honored sales gimmick: "Hot Off the Press!"

The local Topps representative knocked on my door one day and asked me if I was printing 1977 Topps stickers. That's what my catalog seemed to say.

I said, "No! I'm not *printing* them."

"Then where did you get them?" he asked. "They were all sold out in this area."

I said, "They are all sold out because I bought them all."

Here was another guy, shaking his head at me for buying so many baseball cards—just like my dad and Cheryl's dad too!

I struck up a friendship with that sales rep. In fact, he would be somewhat responsible for leading me to the famous Topps-Pacific closeout deal that allowed me to buy unsold Topps trading cases by the thousands. I told him I would like to buy any cases Topps had left over. I knew that, back then, retail stores and candy wholesalers could return cards to Topps

4. Sea Legs and Land Legs

for credit if the cards didn't sell and also get the next product that Topps made.

The rep told me that most of those closeout cases were going to Mexico or a place in California called Jack's Wholesale. (Later, I went to Jack's and bought all of the old cases that they had.)

But about a week after I spoke with the rep, Tom Williams of Topps called me. He was the West Coast regional manager. He asked me what Topps cards I was interested in, and I told him I would buy every case of cards they had left over: baseball, football, hockey, basketball and non-sports.

I think he was stunned.

We made a deal for the case prices and, within a week, trucks full of closeout cases as old as 1968 were showing up. I rented more and more mini storage units. This was the single greatest buy in the history of trading cards—and this deal went on for years. I bought thousands of cases in every configuration Topps made. Most of it, I just stored away, because I was still gone fishing most of the year. But Topps was happy to clean out their old inventory.

I was happy to buy those cases.

We were probably the only two that were happy at that time. My dad, my father-in-law, my friends and my relatives all thought I could surely find a better way to spend my hard-earned money.

5

The Move to Seattle

In the summer of 1977, Cheryl and I were at her parents' house for a family gathering when the phone rang. It was my mother with a message from my brother-in-law, Kris, the captain of the *Bering Sea*.

He was building a new crab boat to be named the *Arctic Sea*. It would be launched in the summer of 1978, and he had a job for me on that boat—if I would move permanently to the Seattle area. I would need to be ready to start working on rigging the crab pots in December of 1977.

This was my dream job.

After all, I was a king crab fisherman, and this was my chance to permanently join the best skipper in the fleet. I said yes even before I asked Cheryl.

When I hung up, I told her we were moving to Seattle.

"When?" she asked.

"Now," I said.

We went home, packed our bags, and drove 19 hours straight through to Seattle. We looked for a house right away and bought one in Edmonds. Because we paid cash, we were able to close in 10 days. While in Edmonds, I also rented several mini storage units so I would have a place to put our card inventory.

We flew back to Phoenix to sell our condo and pack our household belongings into a rental truck. We hired three semi-trucks to ship our Phoenix card inventory to the Edmonds mini storage, where the 1975 Topps Baseball Mini cases had been waiting for more than two years.

Cheryl drove our car, and a good friend and I drove the rental truck back to our new home in Edmonds. That was a very big move, and it changed our lives. But there was even bigger news:

I was going to be a father!

Once we were settled in our new home, I got my trading cards organized. We had a big new home, with plenty of space to work filling orders.

There were other perks to living in the Seattle area. The city's new professional baseball team, the Seattle Mariners, debuted in April 1977, and I became a Seattle Mariners fan.

5. The Move to Seattle

And I started to think about fishing. I decided that I would head back to Dutch, to get in on the 1977 king crab season before Kris needed me in December. The 1977 Bering Sea king crab season began on September 15; the projected end date that season was November 20.

When I decided to fish that season, I didn't have a boat lined up, so I flew up to Dutch Harbor and stayed with my sister, Anji. Kris, her husband, was not there, as his boat was out fishing already.

But Anji knew the superintendent at the UniSea cannery really well. She had asked him to please let her know if he heard of a boat that needed a deckhand so she could tell her brother (me). I had slept on her floor for less than a week when Anji got a message: The crab boat *North Pacific* was coming in with their first load of the season, and one of the crew had quit.

I was at the dock when the boat tied up. I went on board and found the skipper and told him who I was and my experience. He said, "Get your sea bag, and welcome aboard."

I said, "I brought my sea bag with me. I'm ready to fish." I spent the 1977 king crab season on that boat. He was a rare skipper who could "smell crab." Our pots came up full all season.

At season's end in late November, we stored our pots and I flew home to Seattle. It had been another great money-making season. I would soon be back with Cheryl and would get to work right away, rigging pots for the *Arctic Sea*.

* * *

Cheryl had been busy filling card orders while I was away, and she was very happy for me to be home. Once I got settled into the routine of working on crab pots, I spent most of my spare time working on our mail-order business. I got back to publishing a new Cramer Sports Promotions catalog, full of our latest card sets and plastic sheets.

The new year began with an actual new beginning: on January 18, 1978, Cheryl and I were blessed with our first child, Rachael Elizabeth Cramer. Like so many oldest children, Rachael had a big job ahead of her, teaching us about our new responsibilities.

Cheryl was able to keep up with motherhood and our mail-order card business during the times I was gone fishing. Our catalog mail-order address was now out of our home in Edmonds.

I did manage to make some cards that year too. Six Pacific Coast League teams signed up with me for card nights at their ballparks. I produced all the cards, and I took photos for the Tacoma Yankees. A great friend of mine, Wayne Grove, shot photos of the other teams.

The biggest change I made that year was renaming our mail-order card business. Cramer Sports Promotions was okay but didn't quite fit anymore. The promotion side of the business had pretty much taken a back seat to the mail-order card sales.

The new name I chose for our business: Pacific Trading Cards.

My theory was this: when we took a crab boat from Seattle to get to the Bering Sea, we went out of the Strait of Juan de Fuca into the Pacific Ocean. We then crossed the Gulf of Alaska (an arm of the Pacific) and entered the rich crab grounds of the Bering Sea. So … the Pacific led to the jackpot of gold in the rich Bering Sea! It was a perfect new name, I thought.

And, later, Pacific Trading Cards became my new jackpot of gold.

* * *

I spent the winter of 1977 through the summer of 1978 rigging 600 crab pots for the *Arctic Sea*.

In early August, Kris came and took a couple of us to the Marco shipyards in Ballard, Washington, where the *Arctic Sea* was being built.

It was a beautiful boat. Blue with white and dark yellow trim, 120 feet long, with big tanks that would hold 250,000 pounds of live crab—all I could think was "We only have to fill that boat four times to catch a million pounds!"

This was going to be a big season for the crew of that boat. I was excited to get back fishing.

Unfortunately, I also learned late that summer that my dad had lung cancer.

* * *

By mid–August, our pots were fully rigged, and we had 250 of them on board the *Arctic Sea*. We were ready to head north to the Bering Sea and Dutch Harbor.

I loaded 2500 decks of my new king crab boat playing cards on board to take to Dutch. I would try to sell them to Vern's, Carl's (another store), and the captains and crews of the boats that the cards depicted.

I said my goodbyes to Cheryl and Rachael for another season; I would be gone for four months. I boarded the *Arctic Sea*, and we left from Fishermen's Terminal in Ballard. It took about eight days to cross that big ocean, traveling at 10 knots.

When we got to the dock in Dutch, I got some cases of my new crab boat card decks off the boat and showed them around. Everyone I showed them to loved them—and bought them! I sold all of the 2500 decks I brought up with me within a few hours.

When I saw fishermen playing cards on their boats before the season started, I saw that they were playing with my cards. And more people wanted them, so I had Cheryl ship more. We had a winning hand!

5. The Move to Seattle

The Arctic Sea going through the Ballard Locks in 1978, me getting one last look at Cheryl and Rachael. I wouldn't see them again for five months. I'm on the stack of crab pots on the stern of the boat (Cramer Family Archives).

In 1978, when the cards debuted, fishing crab in the Bering Sea was big business. That year, a fleet of more than 200 boats set out on those cold, rough, dangerous waters. Every man on board wanted to catch a share of the year's quota, set at more than 130 million pounds of king crab.

There was no quota per individual boat. Each boat raced to the crab grounds, often staying out in the Bering Sea for days or weeks at a time, catching and filling its tanks with king crab.

The 1978 crab season was fantastic for the *Arctic Sea*. We put in well over a million pounds of king crab, and the crew shares were … well, it was the height of the king crab fishing boom.

We were rolling in dough!

We crewmen often talked among ourselves about what we were doing with all the money we were making. Some said they were going to invest in real estate; others said they were saving to buy a boat. One guy said he was buying bonds. When it was my turn to talk, I said, "I'm buying baseball cards, thousands of cases of baseball cards." By this time I was also buying thousands of bulk closeout cases of cards directly from the Topps plant in Duryea, Pennsylvania.

That raised a few eyebrows! None of those guys thought that was a good idea.

Me in 1978 with a big king crab on the crab boat *The Arctic Sea* (Cramer Family Archives).

In reality, not many king crab fishermen invested their hard-earned money. Sad as it was, many crewmen just simply blew all of it, having a good time. And when they ran out of money, they went back to fishing.

Before the season ended, I learned that Kris was building another boat at Marco Shipyards, a sister ship to the *Arctic Sea*, to be named the *North Sea*. Another 600 crab pots needed to be rigged. I was asked to join the new boat.

That was perfect for me. I could be home for the spring and summer of 1979, working on gear.

I only made two sets of cards that summer: a set for the Phoenix Giants Valley National Bank and a set for the Hawaii Islanders. I was busy rigging crab pots. I did, however, buy several semi-loads of Topps closeouts. With no time to sell them, I just stored them away.

In the spring of 1979, we worked five long days a week on the gear

5. The Move to Seattle

for the *North Sea*. At the beginning of the summer, we put in even longer hours and worked nearly every day, sunup to sundown. It was great, though—I loved it. I always told myself that at least I got to be home every night and spend a little time with my wife and my new daughter.

Of course, later that summer, I had to say my goodbyes to Cheryl and Rachael. I wouldn't see them for five months. But I wouldn't be entirely separated from family on this trip. My brother, Marty, was hired on the boat that year. He had fished on the old *Honey-B* way back when. It was fun to have him on board.

The *North Sea* headed across the North Pacific Ocean to Unimak Pass and the Bering Strait, where we were going to do some exploratory crab fishing.

During the four-day trip, when Kris and I shared a wheel watch shift, he told me he wasn't so sure I should be spending so much of my hard-earned money buying baseball cards. Kris was a good investor, and it just didn't sound like a prudent idea to him.

Years later, when we were both retired, we talked about that and just laughed. Who knew in the 1970s that baseball cards would grow into a billion-dollar industry? Oh! Maybe I knew?!

We baited and launched our deck load of exploratory pots in the Bering Strait. When we pulled the pots the next day, they came up full of completely full-grown *miniature* male king crab!

The whole crew, including me, was surprised that we'd caught miniature crab, only about four inches across the back. Canneries weren't interested in buying them, so nothing ever became of that Bering Strait crab fishery.

Even if our exploratory fishing wasn't as successful as we'd hoped, we enjoyed perfect weather up there. That was the only time I ever hauled crab pots with no rain gear on and wearing only shirt sleeves. It never got dark that far north in the summer; the sun was up all 24 hours a day.

On one of those days, we got to witness a total eclipse of the sun, the most beautiful thing in nature I have ever seen. When the moon crossed over in front of the sun, it was so close to us, I felt like I could touch them both.

We started the long trip back to Dutch to get ready for the upcoming 1979 king crab season. When the season started, Kris got us on the crab right away, as he always did; he was a rare captain that could smell crab. We quickly loaded the *North Sea* with 250,000 pounds of crab and headed to the UniSea cannery in Dutch. We were the first boat in the fleet to come in with a load.

It took about 24 hours for the cannery workers to unload the crab. As soon as we were unloaded, we dropped lines and headed back to the

The three "Sea" boats—*The North Sea, The Bering Sea* and *The Arctic Sea*—in 1979. I worked on all of them; they were the highline boats of the crab fleet (Cramer Family Archives).

Bering Sea crab grounds, 24 to 36 hours out of Dutch. We tidied up the deck and battened down the crab tank hatches on the way out of the harbor; it could get rough as soon as we passed Priest Rock.

About 30 minutes before we arrived on the gear, Captain Kris came over the loudspeakers and woke up the crew. We jumped into our oilskins, put on our boots and gloves, and went out on deck to ready ourselves to haul gear.

I swung out the power block over the port side and locked it in place. The hydraulic wheel pulled the polyline rope that was attached to the crab pot, lifting it off the floor of the Bering Sea.

There was always some anticipation when we hauled our first string of gear. This was a different era in crab fishing. If the pots had 100 or more big keeper crab in them, we probably would set the pots back in the same spot and get our tanks filled in quick order. If the pots had fewer than 100 keepers, we would most likely put the crab in our tank, then stack the pots on deck to move them to richer crab grounds.

Based on the amount of crab in the pots, Kris could tell which way the crab schools were moving, and he was able to keep us on the schools all season long. That man could catch crab. He was incredible, the best skipper in the Bering Sea crab fleet.

It took us only a day and a half to fill the tanks with our second load of the season. We had another 250,000 pounds on board and headed back to town to unload. The crew was very happy. We had all just made a nice chunk of change, but we were all exhausted from the work (even though we each got a couple of hours of rack time during the trip).

We would celebrate this fast money-making trip by eating a great dinner of roasted duck, potatoes, and frozen vegetables on the trip back to Dutch. The cook had thawed out six one-and-a-half-pound ducks, one per man. Believe me, after a trip like that, we could eat plenty of food, and a whole duck was a fine meal.

We could smell the ducks cooking in the galley oven, and that made us even hungrier. Finally, the cook said dinner was ready. We were starved. We sat down at the galley table, which was covered in a green rubber mesh to keep our bowls and plates from sliding.

I took this photograph on *The North Sea* in 1979. **We were catching crab and dumping them out of the pots with a hydraulic pot rack. Making big money!**

We dove into our absolutely delicious, crispy duck dinner, cooked to perfection. Kris always took the first wheel watch, to let the crew eat first. He really respected his crew and knew we were hungry from the countless hours of hard physical labor.

Any man who fished king crab during those heydays knows that a crew could consume its dinner in record time—I mean wolf it down! Those ducks were going to be gone in a matter of minutes.

Our engineer finished his dinner first and went up the wheelhouse ladder to relieve Kris on the wheelhouse bridge, so Kris could come enjoy his crispy duck. (It was one of Kris' favorite meals.)

Around that time, the weather had come up, and the *North Sea* was pitching and rolling a bit in the swells. We had to hang on to our plates and try to eat moving duck and potatoes sliding around on our plates. But not a problem; we were used to it.

Kris came down the wheelhouse ladder, which was about 12 steps, saying in his Danish accent, "That duck smells delicious." As he got to the bottom step, the boat took a hard pitch to starboard.

Just at that moment, the cook opened the galley stove door to retrieve the last duck for Kris. When the boat pitched, the duck shot out of the oven and flew through the cook's legs, skidding and sliding across the galley floor right past Kris on the way to the head. The boat rolled. The duck jumped the galley floorboard and zipped into the head (no one saw it, but we all knew that duck was making a beeline around the toilet: it was the only way out of the head!) As the boat rolled back to port, the duck came shooting back out of the head, around the cook's feet—and ended up right at the base of the wheelhouse ladder where Kris was standing on the bottom step. He looked down at that duck in total astonishment.

We were all stunned, and the cook was devastated. It all happened so fast! We just sat there at the galley table, looking at Kris.

Then Kris broke the dead silence with his Danish accent. " Is … that … my … duck?" And that's all he said.

It was just too funny. We all burst out laughing. We had just seen a cooked duck make an impossible journey through the boat galley—and Kris handled it so well!

He had a cheese and salami plate instead of his duck dinner.

We still laugh about that, 40 years later.

6

The Million Dollar Topps Deal
Game Changer #1

We got into Dutch late in the day. Before we even landed at the UniSea cannery, we had the first tank cover off to start unloading.

I had about an hour during that time to call Cheryl from the cannery's newly-installed phone. I didn't have much contact with her during the season; a couple of letters came through, and a rare phone call was a treat (landlines weren't easy to find up north, and there were no cell phones back then). I finally got through, bad connection and all.

Cheryl was crying.

She was pregnant with our second child, and three semi-truck loads of Topps closeout cases had come in the last week or so. She couldn't unload them on her own and was running out of friends to come and help. She had also rented the last mini storage unit the facility had available. She said, "Mike, you need to do something!"

I went back to the *North Sea* and pulled out my *Trader Speaks*. I wrote up a quarter page sales ad, listing some of the cases I knew we had in those storage units. I wrote a check for the ad and mailed it from Dutch Harbor.

The ad appeared in *The Trader Speaks* late that autumn. By then, the crab season was nearly over; it had been an outstanding season for the *North Sea* crew.

I was able to call Cheryl. Unfortunately, she had a new problem:

So many orders for cases had come in from the ad, she couldn't possibly fill them.

She needed help.

I said, "Hang on! I will be home in about 10 days." Because my wife was pregnant and my dad was sick, Kris said I could fly home instead of riding the boat to Seattle.

This little story was actually the ultimate game changer for Cheryl and me. Our lives would never be the same.

I returned home just after Thanksgiving to my wife and little daughter, who didn't know who I was. We went and visited my dad and mom, then I got to work filling those case orders.

Buying all those cases of Topps cards was paying off.

Having just come off the crab season, I could work long hours with little sleep—and I did. I worked night and day, shipping cases to collectors and to dealers. These entrepreneurs were just starting to open card stores all across the country, for this was the moment the trading card business was starting to really blossom. The dealers with shops needed card inventory, and I had plenty to offer.

I look back on that time in my life and realize: if that ad I ran hadn't produced many sales, I probably would have become a crab boat skipper. And that would have been a great career for me. But, as Joe DiMaggio once said to me, "It's funny where your fate takes you."

By early February of 1980, the *North Sea* was ready to head back to Dutch for the winter tanner crab season. I had to tell Kris I wasn't coming, I was too busy with my baseball cards.

I couldn't believe it, and he couldn't believe it, either. I finally had my crab fishing dream job, but I was giving it all up for baseball cards.

I told Kris that I would be able to go back to fishing as soon as I caught up with orders.

I never did catch up on filling orders, and the more time I spent on the card business, the busier I got. For the next five years, around king crab season time, I got the itch to go to Dutch—but I was always just too busy.

I never went back to Dutch.

My 10 years of crab fishing had officially come to an end.

* * *

By late February, I finally got caught up filling orders. But our home address was on the Pacific Trading Cards catalog as well as in the ads we were still running. Collectors in the Seattle area (and their numbers kept growing) kept coming *to our house* to buy cards.

We were swamped! I had to get the business out of our home.

I found a retail location near our house and opened a trading card store. We named the store Pacific Trading Cards, Inc. I incorporated the business in 1980.

Shortly after that, we went to visit my parents. After being a crab fisherman and working on the Alaska North Slope, my dad had retired to a small farm in Monroe, Washington. I told him about my card sales that

6. The Million Dollar Topps Deal

Pacific Trading Cards' store grand opening in 1980. It was a hit! More than 1,000 people came to the store that day (Pacific Trading Cards Archives).

year and said I was so busy with the business I probably wouldn't get to go fishing again.

"I'm sure glad we didn't throw away those trunks of cards you had in Dutch Harbor," he said. "I don't know why we didn't toss them."

I was sure happy that they didn't!

* * *

Pete Williams of *USA Today* wrote an article about me in later years, saying that I was the first dealer to make a million dollars in the trading card hobby. That winter of 1979–1980 is when it happened.

I had the new Pacific Trading Cards store running well. I had hired a couple of great people to work there, and that helped free me up. One of my great hires was Ann Ninneman (Ann Hicks).

In the early days of the store, Ann came in every week, always with exactly $2 to spend. She looked about 15 years old. One day she said to me, "Can I work here?" I smiled at her and said, "Sure! Do you want to start now?" She said, "I have to call my mom first."

Ann started work at Pacific Trading Cards and stayed for 14 years. She was a key factor in the early growth of Pacific, managing the retail store and mail-order catalog.

Another key person that joined Pacific early was Rae Randall. Rae started as our shipping clerk, mailing our orders to collectors all over the country. When Pacific grew big enough that I needed a secretary, she became my secretary, and worked until 1996 when she married and left to raise her family.

I hired my sister Kathi to work in my store, and she really didn't know much about baseball. On her first day, I asked her to make a store display for the new Major League Baseball mini helmet coin banks we had just gotten in. That same day, a customer walked into the store to buy baseball cards and asked her if we had any Ernie Banks.

She had baseball helmet banks on her mind and answered, "No, we don't have any Ernie Banks, and we don't have any Berts, either."

It took a minute to dawn on both the customer and me what was happening: *Sesame Street* was really popular at the time.

I realized then that I needed to hire people with at least some knowledge of sports!

In April of 1980, our second daughter, Angela Kathleen, was born. I had a growing family, and I was happy to be there with them, not fishing in Alaska.

Also that spring, a very tall man named Phil Roth walked into the store and introduced himself. He was to become my new outside accountant and CPA and a key figure in the future of Pacific Trading Cards for the next 25 years.

I didn't have to promote the new card store; it was such a novelty that it promoted itself. The *Seattle Times*, the *Seattle Post Intelligencer* and the Everett newspaper all sent reporters out. We received a windfall of publicity, and a regular stream of new customers quickly became regular customers.

Early that spring, a new collector who walked in looked somehow familiar....

It was Seattle Seahawks quarterback/coach Jerry Rhome.

We struck up a friendship, and he was able to get the hottest player in Seattle sports history (up to that time) to appear at Pacific Trading Cards to sign autographs: Jim Zorn.

More than one thousand collectors lined up inside and outside of the store to get Zorn's autograph that day. Store sales went through the roof after that.

Jerry Rhome also got me jerseys to display in the store, game-worn by Zorn and another player named Steve Largent. (Jerry told me then, in 1980, that Steve Largent would be a Hall of Famer someday. Rhome was 100 percent right on that.)

In May of 1980, we moved the Pacific offices into a warehouse across the road. I was finally able to get my inventory of card cases out of the mini storage units and all under one roof!

6. The Million Dollar Topps Deal

In August of 1981, I got a call from my mother. My dad had taken a turn for the worse.

At that time, I was just happy I'd had that one season with him on the *Shellfish* in 1974 and that he was also able to finally see that I could actually make a living from baseball cards.

He died shortly after that.

My mother came to work at Pacific, on the mail-order side. She worked with me for 15 years and got to see and be part of Pacific as the whole business grew by leaps and bounds.

I had hired some great people to work at Pacific, and they continued to free me up so I had time to think up new ideas. I began to think about making cards again. I had collected a mountain of great baseball player photos, and I thought some of them would look perfect on cards.

I came up with an idea to make a 30-card set of Baseball Legends. I picked the players I wanted to use in the set and wrote the copy for the card backs at night. In the morning, I brought my handwritten notes into work and my secretary, Rae Randall, typed them on a typewriter, so they could be sent to the typesetter.

After a week of nonstop work, I had a new card design and was ready to print my Baseball Legends card set. They would have a sepia-tone look that the printer and I developed. Once the cards were all printed and cut, I hired people to collate them into sets by hand.

Mickey Mantle from the 1980 Baseball Legends set. The set has 120 different players and was sold nationwide in wax packs. This card is graded a perfect gem mint 10 (Mike Cramer Collection).

We sold Baseball Legends sets in our mail-order catalog. We also wholesaled sets to the dealers who bought my Topps closeout cases, nine-card plastic sheets and three-ring binders. We shipped cards all over the country; the market was booming. I added 30 new players to the set every year until 1983 and eventually had 120 different players in the full set.

In 1982, I made a few display boxes and cases of Baseball Legends sepia cards. The cards were very popular, which pleased me but really didn't surprise me. So I designed a retail display box. I took five different cards, placed them in a printed wrapper, folded the wrapper by hand, and taped the pack shut. I made 36 such packs, then placed all 36 in a display box. Sounds simple? Making just one box was. But when I put a few Baseball Legends boxes on sale at the Pacific Trading Cards store, they sold out immediately.

I could tell I had something here. I needed to make many more of those boxes.

So I got a big, wide, long table and placed stacks of each of the 60 individual players we had made cards of at that time on the table. Then I had some of my workers—and nieces and nephews—go around the table, pick up five different cards and place them on a tray. Other people would wrap the five cards and tape the pack shut. By doing this over and over, we were able to produce, in a month's time, 50 cases of cards: five cards in a pack, 36 packs in a box, 12 boxes in a case.

During that time, I had gone to one of the local candy wholesalers to buy Topps cards and had picked up a magazine actually named *The Candy Wholesaler*. All of the candy wholesaler brokers in America were listed in the back, region by region. They sold candy and trading cards to retail stores.

I decided to see if I could get some of these brokers to sell my Baseball Legends cases.

I sent sample Baseball Legends boxes and sales information to three New England area brokers. Within two weeks, the brokers had faxed orders into Pacific Trading Cards—for the 50 cases I had in stock.

And they wanted more.

I didn't have any more, and I had to tell each broker that I was sold out but that I would get back to them for the next selling season.

Now I knew I *was* onto something big. If I could make a lot of Baseball Legends cases, I could easily sell them. But I couldn't make more cases the way I was doing it; that would take forever. I needed a machine to wrap packs, like Topps used. I knew the machine that Topps used could tuck and fold a wax wrapper around the cards.

I had to find that machine.

7

The DF-1 Card Wrapping Machine

Game Changer #2

I had no master business plan: no business model, no budget, no financial backers—

—and no idea what I was doing.

But I wanted to be able to package my baseball cards in wax wrappers. I was going to have to figure out how to do it on my own, and nothing was going to stop me.

I had eaten a Mountain Bar that week. This candy bar was made by the Brown & Haley Candy Co. in Tacoma, Washington. The bar had a folded wrap, like Topps used for their trading cards.

I called Brown & Haley and got put through to the owner. I explained that I was looking for a machine to wrap baseball cards, a machine like the one Brown & Haley used to wrap candy bars.

Astonishing as it sounds, the owner said, "Oh, we have two of them, and we are phasing them out."

I said, "Can I come and see you?"

He said, "When?"

I said, "I'll leave right now."

The wrapping machines he had were Package Machinery's DF-1 die-fold wrappers. I later learned that these were the same machines used by Topps, Fleer, and Donruss to wrap their trading cards.

Needless to say, I bought the two machines—for only $2500. Brown & Haley even threw in the manual, some parts, and a couple of old rolls of wrap they'd used on the machine. But, the owner added, "you will have to learn the machine on your own; we can't help you there."

I called Package Machinery in Massachusetts. I was told they no longer made that machine and didn't even service them anymore.

I really was on my own.

The very first DF-1 wax wrapper machine I converted to wrap my Baseball Legends cards. At the time of the photo we were wrapping Pacific *Leave It to Beaver* cards (Pacific Trading Cards Archives).

I had a trucking company haul the machines to Edmonds and put them in place on my warehouse floor. The machine was 20 feet long. I cleaned off all the candy grime and painted the machine gray. I had to add 220 power to the electrical panel, which luckily happened quickly.

I began to study the equipment manual—and I mean *study*. I memorized it in a few days, so I would know what that machine was supposed to do in order to wrap a package. I was ready to make it wrap baseball cards.

I studied the mechanism carefully, identifying the functions of all of its parts. I imagined how it wrapped the candy. Comparing what I had read in the instruction manual with what I could physically see, I surmised that a 12-foot lug chain picked a single card from a gravity feed. At Brown & Haley, employees would then manually put a candy on top of each card. Then card and candy would be carried by lug chain to a small elevator, which lifted and placed both into a small metal box. Here, wax wrap was fed over the candy and a rotating knife cut the wrapper to size.

Next, "tuckers" came in from the sides, folding the wrap on the ends. A back plate came in and folded the back side and, finally, the package was pushed by a "pusher" that folded the last side while moving the pack to a hot plate to seal the wax wrapper.

The next pack would nudge the finished one off the hot plate onto a

7. The DF-1 Card Wrapping Machine

1982 Baseball Legends pack and 1985 wax pack of Pacific Baseball Legends. Pacific grew from hand-wrapped packs to machine-wrapped packs (Pacific Trading Cards Archives).

"pack-off belt," which moved packs to a human worker, who placed them in display boxes.

Marveling at the whole operation, I had a sudden revelation:

I knew why baseball cards came in wax packs! Wax could be sealed with heat—*no tape, no glue!* Wax packs saved materials, and labor, too!

I later verified this hunch, learning that early gum companies with baseball card premiums, like Goudey and Play Ball Gum, Inc., often wrapped their products with a machine first designed to individually wrap caramels. Later, companies like Leaf, Bowman and Topps, which prominently promoted trading cards, converted the candy-wrapping machines to seal cards in a wax pack:

The card collector's coveted wax packs.

Now I was reliving baseball card history. I just needed to convert my DF-1 machine from wrapping small candy bars to wrapping a stack of 2½-by-3½-inch baseball cards.

This was not going to be easy. I didn't know what I was doing; no one was going to help me figure this out. So—

I just got to it. I knew if I could make that first machine work, I could wrap my cards.

I started with the card feeding hopper and was able to open it up to my baseball card size. Then I removed the card pusher plate that pushed a single card. I took that plate to a machine shop and had the guy there mill a duplicate plate—except this was as thick as a stack of eight cards. That way, the machine could push eight cards onto the feed chain.

That part went smoothly and, after a week, I could hand-crank the machine and feed my eight cards from the card hopper onto the track.

Next, I pulled out the brass folding box, and had it rebuilt to accommodate my 2½-by-3½-inch cards. (What a great machine shop!)

When I cranked open the folding box well on the machine to put in the new folding box, I suddenly realized *why* a modern baseball card measures two-and-a-half by three-and-a-half inches. It wasn't because Topps, in 1957, decided to save money and make cards smaller than they had before or any of the other reasons people have speculated over time.

It was simply this: two-and-a-half inches was the maximum width the DF-1 packaging machine could wrap! It could wrap a longer card (which Topps did in 1968 with their basketball cards), but the width could be no more than two-and-a-half inches.

From 1952 to 1956, the standard size of a trading card was two-and-five-eighths by three-and-three-quarter inches. Those cards were wrapped on a

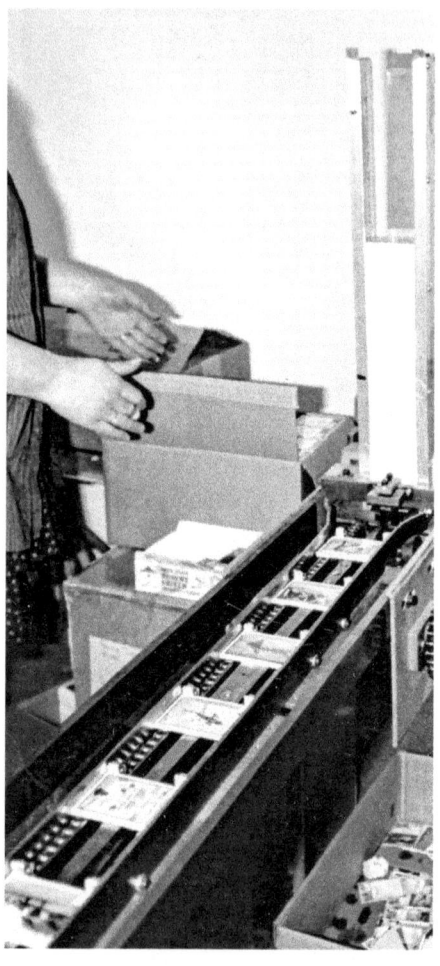

1992 DF-1 wrap wrapper gravity card feeder. The feeder fed eight cards at a time onto the lug chains; the cards were carried into the wrapping machine. It took hundreds of moving metal parts to wrap card cards. The machine had to be timed perfectly so the cards were safely wrapped (Pacific Trading Cards Archives).

7. The DF-1 Card Wrapping Machine

This brass metal box from the DF-1 wax wrapper folding box may be the only one left in the world. The box helped form a wax wrapper over a stack of trading cards (Pacific Trading Cards Archives).

machine made by Lynch Package Machinery; it operated much like the DF-1.

Wrapping 40 to 50 packs a minute, the Lynch was the baseball card industry's choice until Package Machinery introduced their DF-1 in the mid–1950s. The DF-1 could run 100 to 120 packs per minute. If it meant greater speed and capacity, card manufacturers were more than willing to change the size of their cards to fit the new machine.

Topps, Fleer, Donruss and Philadelphia Gum all began using the Package Machine DF-1 wrapper to package their trading cards.

I realized: this DF-1 packaging machine changed the trading card industry forever.

And I was ready to plug the machine into the 220 power and give it an actual go.

I loaded a roll of old candy wrap on the machine and turned on the electric eye (this told the DF-1 when the rotating knife should cut the wrap to size). Then I loaded some cards into the hopper and hit the "start" button.

The machine rumbled to life.

I gently eased back the clutch, and eight cards appeared in the chain feed lugs. One stack after another, they headed into the machine, rode up the elevator into the folding box, got wrapped, pushed out onto the hot plate, and went onto the pack-off belt.

Wow. This was it. This was it!

I made a few adjustments and, a few moments later, the machine was spitting out packs of cards, wrapped in Mountain Bar candy wrap, at a rate of 100 per minute.

I shut off the machine and ran into the office, yelling, "That machine works! We're never going to look back now!"

It was the most important moment ever in the evolution of Pacific Trading Cards. I knew I had it—I knew that I could make cases of baseball cards!

And only I knew, at that very moment, that Pacific Trading Cards was evolving from a trading card store and mail-order business into a full-blown manufacturer of trading cards, destined to compete at the national level.

Collector that I am, there were many times over the years I just looked in amazement at my big, noisy metal machines, with their hundreds of moving parts, wrapping my beautiful cards with such care that, years later, a Pacific card could be awarded the highest condition grade possible—a #10.

* * *

During this time, Cheryl and I had our third child, a boy, Cory Michael Cramer. I had a son! Cheryl was busy with our three children, and I was busy at work.

I had the DF-1 machine up and running in two and a half weeks. I knew right then and there that I could produce my Baseball Legends cards. But the printing and collating of the cards was holding me back; the process still involved too much handling of the cards, too much time-consuming labor.

I called my old rep at Brown & Bigelow, the company that had printed my crab boat playing cards in 1978. I asked for advice, and he told me he had heard of a new machine just out. It could take a sheet of 110 cards, slit it both ways (vertically and horizontally), and stack up the cards in a complete set that then came out on a conveyor belt.

Wow! I needed that machine! Or, at least, I needed access to one.

I called the Rollem Company that very day. Their amazing machine, the Slipstream, was going to revolutionize the trading card manufacturing process. Card sets could now be cut and collated perfectly in one clean step.

But.

It was too expensive for me to buy at that time. So I asked the Rollem representative if they knew of a printer that had one. He said yes, Rollem had just installed a Slipstream in Dallas, Texas, at the Yaquinto Printing

7. The DF-1 Card Wrapping Machine

company. I called Yaquinto and got right through to Tom Yaquinto. He said his company used their Slipstream to cut and collate board game cards.

And yes, we could hire them to print, *cut and collate* our trading cards into sets. They would then ship the finished cards to Edmonds, where we would package them in wax packs.

Another Eureka! I had my collating problem solved!

Pacific had a relationship with Yaquinto Printing from that time on. Over the next 20 years, together we really pushed the envelope for manufacturing trading cards.

I now had a printer and a collator for my Baseball Legends cards. I worked next on finding a supplier for wax wrap.

I called my old friend at Package Machinery Company. I told him I had a couple of their DF wrapping machines and needed a supplier/printer for wax wrap. The man I talked to said there was only one maker of wax wrap: Bomarko in Plymouth, Indiana. He said Bomarko made everyone's wax wrap: Topps, Fleer, Donruss, even Tootsie Roll. He gave me Bomarko's phone number; I called right away, and the lady I was put through to was one of the most helpful people I ever worked with. When I explained that I was going to wrap baseball cards on a DF-1 wrapper, she knew exactly what I was talking about. She said, "I will send you a template for your artwork, and we can make your wax wrap."

After I had to figure out all of the other facets of card manufacturing from scratch, she made that last part a breeze.

Eureka! I had found my wax wrapper supplier.

I was moving along well, and within six weeks, we had cards, wrappers, display boxes, corrugated boxes, tape, and sales sheets. Everything was designed and ordered and starting to arrive in my warehouse.

In December of 1984, I began to package, on my own machine, the first Pacific Baseball Legends wax box produced for mass retail.

The first boxes that came off the line were sent as samples to the Pacific broker reps in New England and then to other prospective brokers across the country. By February of 1985, I had brokers representing Pacific and selling our Baseball Legends in every state.

The orders flooded in. I had to get my second packaging machine up and running, and I even managed to buy a third. I was hiring employees and training them to run the packaging machines—but if a machine broke down, only I knew how to fix it.

Even so, I thought, this is incredible: I have a factory! There was plenty of room in the baseball card market, selling to retail stores, and I had found it. I had my foot in the door!

I would refine and grow my baseball card retail sales for the next couple of years.

* * *

In 1986, things were going very well for Pacific. I was also still adding to my personal card collection and was a member of the Washington State Sport Collectors Association. This group of collectors got together once a month to trade cards and sports memorabilia.

Each year, the club held a sports card show. Collectors and dealers could buy tables and sell their sports memorabilia to anyone attending the show. As president of the club, I was in charge of the 1986 show, scheduled for June at the Seattle Center.

I wanted to boost attendance. So, at one of the club meetings, I proposed to the members that we have Joe DiMaggio as our guest. He would sign autographs at the show, and we would sell tickets for his autograph.

This was a novel idea back then; autograph guests at card shows was still a new idea. Of course, it would be expensive to bring Joe DiMaggio in. But I thought we could pull it off with the ticket sales for his autograph, table space fees and admission tickets.

Only one other collector besides myself thought this was a good idea.

Some of the club members said I was going to bankrupt the club. Some demanded that, if it didn't work, I would have to pay up. I just said, "Fine." I knew it would be a success.

Joe DiMaggio had attended only one card show prior to that date, and I knew the organizer of that show. He provided me with the contact information for DiMaggio's agent, who helped me secure the Yankees legend's attendance at the Seattle card show. I was Joe DiMaggio's contact person for his time in Seattle.

My youngest son, Michael Ross Cramer, was born three days before Joe DiMaggio was to arrive for the show. We had flown Cheryl's mother up from Phoenix to help with the kids, but I was up to my ears in alligators right about this time.

The Friday afternoon before the show, Joe DiMaggio arrived at Sea-Tac Airport on Alaska Airlines.

I met him at the gate. He looked very dapper in his suit and tie. As we walked from the gate, people recognized him immediately, waving and calling out his name.

Several people shouted, "I have your coffee pot!"

(More than 10 years before, the Mr. Coffee company had hired DiMaggio, one of the greatest and most popular players ever, to promote their new automatic drip coffeemaker, which made a good "cup of joe." In 1986, DiMaggio was still seen in TV commercials every day across the country. Younger folks who had never known "Joltin' Joe" instead knew the slugger as "Mr. Coffee.")

7. The DF-1 Card Wrapping Machine

I drove DiMaggio to the Seattle Sheraton Hotel. On the way, I told him about my booming card business. He talked of his playing days in the Pacific Coast League back in the 1930s, when he played for the San Francisco Seals, and how he'd loved coming to Seattle then to challenge the Seattle Indians.

We arrived at the Sheraton and went to check him in. I noticed a crowd quickly form around us, people asking him for autographs and just acknowledging his presence. He was a real celebrity.

I got him checked into his room while he signed a few autographs. Then I said, "Joe, I will pick you up at 9 a.m. tomorrow."

Joe looked at me and said, "No, you won't. We're going to dinner!"

I said, "Wow! That works."

We went to an Italian restaurant in Pike Place Market.

The owner was totally excited and sat us at the center table in the busy restaurant. Heads were turning; people had noticed that Joe DiMaggio was in the restaurant!

Within a minute of our sitting down, people were coming up to our table, asking Mr. DiMaggio for autographs and just wanting to say hi.

Joe looked at me and said, "Mike, help me out here. Tell the people that when we are finished with our dinner, I will have time to talk and sign some autographs."

So, for the next 10 minutes or so, I told anyone that approached our table that Mr. DiMaggio could see them after our dinner. Word got around, and the people left us alone to enjoy our meal.

We sat talking about everything from baseball to movie stars. I absorbed everything he said, so many wonderful stories, about which he observed, "It's funny where fate takes you."

I knew all about the fate part. I felt I was experiencing some of it right then.

For our dinner, he introduced me to tidbits of traditional Italian dining. Ossobuco is one of his favorite dishes; I ordered it and love it to this day. He also showed me how to eat good Italian bread. You just eat the crust with butter and peel away and toss the soft part. I still eat bread that way, 35 years later.

When we finished our dinner, Joe said, "Mike, you can tell the people that I can see them now."

Some people had finished their dinner long ago but were still waiting, having an extra drink or two. I stood up and made the announcement. To my astonishment, Joe sat there for the good part of an hour, talking baseball and signing autographs (mainly on napkins) with every person in that room that wanted to see him.

He was a class act.

I finally got him back to his room about midnight. I told him I would pick him up the next morning for breakfast and the card show.

I drove all the way home grinning my face off! For a baseball fan, that evening I had with Joe DiMaggio was one of the ultimate prizes.

The next morning, I met him at his room, and we walked to the Seattle Center food court for coffee and a doughnut before the card show.

When we got to the hall where the show was being held, we saw more than 1000 people lined up to get in. Joe looked at me and said, "Mike, I'm not going to have time to sign for that many people. I have a flight to catch at 5:30!"

I said, "No, no—remember? We sold tickets for your autograph. Only those people can get in line to get your autograph."

He asked, "Then why are so many people here?"

I told him, "To see you and attend the card show."

He signed autographs for all the people that had an autograph ticket and finished about half-hour earlier than we had planned. "Mike," Joe said, "I can sign a few more if you'd like to sell some more tickets."

I made an announcement that we could sell more autograph tickets, and they were gone in a few minutes.

Our mission had been accomplished! The card show was a huge success. A record number of collectors attended, and Joe DiMaggio was an overwhelming hit.

I took him back to the airport and walked him to his gate. Saying goodbye, I felt like we were newfound buddies.

On my drive home, it finally sank in: I had just spent most of two days with the greatest living baseball player at the time, Joe DiMaggio.

* * *

I wanted to make cards of Major League Baseball players. I had a card factory, and I was ready for my next adventure.

Sales for Pacific Baseball Legends were strong. My sales brokers were confident that, if I could make cards of current players, retailers would buy. So in 1987, I contacted the Major League Baseball Players Association and applied for a license. The MLBPA was interested.

I flew to New York to meet with the head of licensing. Shortly after, Players Association licensing board members visited Pacific. Within weeks, I received by mail a license agreement for review.

I thought I was going to get a license to make Major League Baseball cards. However, within a few days, I got a call from the Players Association, saying they were suddenly extremely busy and my license would need to be put on hold.

In the meantime, a new company, Upper Deck, received a license before Pacific.

7. The DF-1 Card Wrapping Machine

June 21, 1986, Joe DiMaggio signing autographs at the Seattle Card Show with me assisting (Pacific Trading Cards Archives).

Such is the way things go. But I still have the unsigned license agreement as a souvenir, and the 1987 prototype baseball cards that Pacific produced still exist.

That year, I also applied for an NFL license with the NFLPA, but nothing became of that, either.

However, in 1987, Pacific did obtain a license to make Major League Indoor Soccer cards, a relationship that would last for six years, until the league folded in 1994.

Meanwhile, Pacific brokers sold way more cases than I could deliver of that first series of sepia Pacific Baseball Legends. I only had three card packaging machines and realized that was not enough to keep up with the demand for all the products we were making, like our *Leave It to Beaver* card set, based on the iconic 1950s TV sitcom.

In 1988, Pacific produced a color set of 110 Baseball Legends. We were able to get a license for these players, and the sepia Baseball Legends, from the Baseball Players Alumni Association. We got our first Major League Baseball Properties license in 1988, and this one-two punch put us over the top. I knew Pacific was one step closer to getting a license to produce current major league baseball players.

The manufacturing of trading cards had taken over the company. To streamline the work, I set up the grid system for the 110-card printing sheet. The system remained part of Pacific operations.

There were no books or manuals on how to produce baseball cards, and the few existing manufacturers certainly weren't going to tell me their secrets, so—I just had to figure it out.

And I did:

After assigning players numbers up to 110 (the number of cards that fit on each printer's sheet), I chose and numbered each player's photo. Then I compiled his bio and statistics for the card back, each with his previously-assigned number. Next, a secretary typed my words to send to the typesetter, then each player's photo and typeset information were sent to a color separator. Print film was then made and sent to the printer. Nowadays, everything printed is compiled on computers, going directly from computer to press. This saves mountains of printing film, labor and time—and still produces quality that could not be attained the old way.

About that time, I found and added a fourth packaging machine. With all of my production problems solved for the time being (and with Yaquinto printing, cutting, and collating my cards), the Edmonds team started to package our 1988 Pacific card products.

We were rolling! When McCorys, an East Coast chain store with 1300 stores, ordered from us, we were able to produce and ship—on time—enough cases to fill their order as well as almost all of the orders our Pacific brokers faxed in.

I had more good fortune come my way in the fall of 1988. My secretary, Rae, informed me I had a call from Ron at Berkley Publishing Co. in New York City.

I knew what Berkley was. I had read the current bestselling Tom Clancy novel, *The Hunt for Red October*. It was one of my favorite books, and Berkley was the publisher.

That phone call changed Pacific Trading Cards, Inc. forever!

Berkley was having incredible success with the Tom Clancy novels and had opened up tremendous distribution channels in magazine and newsstands all over the United States. They had a powerful hands-on sales force in every state in the country, selling books to all the stores that carried books.

7. The DF-1 Card Wrapping Machine

Berkley was looking for a new product that their sales force could sell to all these stores. They had done some research and decided to try to sell baseball cards to the tens of thousands of stores and magazine wholesalers they called on.

Ron was looking for a trading card company Berkley could represent. He had bought some packs of our 1988 Pacific Baseball Legends cards in a store in New York and had fallen in love with them. He thought Berkley could do well with them because he didn't see them in that many stores and knew we could sell more with their help.

I was most intrigued and interested. Collaborating with Berkley would be well worth the commission we'd pay on orders they sold. Ron's only concern? If they got a lot of orders, could Pacific deliver?

I said, "Yes, of course—we have a factory!"

I made a deal with Berkley, and they delivered.

It was huge. Orders came in, not only for Pacific Baseball Legends, but also for our entertainment cards. The next year, Cheryl and I went to the Berkley national sales convention in Puerto Rico, and Pacific was the hot topic of the convention.

The relationship with Berkley was a game changer and put Pacific on the map. With the Berkley sales force, our Baseball Legends wax boxes and other Pacific products were being placed at the checkout counters in tens of thousands of stores and magazine stands—and the cards were selling out.

Combine that with our candy broker sales force, and we had instant sales and distribution to retail stores across the country for every trading card product we produced. What Pacific needed now was a major trading card license. MLB baseball, NFL football or NHL hockey—we were ready!

During the time the 1988 products were being produced, we included a series of cards from the movie *Eight Men Out*. That card set was licensed by the movie studio and also by Major League Baseball Properties. We made wax boxes, and they sold incredibly well through our massive retail distribution system.

Incredibly, almost none of our Pacific products were sold through baseball card stores at this time.

We were growing, and I saw two more big problems coming.

Although I had hired very capable people to run the card packaging machines, if one broke down, I was still the only one who could fix it and get it back on line.

My second problem was even bigger. The 7000-square-foot warehouse and offices we were in were bursting at the seams. We needed a much bigger space to work in.

I'd started preparing for this problem more than a year before, when I purchased some land and hired an architect to draw up plans for a new building for Pacific. Everything was in place. All that needed to be done was to start the ball rolling.

Within a couple of months, we had architectural drawings ready for our new headquarters.

8

The Kid and the Candy Store

Seattle Mariners fans were buzzing in the spring of 1989.

A player had finally emerged that Mariners fans could sink their teeth into. At spring training that year, a player named Ken Griffey, Jr., was having tremendous success, and there was talk he might make the team.

In the 13 years of the Mariners franchise, no player had ever shown such promise. Griffey was a phenom, and many of us saw it.

One day in March, I walked over to the Pacific card store to see my store manager, Ann Ninneman. As we talked, she said, "You know, that Ken Griffey, Jr., guy has everyone's attention. We need to make something with him on it to sell, like a pencil or a key chain or something."

I knew she was right, and her words got my creative juices flowing. I looked into our display case and saw a Reggie Jackson candy bar we had for sale.

I turned to Ann and said, "We're going to make a candy bar of him."

She stared. "What? How are you going to do that? We don't make candy."

"I don't know how we're going to do it yet, but I'm going to figure it out," I said.

I walked back across the street to my office, and by the time I reached it, I had a plan.

I would make a chocolate bar with Griffey's image molded on it. I could wrap it on the same DF-1 machine we wrapped cards with, using a silver food-grade paper—like a Kit Kat bar! We'd finish by folding a printed color paper band with Griffey's picture around the bar.

I called the Mariners office, and was able to get the name and phone number of Griffey's lawyer, Mr. Brian Goldberg. I called Brian right then. He answered, and I explained my crazy idea: I wanted to make a Ken Griffey, Jr., candy bar.

Brian said, "A candy bar? Ken hasn't even made the team."

I said, "That doesn't matter. He will make the team."

Brian said, "A candy bar? Are you sure?"

I said, "Yes! Seattle fans can't wait for him to play here, and when he does, the roof is going to blow off the Kingdome from all their cheering."

He said, "Okay … let me talk to Ken. I'll get back to you."

I said, "Brian, I need to move fast."

A couple of days later, Brian called, and we made a deal.

It was Griffey's first endorsement ever. And I've always remembered how Brian said, "Good luck with that, Mike."

I moved quickly, putting all my efforts into making a candy bar.

I grabbed a couple of sheets of paper and designed two color wrappers, one blue and one yellow, the Mariners' team colors. Each design had Griffey's picture. Then I made a paper prototype, a "mock-up bar" (which I still have).

Next, I called a small, local candy company that made chocolates for the Northwest market. I told them about my idea and explained that I wanted to make a pure milk chocolate candy bar the size of a baseball card. I wanted a baseball player's image molded into the chocolate, so I needed someone who could make a mold. The company said it could make a mold and could even mold all the actual bars.

Eureka! Another problem solved!

We got a candy bar mold designed and made, and we poured some chocolate prototypes. I rejected the first prototype because it didn't have enough image relief, and Ken Griffey, Jr., didn't stand out well enough. But it tasted good; I ate that prototype!

The next mold effort looked really good and, on March 15, we ordered enough bulk milk chocolate from Ghirardelli Chocolate Company to melt and mold 2500 bars (at our special size, each bar weighed 1.625 ounces).

This was going to be a novelty bar, and we would sell them at the Pacific Trading Card store.

Everything was in motion. I even formed a subsidiary of Pacific Trading Cards, Inc., named Pacific Candy Company. We were moving fast.

The milk chocolate was being pumped into the molds by March 25.

And just as I'd predicted, when the Mariners came north from spring training, Ken Griffey, Jr., had made the team.

Fans in Seattle were excited like they'd never been before. Griffey appeared in his first major league game on April 3, 1989, and had his first hit that day. On April 10, he hit his first home run.

Fans were going wild. This phenom player was doing it! Seattle had its first true baseball superstar in the making!

By April 20, after I got approvals from Brian Goldberg, we printed the Griffey Bar wrappers and a candy bar promotion card to go in each retail

8. The Kid and the Candy Store

box. For, in the midst of all the new challenges, we also did what we did best: designed a baseball card.

One week later, we were wrapping the Griffey Bars in silver food-grade foil on the DF-1 baseball card wrapper that I had converted to wrap chocolate bars.

A crew of workers put the color wrappers on by hand, one bar at a time, sealing each with a dab of glue. We put 24 bars in each display box. Ann put the new bar on sale in the Pacific Trading Cards store that day.

They sold as fast as we could wrap them.

On the top of each packed box of candy bars, we placed our promotional trading card. Some collectors say it is Griffey's first card in a Mariners uniform. And it actually was. The card wasn't wrapped, just placed on top of the bars in the candy box. Whoever opened the box or got there first got the card. Not a great system, but that is what we did. Those cards are very scarce nowadays.

I was so exhausted and excited by then—but I knew I had a winner. To celebrate (and because I was exhausted!) I went into our offices and had my first-ever drink.

Of coffee.

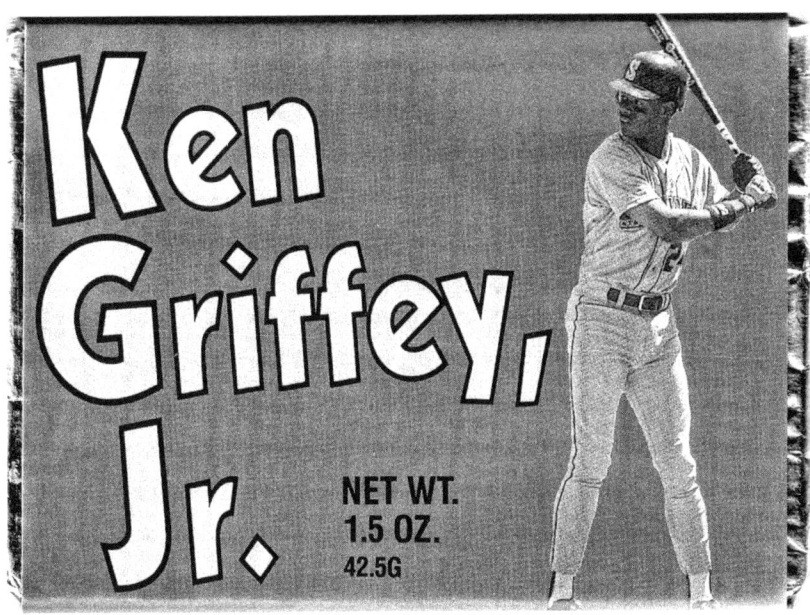

Ken Griffey, Jr., Bar blue wrapper, 1989. This milk chocolate candy bar was molded with Ken Griffey, Jr.'s, image on it. It was a mega hit in the Seattle area, where "Ken Griffey" played (Pacific Trading Cards Archives).

I had never drunk coffee, even all the time I fished crab. But once I drank that first cup, I realized why all the crab fishermen lived on coffee.

I knew I could sell more Griffey Bars. I called my brother Marty who was, at that time, the operations manager for 20 Andrew's Hallmark Stores in the Seattle area.

"I made a candy bar for Ken Griffey, Jr.," I said, "and they are flying off the shelves at my store."

He said, "You made a what?"

I said, "A Griffey Bar! You should sell them in your Hallmark stores." Once he had them in the stores to sell, I would send a press release out to the Seattle media.

Marty said, "Let's do it."

I delivered 40 boxes to him the next day, and he got them on sale in all his stores. Then I sent out a press release to the Seattle media. The headline read, "Mariners Rookie phenom Ken Griffey, Jr. is so good, he already has his own candy bar."

The media went nuts covering the story.

Local sportscaster Tony Ventrella visited the Ballard Hallmark store and did an interview with Marty's wife and store manager, Michelle Cramer. The interview was broadcast on the 5 o'clock news that evening.

The Hallmark stores sold out that evening. We replenished their stores the next day, and those Griffey Bars quickly sold out too.

I knew this was big and ordered more chocolate and raw materials. Ten thousand more Griffey Bars went into production. To my astonishment, that still wasn't enough. All of the Seattle media outlets began to talk on radio and TV about Ken Griffey, Jr., and his candy bar, every day. He was a phenomenon—and so was his candy bar.

That's when I called a good friend who owned a packaging machine business. I explained what I was doing and said I needed a machine to automatically wrap a printed wrapper around a candy bar, like a Kit Kat bar.

He told me he knew of a packaging machine that could do that, once he converted one for me.

"When do you need it?" he asked.

"Right now!" I said. "I have orders for over 500,000 bars."

He said, "I'll get it converted, ship it to you, and fly up from San Francisco to get it up and running."

I ordered the color wrap in rolls to the specs he sent me for the machine. He had that machine on my floor, up and running, in just two weeks.

Orders were pouring in. The bar was consumable, so people were eating them and then buying more. The press interviewed Griffey about his candy bar.

8. The Kid and the Candy Store

Griffey said he was allergic to chocolate!

The press went nuts with that story.

And sales went through the roof!

The president of Associated Grocers called me. They wanted Griffey Bars in all the grocery stores they supplied—and they wanted them *now*. They would bring the bars in through the produce department, because that let them circumvent paperwork and red tape, and get the bars to their checkout counters immediately.

We produced Ken Griffey, Jr., bars day and night at Pacific. During the run, Griffey's parents visited Pacific's candy bar production site, and I got to meet them. Ken Griffey, Sr., at the time a Major League Baseball player near the end of a long career, would make history with Ken Jr. the following year when they became the first father-son duo to be major league teammates. (When Ken Sr. signed with the Mariners, the press—and the public—started calling his son simply "Junior" and, sometimes, "The Kid.")

When the whole venture finally wrapped up two years later, nearly one million Ken Griffey, Jr., bars had been produced and sold. People in the Seattle area consumed a lot of milk chocolate Griffey Bars! The best part was that Junior lived up to his billing and now is in the Baseball Hall of Fame.

I'm told his Pacific Griffey Bar is on display there too.

When I met Brian Goldberg a few years later and the subject came up, he just said, "Who would have thought?"

And smiled.

I did too.

* * *

In 1989, right after the Griffey Bar, Pacific produced a football card set featuring Seattle Seahawk Steve Largent, a future Hall of Famer. The set was licensed by Largent and by the NFL.

That set was a big seller (the Seattle area Hallmark stores sold a majority of them). Steve Largent became a good friend of Pacific and made several appearances at our functions.

When Steve Largent retired, he was the greatest wide receiver the NFL had ever had.

Pacific also began a five-year relationship with Oroweat Bread in 1989, producing a set of NFL-licensed Seattle Seahawks player cards. Oroweat distributed these in the Seattle area, one card per bagged loaf of bread.

In October of 1989, I was following the San Francisco Giants very closely. If they beat the Chicago Cubs in the playoffs, they would go to their first World Series since 1962.

I decided that, if the Giants made it, I was going to attend the World

Series in San Francisco. I called my great friend, Wayne Grove, an old buddy I first met in Phoenix back in 1975 when he got a baseball card of me. Wayne was a card collector and a sports fan, with his own sports memorabilia shop in the Dallas area. Wayne wanted to go to the World Series, too, and we were able to get great seats for games 3 and 4 at Candlestick Park.

We found lodging in San Mateo, 15 miles south of San Francisco, booked everything, and were all set. A couple days later, we met up in San Francisco for the San Francisco Giants vs. Oakland A's World Series matchup, Game 3, on October 17, 1989.

This was as good as it gets: two longtime baseball card collectors at the World Series! Wayne and I got our rental car and drove to Candlestick Park early for the 5:30 game.

We had ample time to each get a beer and a hot dog and to find our third base–side seats. The seats all around us were filling in with noisy, excited fans. With just three minutes before game time, Giants fans were cheering and stomping their feet like I had never witnessed before. I had been in the Kingdome in Seattle, surrounded by cheering and rumbling and stomping, but this was crazy! I thought, if they don't stop this noise, they are going to shake this stadium apart!

Then, suddenly, it felt like the seats we were in surged out from under us, toward the field. I looked up. The stadium lights were twisting and turning and waving back and forth. I looked over at Wayne and he said, "Earthquake." We looked in the distance outside the stadium and saw smoke.

I looked at Wayne. "This ain't good."

A magnitude 6.9 earthquake had struck the Bay Area, causing significant damage to both Oakland and San Francisco. Power was knocked out. Candlestick Park suffered damage to its upper deck, as pieces of concrete fell from the baffle at the top of the stadium.

Needless to say, the game was called off. Wayne and I made our way out of the stadium with the rest of the stunned crowd. We found our rental car and decided to try to get back to our hotel in San Mateo.

Most of the roads were closed—and it was getting dark. The street lights were out everywhere, and we had to take back roads and side streets, slowly making our way south.

Soon it was pitch black. There was no power at all.

We knew we were on the right road to the hotel, but the going was slow. Finally, nearly four hours later, we saw lights in the distance for the first time that night. As we got closer to the lights, we saw our hotel was in the only four-block section of San Mateo that had power—the only power for miles and miles.

8. The Kid and the Candy Store

Wayne and I checked into our rooms, and I had the feeling God was watching over us that night. We spent a couple of days in that hotel, until San Francisco International Airport opened and we were able to fly back home.

* * *

I had seen the writing on the wall: Pacific was growing, taking on ever-expanding challenges and, like any living thing, it needed space to grow.

I had purchased three acres of land on Highway 99 in Lynnwood, Washington. I'd hired an architect to design a building, my building, with offices, manufacturing and warehouse space, loading docks, and plenty of parking for employees.

Construction had been going on while I wrestled with candy bars and earthquakes. And, in the fall of 1989, Pacific moved into our new 60,000-square-foot facility.

We were a growing company!

I still needed to find a production engineer to take care of our packaging machines and run the factory. I was overloaded.

About that time, I found out that a candy company in Los Angeles was closing down and selling their equipment. I flew down to Los Angeles to talk to the owner and asked him who kept his manufacturing equipment running, including the two DF-1 wrappers that they used.

"Whoever it is," I said, "I need to hire that person!"

The owner promised to have his former production manager call if he was interested in the job.

I bought those DF-1 wrappers and had them shipped to Pacific to be converted to wrapping cards.

Not long after I got back home, I received a call from a man named Felix Mendez.

We talked for a while, and I told him that Pacific had DF-1 wax wrapping machines that we were wrapping baseball cards on, and I needed a production manager who knew those machines.

He said, "I can do that." I made him an offer, and he moved his family up from California.

Felix was at the new Pacific factory working two weeks later. He was a perfect fit for the company and took that big production load off my shoulders. I could then concentrate on new ideas and developing new products.

The timing couldn't have been better. Just after we moved into our new facility in 1989, I got a call from former major league player Frank Torre. He asked if Pacific was interested in a license to make baseball cards for the new Senior Baseball League just starting up in Florida.

I said yes and signed the license. Then I called a good friend who lived in Florida. We made an agreement, and he got to work taking Senior League player photos for our new card set. We printed the cards, made wax cases and, to everyone's surprise (including mine), they sold very well. Berkley was, in part, to thank for the great sales.

As might be expected in a growing company, I kept encountering new issues. Like the fact that Pacific had only four DF-1 card-wrapping machines and, with our growing production volumes, that just wasn't enough equipment to keep up.

I couldn't find any surplus DF-1s, because Fleer and Donruss had bought up all the DF-1 wrapping machines as candy bar manufacturers phased them out. Donruss, I learned, had more than 50 DF-1 trading card wrappers on their floor in Memphis. Moreover, Donruss had purchased all the DF-1 parts from Package Machinery Co., including the molds used to make those parts, when Package Machinery stopped making the DF-1. (Luckily for Pacific, the chief engineer at Donruss, Jerry Adams, became a good friend, and he often sent me a spare part when I needed one. Jerry understood my eagerness to keep my card wrappers running.)

As my search for more machines continued, I called my old contact at Package Machinery Co. to see if he could offer any leads. What timing! Just that day he had heard that Hershey Candy Co. was phasing out some of the DF-1 wrappers they had been using to wrap Reese's Peanut Butter Cups.

I had to get those machines.

I made a call to the Hershey Company in Hershey, Pennsylvania, and got through to the plant manager. He told me he had six DF-1s in Hershey and five more for sale at the Oakdale plant in California, all painted green.

I flew down to Oakland, California, then drove 86 miles to the Oakdale plant to take a look at the five machines there. I liked what I saw and made a deal to buy all 11 DF-1s and several crates of parts. While I was there, I got a quick tour of the candy line making Hershey candy bars. Needless to say, it was fascinating.

I had 11 more wax wrapper machines. They were shipped to Pacific.

Felix and our mechanics got to work converting the machines to wrap trading cards. Soon, we had 18 fully-running trading card wrappers on the production floor at Pacific.

Then, in our machine shop, Felix and I designed fully-computerized pack-off belts for each of the DF-1 wrappers. This four-foot belt shingled the card packs, and when the electric eye counted nine packs, the belt jogged ahead one inch. This allowed the person putting packs into display boxes to just pick up nine packs, no counting. Before we built these belts, it took two people to pack off a machine; now one person could easily do it.

8. The Kid and the Candy Store

Eight lines of DF-1 trading card wax wrapping machines at the Pacific factory in 1991. These were the machines used to wax wrap trading cards. We had 18 of them wrapping cards (Pacific Trading Cards Archives).

Because of our increased card wrapping capacity and our new pack-off belts, we could now produce and release more than one product at a time, and use fewer people to do it.

I still wanted to give the candy bar venture another go. I called the Major League Baseball Players Association to see if they could provide me with names of the agents for Tony Gwynn and Wade Boggs, two players I thought deserved to have a candy bar. After all, great baseball players had their own candy bars. Like Babe Ruth had a candy bar (sort of…).

To my surprise, the agent for both players was Matt Merola. A quick call to him and Pacific Candy Co. had two more candy bars in production: the "Wade Boggs .352 Bar" and the "Tony Gwynn Base Hit Bar." Both bars sold well.

However, I realized that shipping candy bars from Lynnwood, Washington, to Boston and San Diego in the summer could cause problems. Chocolate melted, so it had to be shipped on refrigerated trucks, and that was expensive.

Too expensive. I did have fun making candy bars and overcoming the challenges to do so. However, we didn't make any more candy bars after that.

Meeting and working with Matt Merola was one of the best things that came out of the experience. One day Matt called me and said, "Mike, can you do anything with Nolan Ryan or Tom Seaver? I represent them too."

I said, "Yes! I would like to make baseball card sets based on their careers." I added, "I will make the Nolan Ryan set first and, if it works, I'll make a Tom Seaver set."

Needless to say, the Pacific Nolan Ryan set worked really well, and we followed up with the Tom Seaver set the next year.

In the 1980s, I started noticing old, classic TV shows cropping up on new cable television channels. I remembered the success of our 1986 *Leave It to Beaver* set and realized trading card sets had never been made for some of the classic shows.

Wait! This looks like a job for....

Yup, you guessed it.

On one of my trips to New York, I visited CBS/Viacom. They let me peruse their photo library files in the basement archives. I found a treasure trove of photos, enough to produce card sets for *I Love Lucy*, *The Andy Griffith Show*, *Gunsmoke*, *The Wild Wild West*, and *My Three Sons*. I acquired the trading card rights for all of these shows.

The first classic television card set we produced in 1990 was *I Love Lucy*. It was the very first "parallel set" of trading cards ever made. The 110-card set was printed once with pink-bordered cards, then a "parallel set" was printed with silver-bordered cards.

In 1993, Nolan Ryan (left) and Tom Seaver proudly posed with their Pacific cards. This was so much fun, we made a card out of the photograph. This card is graded a perfect gem mint 10 (Mike Cramer Collection).

8. The Kid and the Candy Store

Andy Griffith and *I Love Lucy* cards were hits, but *Andy Griffith* was a mega hit. We made three series of cards on that great show over a two-year period. Pacific then got so busy with other projects that *The Wild Wild West* and *My Three Sons* were put on the back burner, and ultimately were never produced. What a shame.

Thirty years later, while cleaning out my attic, I found the original photos for those two projects. For an instant, I thought, "I should make card sets from these photos…." Then I caught myself, smiled, and put them back in the box.

The moment was a waking version of a recurring dream I still have sometimes. I dream I have a great new card design, and I have to get it into production right away, before the other card manufacturers hear about it and copy it. I rush into Pacific to start the design process, when suddenly I realize: We no longer have a factory to produce trading cards! How will we—

The 1991 Pacific Nolan Ryan set was the first use of prism foil on a trading card. We printed several different varieties of prism foil on this seven-card insert set (Pacific Trading Cards Archives).

Every time I have that dream I wake up, smile and roll my eyes, and then go back to sleep.

* * *

In February of 1991, I began to produce the first set of our immensely popular Nolan Ryan cards. I had an idea in my head of how I wanted the cards to look. The idea just came to me; I didn't have a design team or anyone to help back then. I just took out a pencil and sketched my idea on a piece of paper. Then I turned it over to a lady who worked with me, who took my rough sketch and made a usable card design out of it. Meanwhile, I was compiling photos of Ryan, writing all the card backs and attending to the wrapper, retail display box, and all the other details of the project.

We sent Pacific Nolan Ryan sales material to our sales force. We found that Nolan Ryan was very popular in most of the United States, but most popular in New York and California, states where he had played, and Texas, where he was currently playing.

By late March, Pacific was printing and shipping Nolan Ryan Texas Express baseball cards. Sales were quite good, and about what I had expected.

Until May 1, 1991. That day, I received a call from one of my employees. "Are you watching?" he asked.

I said, "Watching what?"

He said, "Turn on your TV. Nolan Ryan is in the seventh inning, and could pitch his seventh no-hitter. All the TV stations are covering it."

I turned on my TV in time to see the 44-year-old fastball pitcher Nolan Ryan pitch his record seventh no-hitter.

I think I was as thrilled as he was.

The next morning, I arrived at work early and checked our four fax machines for orders, as I did every morning. This morning was different: all four fax machines were out of paper.

Orders for Pacific Nolan Ryan cards spilled onto the floor, orders from our sales brokers and from Berkley. I quickly loaded more paper into the fax machines, and more orders came streaming out onto the floor.

The Pacific Nolan Ryan cards were a tremendous seller, thanks to Nolan's seventh no-hitter. We also designed and produced a Pacific Prism Nolan Ryan insert card set. This was

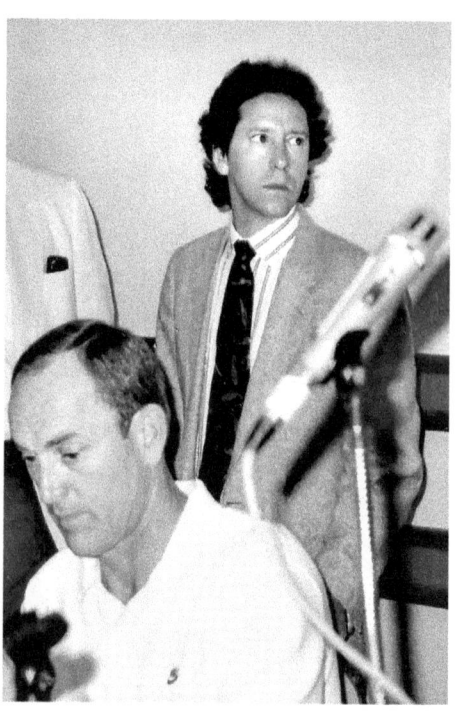

Nolan Ryan and me, June 12, 1991. Nolan signed autographs after his Pacific sales conference talk in Dallas. His Pacific Nolan Ryan cards were hot (Pacific Trading Cards Archives)!

8. The Kid and the Candy Store

not only our first use of a Prism card in a Pacific product, but the first time any card company had made a card like this: laminating a prismatic foil onto the sides of a trading card. This was innovative. The cards had pop! We made several parallel sets of that Nolan Ryan insert, each set with a different style of prism foil.

The success of the Pacific Nolan Ryan cards led to a second series the next year, and Nolan himself provided us with several photos of his younger days.

Pacific also produced, printed, and packaged several Nolan Ryan promotional card sets for other national companies: Advil, McCormick & Company, and more.

Later that summer, I got to meet Nolan Ryan when he attended our Pacific sales meeting in Texas. He gave a great speech and helped promote his Pacific cards; he was a true gentleman.

As long as he wasn't throwing fast balls at you.

9

1991 Pacific Plus Football Cards

I focused on acquiring more licenses to make card products. About that time, I received a call from Frank Torre. He wanted to know if I wanted to renew my Senior League license for a second year. Of course I did!

Several card companies made Senior League cards that first season, including Topps. Frank may not have been surprised that Pacific was the only card company to renew the license for a second season; he told me that Pacific had out-sold Topps and the other first-year companies. The Berkley sales force was an enormous asset.

Frank and I had a really good conversation, and I let Frank know that Pacific was looking to acquire more licenses to produce cards for Major League Baseball, the NFL, the NHL, and movies and TV shows.

Frank said, "I'll come out to Pacific and visit you. I think I can help."

He called me a few days later and told me he was coming and bringing along another fellow who could help get Pacific more licenses. I was excited! Frank Torre was a former major leaguer; I had baseball cards of him. Frank hit two home runs in the 1957 World Series with the Milwaukee Braves.

A week or so later, Frank arrived at Pacific with a man named Victor Temkin. Victor was a former assistant U.S. attorney; after that, he had worked at Bantam books and had been CEO of Berkley Publishing. He was also the former head of MCA-Universal Studios licensing. He had licensed *E.T.*, *Jaws* and many other movies for Topps trading cards.

After a quick tour of Pacific, Frank and I sat down to talk about licensing baseball, football and hockey. He thought that he could help get Pacific an NFL card license right away. I was overjoyed. That would be a big boost for Pacific, and I was ready to go.

Then Victor sat down with me, and we talked for a long time. He was flabbergasted when he learned of my relationship with his old company,

9. 1991 Pacific Plus Football Cards

Berkley. Then Victor put his cards on the table: not only could he help Pacific get licenses, but he could also help me a great deal as a consultant.

I knew he had mountains of business experience. I agreed right away; he would become my consultant and, with his wealth of knowledge, I would learn more than I'd ever imagined. In the process, I made a lifelong friend.

That summer, 1990, I learned that the NFL Players Association would grant Pacific a 1991 license to begin printing and marketing football player cards. Eureka! I was overjoyed: we had a major sports card license!

This was a game-changer for Pacific.

Right after that, Frank Torre and I met up in New York to visit NFL Properties. We needed another, additional license that would let us picture NFL team logos on the cards.

Pacific had been a licensee of NFL Properties since 1987. We figured getting the license from NFL Properties for our 1991 Pacific Football cards would be no problem, as Pacific was already a licensee of NFL Properties for two previous trading card projects, Steve Largent and the Seattle Seahawks Oroweat Bakery promotion. And Pacific had proven retail store sales and distribution.

I knew that a line of NFL cards from Pacific would sell in the vastly undersupplied retail football card market; at that time, only Topps, Fleer, Score and Pro Set were making NFL cards. I thought getting a license for our new NFL player cards would be a piece of cake.

Frank and I were stunned when the NFL Properties directors said no.

They said no—but it didn't feel right to me. I thought something smelled a little fishy.

Frank and I left the meeting very disappointed. Frank said, " Do you have a good lawyer?"

I said no.

Frank said, "I think you're going to need one."

Back home, I called my CPA, Phil Roth, who recommended a Seattle lawyer who recommended a specialist in trademarks and intellectual properties rights: a bright, new lawyer named Mike Kipling.

After I explained my situation to Mike, he did some research and told me that Pacific would be able to make football cards of NFL players in their uniforms. We could show logos when they were part of the players' uniforms but not print the team logos anywhere else on the cards.

However, to avoid any litigation once we printed and sold our cards, Pacific would have to sue NFL Properties beforehand. This would force NFLP to promptly acknowledge that our cards were licensed.

Our lawsuit followed. After depositions in Seattle and New York City, the hearing was scheduled in Seattle. As I was driving there to meet with

Mike and his team just before the court proceedings, the phone rang in my car.

It was Mike. "I just got off the phone with NFL Properties," he said. "They are sending you an NFL Properties license. The lawsuit is settled."

This was the best news ever! It had been a grueling six weeks. I had never been through anything like that, making the sorts of choices I had to, to determine the outcome. But I wanted to make cards, and nothing was going to stop me. It was just my fate.

About three years later, Frank and I found out why we were initially refused a license. There was really no problem with Pacific Trading Cards. What we learned was that the NFL licensing directors each had a personal investment in Pro Set Press LTD, a trading card printer owned in part by the once-high-flying football card maker Pro Set.

Both Frank and I were shocked when we learned of this conflict of interest. Neither of us were surprised when those involved ultimately resigned.

But I think Pacific got a bad reputation among the major sports licensing entities because of that situation. At the beginning, other licensors only knew that Pacific had sued NFL Properties. They could easily have assumed that Pacific was somehow at fault, that Pacific was risky and difficult to work with. They couldn't have known the true circumstances of why we brought a lawsuit.

That licensing step took a little longer than expected, but we prevailed and were granted the NFL Properties license to go with our NFL Players Association license. We launched our 1991 Pacific Plus NFL Football card brand shortly after that.

It was a win/win for Pacific, NFL Properties, and the NFL Players Association: over the next 12 years, Pacific produced and sold millions of dollars' worth of football cards and paid millions of dollars in royalties to the league and players.

I became busier than I'd ever been making cards. All the steps I had learned years before about how to make cards were the same, but now everything was on a much bigger scale.

In early 1991, Pacific received permission to print prototype cards of 10 different current Major League Baseball players in both English and Spanish. Then we went to see the MLB Players Association in New York to apply for an official license—but to no avail.

We continued applying for the next two years. My dream of making cards of major league baseball players was still alive, and I was not going to rest until I could make it happen.

* * *

9. 1991 Pacific Plus Football Cards

In early summer, Pacific began to package 1991 Pacific NFL Plus football cards and ship to retail stores.

Our football cards were very popular. It was a big set, with 660 different football player cards, and it included a really popular insert set I named "Pacific Picks the Pros." Twenty-five of the top football players of 1991 were in the insert. We designed and printed that set with gold foil, then made a parallel set with silver foil.

Pacific was definitely first with parallel cards. We discovered that parallel sets created a real win/win situation: because parallel cards were included in most of our products, but printed in limited quantities, collectors found a new thrill of the chase and a new satisfaction when they found a parallel card in a pack. We found this to be really good for our sales.

When we were picking players for our 1991 set, we had photos of a journeyman football player named Cap Boso. We had lots of players to choose from, but I said, "Hey! With a name like Cap Boso, this guy has to have a card made of him." His 1991 Pacific Football is the only NFL card he has. And he did become famous—as a player with special powers in a Nintendo game, Tecmo Bowl!

To date, more than 30 years later, that 1991 Pacific football set has 55 players that have been inducted into the Football Hall of Fame. One of those cards is a Brett Favre rookie card that I included in the second series set at the insistence of a trusted Pacific football card advisor, Chuck Bennett.

Chuck lived in Hattiesburg, Mississippi, and also worked at the University of Southern Mississippi. He had watched Favre play and told me I must make a rookie card for him. That was excellent advice, and I learned a great deal from it, mainly, if you're

1991 Pacific Picks the Pros. This card concept evolved into Cramer's Choice Awards in 1994 (Pacific Trading Cards Archives).

making trading cards, you must learn and study the players, especially newly-signed players or even unsigned players. Some of those guys will spend years in the minors before getting called up to the major leagues and becoming an official "rookie." Others show so much promise, they go straight to the bigs. Card makers sometimes gamble when they make rookie cards. Will their picks really get called up that year?

I had a good eye for football talent. I don't know why; I think it was just my calling. I did study the players and their habits, but why could I "pick them"? The only answer I can come up with is that I was lucky—or maybe it was just in my bones.

Making cards gave me the desire to follow players, to really pay attention to them. Like Chuck Bennett said, rookie cards were extremely important; they could drive the sales for an entire product line, especially if your trading card company is the only one with a card for a hot new rookie.

After Pacific received its football license, a license was also given to Upper Deck and several other card companies. The market got crowded, with nine manufacturers of NFL cards that season.

Pacific held its own because of the extremely strong retail store distribution we had. When the dust cleared after one crowded season, Pacific, Pro Set, Topps, Upper Deck, Fleer and Donruss were the major manufacturers left standing in the packed football card market.

At the 1991 National Sports Collectors Convention in Anaheim, California, Pacific brought in *The Andy Griffith Show* stars Hal Smith ("Otis the Drunk") and George "Goober" Lindsey to sign autographs in our booth. There were dozens of sports stars signing at that show, including Sandy Koufax, Brooks Robinson, Jim Brown, Bart Starr and Bobby Hull. But just like the sports stars, Otis and Goober had long lines of fans all day. A couple of the sports stars even came to get Mayberry autographs!

Summer changed to fall and, by late 1991, Pacific had so many employees, we had to hire employees to be in charge of hiring employees! We were busy and, again, I was up to my ears in alligators!

I needed more help. Coincidentally, my brother Marty happened to be in between jobs and asked if I needed help.

I said, "Oh, boy, do I!"

Marty came to work right away and quickly became my director of operations at Pacific. He later became vice president of the company. Together we attended Super Bowls, World Series, MLB All-Star Games, National Sports Collectors Conventions, and many other events where Pacific Trading Cards, Inc., was promoted. Marty was with me for five great years, until he left to start his own retail furniture company.

During the 1991 season, I hired several sports action photographers to shoot NFL games exclusively for us. I knew a trading card was basically just a photo, and I wanted the best photos we could get for our cards.

As a NFL licenser, Pacific could send out our photographers to be on the sidelines and shoot any NFL game for Pacific. They would shoot the game with photo/slides film and overnight the film to us with a game roster. We processed the photos, identified the players in the photos, and filed them in our photo library for future use on cards.

One of the photographers that joined Pacific that season was Jack Wallin. His work stood out among the group we hired. He had, up to that season, never shot an NFL game but was a seasoned Major League Baseball photographer shooting out of Wrigley Field in Chicago, where he lived.

I took charge of the Pacific photo department and, at that time, either myself or my secretary, Rae, talked to the photographers one on one before and after each game. I talked to Jack a lot. He was excited and enthusiastic, and he loved this job. He said, "Being on the sidelines, shooting an NFL game—it's a gigantic rush!"

Immediately, I wanted to learn more. I wanted to learn how to shoot, so I could photograph a game! Jack told me where to buy Canon cameras (you had to have two in case something happened to one). The same outlet sold the long white Canon 400mm lens, light meters, and other parts I would need.

Jack taught me light settings, how to use the light meter and, most importantly, where to position myself on the sidelines to get the best shots of the players. All of this schooling was done over the phone. I listened to every word Jack said, etching it in the front of my brain.

I ordered all the camera gear, and it arrived about a week later, on a Thursday. I immediately unpacked all of it. I mounted the camera onto the lens, loaded up the batteries, and shot a few photos. The camera could take seven frames a second, and it had autofocus. If Emmitt Smith ran the ball at me during the game, I could get 36 photos in a few seconds before the roll of film ended.

I was excited and had my secretary book me for the San Francisco 49ers vs. Dallas Cowboys game three days later. I boarded a very early flight to San Francisco that Sunday morning, took a taxi to Candlestick Park, picked up my game pass, and entered the stadium.

There were a couple photographers already in the stadium and, in talking to them, I revealed to them it was my first game. They asked, "How much film did you bring?" I said, "Thirty-five rolls of Fuji 100 slide film."

I did not tell them that I had picked up this camera for the first time three days ago.

Then I got the schooling on how not to get killed on the sidelines.

When you shoot on the sideline, you kneel. You're looking through a long lens focused on one player, not the game. The other guys said, "If your lens fills up full of a player, get the hell out of the way, because that player is about to run over you!"

That was good advice. It happened a lot, and I learned to bail out pretty quickly when I needed to!

One time, at an Oakland Raiders game, a photographer right next to me couldn't get out of the way in time, and he took a knee right in the chest from a running back. His camera and lens went flying, and the lens broke off in two pieces, exposing about a million colored wires.

I shot that first game and survived—and it *was* a gigantic rush. I was hooked!

I flew home that night with my 35 rolls of film (I did shoot all the film I took with me). I developed it all the next day, and I had some beautiful photos of NFL football players. The lighting at Candlestick Park was as perfect as it can get, and Emmitt Smith ran the ball my way several times. We had plenty of his photos (and other players' photos) from the two teams I'd shot to publish on our cards.

I liked shooting NFL games so much, I shot photos 14 weekends that season. In fact, every NFL weekend after that for the next seven years, I was at a game somewhere. Sometimes, Cheryl went with me. One time, we flew to Buffalo early and went to Niagara Falls. I shot the Buffalo Bills game on Sunday and, not long after, I bought a second set of camera gear. After that, whenever Cheryl went with me, I got her a pass, and she shot a few games with me.

She didn't like the sidelines that much, so I had her go to the bench and shoot headshots of the players for the backs of the cards. We used some of her photos and, 25 years later, when our grandson Ryder was collecting football cards, Cheryl gave him some football cards with player photos his grandmother had taken.

Ten-year-old Ryder was very impressed. His grandmother was famous—an NFL photographer!

In February of 1992, Pacific attended the NFL Experience at the Super Bowl in Minneapolis, Minnesota. Cheryl, our daughter Rachael and I went, along with several Pacific employees. It was a cold winter in Minneapolis, with snow piled 12 feet high on some of the roads. Fans braved the temperatures and, in spite of the weather, the NFL Experience was busy.

We brought in the great Seahawks wide receiver Steve Largent to sign autographs in the Pacific booth. Largent held several NFL records when he retired in 1989 and was very popular.

One of the other card companies brought in a very young player named Emmitt Smith to sign at their booth. Steve Largent had been

9. 1991 Pacific Plus Football Cards

Emmitt Smith (left) and Steve Largent at the Pacific Booth at the 1992 Super Bowl Card Show in Minnesota—two of the NFL's greatest players, both are in the Hall of Fame (Pacific Trading Cards Archives).

signing in the Pacific booth for a few hours and always had a line of people waiting. In the afternoon, I was sitting next to Steve helping fans through the line when I looked up and, to my astonishment, I saw Emmitt Smith waiting in our line. He had taken a break from his signing and wanted to meet Steve.

I whispered to Steve, "I believe Emmitt Smith is in our line." Steve glanced up from his signing, saw Emmitt, and immediately jumped up to go greet him. It was one of the most spectacular moments I ever had the privilege of witnessing. They both had big smiles. Then Emmitt and Steve decided to sit down in our booth so Steve could continue signing autographs for the fans while they continued talking.

Within a minute, the fans realized that Emmitt Smith was at our booth and lined up for his autograph too. We had two lines going. Steve and Emmitt were both signing away, chatting between themselves and with the fans.

It was great! My brother, Marty, and I had the high-fives going. We had the biggest crowd at the show! It wasn't long before the PR director from the other card company came over to see what all the commotion was. That ended our coup.

But for a short 10 minutes or so, we had two of the greatest NFL players ever together, signing autographs and enjoying conversation.

Great as that day was, the story of that feat would actually improve over the years.

Young Emmitt Smith would go on to become one of the greatest running backs in NFL history, and Steve Largent would be elected to the Pro Football Hall of Fame in 1995, his first year of eligibility.

10

Growing by Leaps and Bounds

Running your own business is a never-ending battle. Everything at Pacific was running smoothly in the fall of 1992, but I saw two issues on the horizon.

First, our trading card graphics work was being hired out, which was both expensive and required a large amount of my time to oversee.

Luckily, about that time, Apple Computers released a new computer that could handle incredibly large data files—like the files needed to create trading card templates. The new computer could handle huge files, but was so small itself, it fit on a desktop. One of the programs Apple developed to go with the new computer was a desktop graphics production program.

I wanted to bring our trading card graphic production in-house, under our roof. Then we would have hands-on production of all our trading cards and designs, and we could produce our own printing film to send to the printer.

My retail store manager, Ann (the kid who used to come to spend two dollars on cards every week), was by this time married to a fellow named Rob Hicks. He was a local delivery driver but was dabbling in a new thing called computer graphics.

Rob had helped Ann with the graphics layout for the Pacific Trading Cards mail-order catalog. The catalog was still being mailed twice a year to some 50,000 card collectors, and Ann was running that side of the business. We printed mailing labels on our Ohio Scientific Computer, which was the size of a small refrigerator, boasted a powerful 26 megabyte hard drive, and was considered "state-of-the-art" at that time. (It would soon become a dinosaur.)

Rob came to me and said we should produce the mail-order catalog with desktop graphics. He said he could help me set up not only the computers but also a whole graphics department at Pacific.

I asked, "Once we set it up, who will run it to do the work?"

10. Growing by Leaps and Bounds

This was my card factory: Pacific Trading Cards. We moved into the building in 1989. Every trading card we produced from that point on came through these doors (Pacific Trading Cards Archives).

"I will!" Rob said.

I said, "Do you know how to do it?"

"No," he said. "But no else does, either. It's all new! But I can learn."

Boy, that attitude sounded familiar....

I then asked, "Can we design and compile film for our card sets on the desktop too?"

Rob assured me that we could. And so we bought the Apple computer, monitor, software, and a state-of-the-art photo scanner. Then Rob started on the graphics for the first card set Pacific ever produced on our new equipment: a 110-card set of World War II history.

I liked this new way of doing things. We had a tremendous amount of control over the design and production of this set. I could go down to the graphics department (which was just Rob at that time) and look at a card design on the computer monitor. Changes to the design were a piece of cake: he just pressed some buttons on the keyboard to make changes, and the new look would show up on the computer monitor!

This was a serious game changer for Pacific.

We would no longer have to manually produce our printing film by cutting and pasting physical photos and blocks of text and decorative card borders. This would save both money and countless hours of time from dozens of skilled workers.

I saw the potential and went one step further. I bought the machine that printed out the film used to make printing plates. All of our card sets, wrappers, display boxes, sales materials—everything needed to print our card products was now created in-house at Pacific.

This included our first (and the trading card industry's first) full-card Prism cards, created by Pacific in 1992 and released as an insert in the 1992 Pacific Pro Plus Football. Each card featured a player photo surrounded by a Prism background.

In this Pacific Plus set of 660 football cards, we included a New England Patriots rookie tight end named Ben Coates, card #196. This card became his only rookie card. In 2022, Pacific Pro Plus Football had 38 cards of Pro Football Hall of Fame players; Ben Coates could be a great new addition in the future.

Looking back, I can see that Pacific made cards during one of the best times in sports history. Some of the greatest, if not the greatest, players in their respective sports played during the years Pacific manufactured cards: in baseball, Ken Griffey, Jr., Cal Ripken, Jr., and Nolan Ryan; in football, Tom Brady, Emmitt Smith, Joe Montana, and Kurt Warner; in hockey, Wayne Gretzky, Joe Thornton, and Martin Brodeur. And that's just a handful of the great players we made cards of.

Our sets from over the years are loaded with Hall of Famers. I'm always so pleased when I hear of collectors who search for, then find, specific Pacific cards for their collections. The Cramer's Choice Award cards are still sought-after by collectors—including myself! I still collect them, in PSA 10 grade, when I can get my hands on one. However, I find myself getting outbid for those cards most of the time!

In 1993, Topps came out with something similar to our Pacific Prism cards. Topps called their card a "refractor." They like to credit themselves for being first, but Pacific had released this kind of card one year before, and the cards are out there to prove it.

I still like the Topps brand. Pacific was, after all, a stepchild of Topps. Topps, in its way, helped launch Pacific back in the late 1970s, so … thank you, Topps, for that!

Rob Hicks was the first person I ever met (besides myself) who could pick up a manual, read it, and understand what he was doing. (I've conquered a lot of such challenges, though I still can't figure out IKEA furniture.) Rob learned how to use the Apple graphics software and computers in short order, just by reading the manuals and trying things.

Pacific was designing and producing trading cards like never before. Our pre-press department was starting to grow.

In 1992, Shannon Johnson came to work for Pacific. She was put in charge of our customer service department. Her job, and her crew's main task, was to answer collectors' questions about Pacific products, both by mail and over the phone.

Shannon and her team could also replace cards that might have been damaged in the production process. And when we started to keep records

10. Growing by Leaps and Bounds

of our card products in 1994, Shannon was responsible for the binders we kept on file containing sample cards and production records for each product Pacific made.

We called the binders "The Shannon Books," because her name is on the front of the binders.

Years later, in 2021, I was cleaning my attic and found those binders. They contain a treasure trove of information about Pacific products, and I had kept them. After all, I am a collector, through and through.

Pacific was doing well. We were making soccer cards and NFL football cards, but ... I still had that dream of making baseball cards. There was no getting rid of it. I was a baseball fan, and my dream of making Major League Baseball cards on a grand scale was still not fulfilled. I needed to make it happen!

In the fall of 1992, Pacific was able to meet with the MLBPA to present our ideas and designs for a baseball card license. Marty, Victor Temkin, and I flew to New York City for that meeting. We took along the prototype cards I made in 1991: 10 different baseball players with the cards printed in English, and the same 10 players with cards printed in Spanish. We had a presentation folder with all the pertinent information.

We quickly learned that the MLBPA thought there was no room in the market at that time for us, and so they declined to give us a full license to produce baseball cards. Then we presented our second idea: Spanish-language baseball cards.

The MLBPA had interest in this. Towards the end of the meeting, they told us that their current licensees were talking about making cards in Spanish.

"Yes, they talk about it," I said, "but they don't do it. I will!"

After I said that, they told us they were going to recommend to the players that Pacific receive a license to produce Spanish-language cards for the 1993 baseball season.

My dream came true a few weeks later when I signed that baseball card license. I was the happiest man on the face of the earth!

In 1993, Pacific produced the first all–Spanish-language set of baseball cards ever in the United States, a large, 660-card set. I found the task of making 660 different baseball players cards, along with some insert card sets, totally fun and exciting. I knew the names of all the players and which teams they were on; this was going to be a breeze for me.

I used the same card design we had shown in the licensing meeting. Then all I had to do was find 1200 photos, one photo for the front of each card and one for the back—no easy task. But with the help of my football photographers, who knew all of the baseball photographers out there, baseball photos and slides began to arrive at Pacific. I handpicked every photo we used in that card set.

Writing the copy for card backs was a huge project, but I finished up and sent the copy to be translated to Spanish. Having gotten the card production well under way, I moved on to the packaging and sales materials side. We were ready to print and package in February of 1993. Then I went to Mexico and found a sales broker to sell the product down there. That was a big step.

Pacific released the first series of 330 cards in the spring and the second series a month or so later. I was happy with sales and distribution, and we were able to open up some new markets in Mexico for the product. Nearly 30 years later, that set, produced in 1993, contains 43 players that were inducted into the Baseball Hall of Fame: Robin Yount, Dave Winfield, Nolan Ryan and Ken Griffey, Jr., are among them. Interestingly enough, I see nowadays that more and more collectors are searching out cards of their favorite players from the 1993 Pacific Baseball set.

That year, we got busier than ever before, so I set up eight departments at Pacific. I appointed eight managers to oversee departments including Graphics/Pre-Press, Production, Media, Customer Service, Shipping, Sales, Purchasing, and Accounting.

We became a well-oiled machine. I was able to develop and create new card products while Marty directed the day-to-day operations. We had great employees, some of whom had been with Pacific for more than 10 of its 13 years.

* * *

The second big issue I had to overcome in Pacific's growth was that of our card-packaging lines. Our very capable DF-1 card wax wrappers were becoming dinosaurs. They were slow, and their end product was a folded wax pack of cards. Very nostalgic, but....

I had heard of a new machine that could wrap cards at up to 500 packs per minute. These machines sealed wrappers made of thin, printed plastic material that came on a roll; the machine formed the plastic wrap around the cards, and a rotating hot knife cut and heat-sealed the pack at the proper length. It was called a "flow wrapper" and was fast becoming the trading card industry standard. I knew Pacific needed to upgrade our packaging lines to adopt this machine.

However, this new machine came with a price tag of $250,000 to $400,000 each, depending on the add-ons. That was a whopping chunk of change for a machine. The most I ever paid for a DF-1 wax wrapper was $2,500 and, truth be told, even that had been a bargain. I knew that

10. Growing by Leaps and Bounds

Donruss had paid up to $29,000 for most of their DF-1 wrappers, even used ones.

We had had a good year and did have the cash reserves. We ordered one of the new machines and paid cash for it. In the history of Pacific, I never bought any equipment we didn't have cash to pay for. I didn't want to, and Pacific never had debt.

Later that summer, the new flow wrapper from FMC was on the production floor at Pacific.

The card feed lug track was 32 feet long. Instead of a gravity feed hopper to deliver the cards onto the track, the flow wrapper used an air-driven rotating suction cup system with four suction cups, one for each of four card hoppers.

Each cup gently picked a single card from one of the hoppers. Cards were then placed on the chain and carried into the wrapper at a rate of about 200 per minute. Because the in-feed track was so long, we could have up to 32 card magazines feeding the machine at one time. Up to 32 different cards could be wrapped in a pack at one time (though the average number of cards per pack ranged from two to 12).

The engineers at Pacific had that FMC wrapper up and running in time to help pack 1992 Pacific NFL Football Plus. We still used the DF-1 wrappers for some of the packaging production (that's why there are two different types of packs for 1992 Pacific football). The FMC wrapper was so efficient, we eventually ordered three more.

The beauty of it was I never had to work on those machines. Those days were long gone. My production engineers ran and maintained all Pacific packaging lines.

With our packaging lines all modernized and running perfectly, there was no need to keep the DF-1 wax wrappers, the packaging machines that had helped build Pacific. They had become obsolete. I made the hard decision: we would have to scrap them.

The day we pulled the DF-1 machines off the line brought back a lot of memories for me. I remembered the first time I made that machine wrap a pack of cards and realized there would be no looking back for Pacific. I thought of all the hours I had devoted to keeping them up and running in the early days ... these machines had become my friends.

I said goodbye to each one. I couldn't watch them being loaded on the trucks headed to the scrap heap. Those machines had made Pacific a lot of money and had served us well.

If there is ever a trading card museum, a Package Machinery DF-1 wax wrapper ought to be in it. That machine was part of the history of trading cards. Hobbyists that collect wax packs and wax wrappers never got to see that machine running and probably know nothing about how the wrapper operated until now. However, that machine helped create the iconic wax pack, the prize that wrapper collectors still search for and collect so passionately.

Before we sent the DF-1s to the scrap heap, I had Felix remove one of the brass folding boxes that helped fold the wax wrapper over and under the cards. I still have that folding box as a memento of those days. It could be the only one left in existence. I'm not sure if any DF-1 wax wrapper machines still exist; unfortunately, they were probably all melted down years ago.

* * *

Pacific had been modernized in two crucial areas. We could now move forward to bigger and better days ahead.

The Prism cards we were making as an insert set had become so immensely popular, I decided to make a brand out of it in 1993. The Pacific team had a brainstorming meeting about it.

There, I announced the new football brand name, "Pacific Prism." Then I said, "These cards are so nice, we're only going to put one card in a pack."

No one in that meeting thought that was a good idea.

"No one is going to buy a pack with only one card in it!"

But I knew that, in 1993, the Pacific Prism card design was light years ahead of its time. I just said, "Collectors will buy them, and we are going to make that product."

We turned and burned, and when we launched Pacific Prism NFL Football cards in the summer of 1993, it sold out faster than any product Pacific had produced up until then.

The Prism trading card brand first introduced by Pacific in 1993 was still being made 30 years later by Panini, the company that bought the Pacific brands. I was thrilled to hear the brand was still alive and that, even though the spelling had been changed, Prizm is their flagship brand.

* * *

In the fall of 1993, the MLBPA invited me to accompany them to meetings with the World Baseball Organization in Barcelona, Spain, and personally introduce the Pacific Major League Baseball Spanish-language cards to Spain. Of course, I said yes!

And of course Cheryl went with me, and we made our first trip to Europe together. We brought along a display booth and two cases of Pacific baseball cards.

We set the booth up for two days, in a neighborhood of Barcelona near where a baseball exhibition game was to take place. Dozens of excited,

10. Growing by Leaps and Bounds

courteous kids came to the booth to see what we were doing. We showed them the baseball cards.

The kids had no idea what baseball cards were or what those beautiful pictures were for.

I said, "The cards are for collecting; you save them."

One little boy asked, "Why?"

I said, "In America, kids collect their favorite baseball players, or collect the entire set of cards."

Well, these kids had no idea what Major League Baseball was and didn't know any of the players. However, the kids liked the pictures on the cards and very quickly saw that a lot of the players had Spanish names.

It didn't matter that they had no idea what the cards were; the kids still wanted some.

Years later, I often wondered whatever happened to those Pacific baseball cards in Spain.

The best thing that came out of the trip to Spain was seeing the symbol of the Spanish crown for the first time. Cheryl and I were able to spend some time sightseeing and touring Barcelona, and I noticed the Spanish crown emblem everywhere—on buildings, on lampposts, on billboards....

I liked it.

I had been looking for a new logo for the Pacific card brands and thought a crown would look wonderful. And it fit in well on our trading cards. We would upscale our card designs, printing a crown in gold foil on our cards and on our packaging.

Pacific Crown Collection was born. When our baseball, football and basketball card products were launched in 1994, all of them featured the new Pacific crown.

The new crown logo was a hit with collectors. The beautiful card designs Pacific created that year were instantly successful.

* * *

In 1994, I went to spring training in Arizona to shoot major league baseball player photos for our cards for the first time. We had Jack Wallin and a couple of other Pacific photographers covering Florida, but just one Arizona photographer who couldn't cover all of the teams due to overlapping headshot days. I decided I would help cover headshot days—and also catch some spring training games. How fun would that be? I remembered, when I was a kid, clamoring to go to just one spring training game. Now I would be a participant, on the field taking pictures of Major League players!

Headshot days were at the very start of spring training. About 40 players on each team's spring training roster came out in the morning before practice and posed individually for about 10 different photographers.

Card companies, newspapers, and team photographers were all there taking photos. The photographers lined up, and players just basically went down the line. The first picture each shooter took was of the player holding a piece of paper up to his waist with a number on it: this picture let photographers identify each player from the team roster. Then each player posed left, posed right, and posed with a bat. Next, photographers got six to eight nice headshots of each player. (At Pacific, we used headshots on the card backs and sometimes on the fronts.)

On my first day, I shot the California Angels. I had great lighting that day, soft clouds with the sun filtering through. All of the players on the Angels roster came out to pose. The next day, the Cubs and A's shoot was at the same time, so I took the A's and our other photographer took the Cubs.

It was not so easy that second day. These A's players didn't have numbered signs. So I asked each player to turn around for a shot of his back—where his uniform number was.

It was extremely important to identify who each player was. This normally-easy task was made difficult by the sheer number of players we had to deal with. There's nothing worse than printing a card with all the correct information, then realizing the photo is of the wrong player—and, in spite of all our precautions, it did happen a few times.

I was going through the A's lineup of players very smoothly when I looked through my lens and saw number 25. I took the photo. The player then turned around.

It was A's slugger Mark McGwire.

That was a wow factor! I was shooting photos of one of the greats of those days.

At seven frames a second, I shot the entire roll of 36 photos. He just looked at me and asked, "Did you get enough?"

The next day, I shot the San Francisco Giants. That's when I learned that a few players didn't pose on headshot days. Barry Bonds was one of those players. That's why, when you look at his cards from that era (where headshots were used), you won't find a posed headshot photo of him on the cards. His headshots are virtually all candid shots, taken with a pretty long lens.

Spring training was fun. I enjoyed it so much, I went back for seven years straight.

* * *

A lot of key players came on board Pacific in 1994. We hired a new national sales manager, Bruce Chappelear. Bruce was a former college football player and the former sales manager of the now-defunct card manufacturer Pro Set. Chappelear was truly a game changer for Pacific

10. Growing by Leaps and Bounds

and became a crucial part of our success when we later launched our NHL and MLB trading card brands.

Bruce was very structured and knew our product lines well. His great sales skills helped drive our retail sales for the next 10 years. Under Bruce's leadership, 75 percent of our 1994 sales were through retail stores, from giants like Walmart, Target, Kmart, Toys"R"Us and 7-Eleven to smaller outlets such as news and magazine stands. If a U.S. retail store carried trading cards, chances were good that they carried Pacific.

Our sales to hobby shops lagged considerably behind the retail. To beef up our hobby sales, I hired my good friend, hobby expert Bob Wilke.

I first met Bob when I lived in Phoenix. He was a collector who first contacted me when he got my 1975 Phoenix Giant card. Bob later opened a card store in Phoenix. He had a wealth of trading card knowledge. He moved his family from Phoenix to Edmonds, Washington, to work full-time at Pacific. His help was instrumental in growing our hobby store sales.

That year, Walmart changed its card buying and distribution. This meant no more trips to Bentonville, Arkansas, for our sales crew and me. Instead, Walmart started working through Treat Hobbies, a company that bought our trading cards and then supplied the Walmart stores, replenishing when needed. This turned out to be a boon for Pacific products in Walmart stores.

The face of our new buyer and distributor was Harold Anderson, who had founded Treat Hobby. Harold knew how to merchandise: he came from a family of merchandisers. His family's flagship company, Anderson News, was the largest magazine wholesale company in America.

Harold was a friend of Pacific. He had watched Pacific grow from the Baseball Legends days into a trading card manufacturer with two substantial licenses (baseball and football) and an array of other products. We had a great mutual respect for each other. With as much distribution as Harold and Treat Hobbies had, he would write purchase orders for more than a million dollars for one product.

The beauty of it was none of the products he ordered were ever returned. With Harold, products always sold through at retail. This was excellent business for Pacific, Walmart, and Treat. We had that relationship until Pacific was sold in 2004.

* * *

In the summer of 1994, NFL Properties had its annual licensing meetings in Palm Desert, California. Along with meetings and dinners, a golf outing was offered to attendees. My brother Marty and I signed up to play in the Best Ball tournament, as did several current and former football players.

This was in July—and it was hot. Tournament organizers had cases of bottled Perrier water out on the course to drink, thinking we would be fine to play in that heat.

Not so. By noon, the temperature had reached 107°F. Most of the golfers (including some of the NFL players) were overheated. We drank cases of Perrier. Some of the NFL linemen that were playing—these were big men—were drinking five to six bottles of Perrier, then dumping five to six bottles over their heads in an effort to cool down.

When Marty and I saw that, we started doing likewise. It was just so hot! I bet the golfers that day must have dumped 1000 bottles or more of expensive Perrier water over their heads. Not many golfers finished that round. We certainly didn't.

That evening, we had a great time. We attended the NFL dinner banquet, where the guest speaker was football great Terry Bradshaw. He was an outstanding speaker and also extremely funny.

At the licensing meetings, we met Ken Goldin, who had a reputation as a very smart man and a trading card hobby visionary. He requested a meeting with us. Victor and I had some licensing meetings already scheduled, so my brother Marty went to see what Ken had in mind.

Through his company, Classic Games, Ken had signed enough 1993 NBA basketball draft pick players to make a trading card set. He told Marty he could sublicense Pacific to make a basketball card product. Marty reported the news back to Victor and me.

We were very excited. This would be a new venture for Pacific.

We signed a three-year sublicense with Ken and Classic Games. We would produce only 1500 20-box cases. How do I remember that? Because the production records for 1993 Pacific Prism Basketball still exist, in "The Shannon Books."

We produced our first Basketball Draft Pick product, Pacific Prism, that year. That first set sold through fairly quickly. Future NBA Hall of Famers Grant Hill and Jason Kidd are in that set.

That year, we also made a very popular card set based on the TV show *Saved by the Bell*. The set included a 10-card Prism insert that had a card featuring Screech, a character on the show played by Dustin Diamond. That card became the hottest card in the set in later years.

Our in-house graphics department was up to the challenges that came their way. By this time, four full-time graphic artists were working, designing our cards and producing printing film for our wrappers, display boxes and other card components.

In-house graphics was a very expensive department to maintain, as the technology for desktop publishing kept growing by leaps and bounds. Apple regularly released new computers and monitors that eclipsed the

10. Growing by Leaps and Bounds

technology we had. Of course, we had to buy all new equipment and its accompanying software. Even though the "old" equipment was only a year or so old, it was already obsolete. Sometimes, the software was obsolete after only six to eight months, and we had to buy upgrades.

But every time we upgraded, we could make even better card designs, and this kept us on the leading edge in card designs.

We were always on the lookout for graphic designers who could come to work for Pacific. Cornish College of the Arts in Seattle was the source for most of the designers that came to work at Pacific. Word got out at the school that there were jobs designing and producing trading cards at Pacific. Some extremely talented people applied for jobs, and we had the pick of the best.

Our card designs just got better and better. When our team had a new design ready and up on the computer screens, I would go down and look. Sometimes I would tweak it a bit, but most of the time I would just say, "Wow! Go with that."

These people were talented. The competition was easily 18 months behind us, always scrambling to catch up. Our card designs were way ahead of the game—and we knew it too!

For example, right at this time we developed a way to print cards on crystal clear plastic. Our first set using this new idea was a 20-card insert set in 1994 Pacific Football. We named the cards the Crystalline Collection.

Realizing we could print high quality cards on this new plastic material got my creative juices flowing with new ideas! We figured out how to print and laminate the clear plastic between card stocks, making both a window and a view. We created Pacific Invincible, a card with a player's headshot printed in a clear plastic window, and added it to our baseball, football, and hockey lines. We used this idea over the years for many of our insert cards.

During this time, I was still shooting NFL games on Sundays. I realized that, if I was in San Francisco on Sunday, why not shoot a baseball game in Oakland on Saturday? Or vice versa.

And I did. There were years I worked seven days a week during those months. We had to have great photos to produce great cards, and I was a part of that.

The Baseball Hall of Fame has inducted 41 of the players who are in 1994 Pacific Crown Collection Baseball, and the 1994 Crown Collection Football has 40 players enshrined in Canton, including a rookie card of running back Marshall Faulk.

In 1994, we also introduced Pacific Triple Folders, a new product with an all-new design. Each of the 33 cards in the set had a player photo that folded open to reveal three more photos of the player. The set has 13 Hall of Fame players to date.

We were back on cruise control. We had great-selling products, with Pacific Prism Football as our the hottest-selling brand for the second straight year. I started to concentrate once again on the new, innovative card designs that were keeping Pacific out in front of the competition. After all, a trading card is just a thick piece of paper with ink printed on it—but I wanted to take that piece of paper and turn it into a card like no one had ever seen. Keeping up with the newest technology helped fuel design innovation.

I sometimes thought to myself how easy Mr. Hershey's job was. Around 1900, he designed and made a chocolate bar. The Hershey Company is still making that same basic candy bar some 120 years later. Of course his job was much more than that, but you get the idea.

At Pacific, we made baseball, football and basketball cards, but every year we had to create all new cards for our established brands as well as introduce some new brands (completely different card designs) to go with our reliable flagship products—maybe Mr. Hershey had it easier, but I loved my job.

Almost all of our ideas for card designs came through our monthly design think-tank team meetings, where six to eight people met in the conference room, bouncing ideas off each other and, sometimes, off the walls.

I would often look around the meeting table and see every person consumed in thought, right arms draped over their heads. I'd say, "Look at us!" We'd all start laughing, and new card design ideas started pouring out.

Victor Temkin was great at getting us to explore and expand our ideas and to open our creative minds. He had his arm draped over his head too.

* * *

In 1995, Pacific attended the National Sports Collectors Convention in St. Louis. We set up our big trade show booth, displaying our cards and promoting our products to the dealers and collectors attending.

Cheryl and our four kids came to the St. Louis National with me, planning to spend a day at Six Flags Theme Park.

Frank Torre was in his fifth year working for Pacific and attended the show to help promote our baseball and football cards. He called me before I left, and we agreed to meet in St. Louis a day early to talk. Frank also mentioned that, after our meetings, we would go to dinner at the best Italian restaurant in St. Louis, Rigazzi's, the oldest restaurant in the historic Hill neighborhood.

That sounded fun. Then Frank told me his brother Joe would be there,

10. Growing by Leaps and Bounds 119

along with Hall of Fame pitcher Bob Gibson and former Major League player and announcer Bob Uecker. I asked Frank if I could get some signed Gibson photos so we could hand them out to clients. He said, "Sure, whatever you need." I ordered 25 eight-by-10 color Bob Gibson photos and brought them with me.

Our day-long meeting went well and, at the end of it, we were hungry. I got dressed in a jacket and tie, and Frank and I headed out to Rigazzi's.

When we arrived at the restaurant, we were shown to the table where Joe Torre, Bob Gibson and Bob Uecker were already seated, along with one other man that I recognized immediately: Yankee great and Hall of Famer Yogi Berra! He had grown up in the Hill neighborhood and was in town visiting for the week.

"Meet Mike Cramer," Frank said, "president and owner of Pacific Trading Cards."

We all shook hands, and I was seated at the table with Yogi on my right and Bob Uecker on my left.

This was a dream come true for a baseball fan. For a second, I thought back to my days as a kid collecting baseball cards. This was unreal! I was seated at dinner with five former major league players that I had baseball cards of!

And my next thought was, I'm the only one at this table that has a card of every person sitting at this table—including me!

That's a crazy thing to think of, unless you collect cards, like I do.

They all started talking, and I listened to some great stories. Bob Uecker and Yogi Berra were very funny, but Uecker was at times hilarious.

We ordered, and when I was halfway through my salad, Yogi turned to me and said, "So, you own a card company. How did you get into that business?" He and Uecker listened as I told a short story of how I started as a card collector, fished king crab, then grew my hobby into Pacific Trading Cards. They were both very interested, and Bob said, "Mike, you should write a book."

That's the first time I ever heard that.

Then Yogi said, "You must be rich."

I said, "Well, I'm not rich, but I do okay."

He said, "You have to be rich! I've signed so many of your Pacific Baseball Legends cards."

Bob Gibson heard that and said, "I'm on a Pacific Legends card."

Joe and Frank chimed in, saying they were each on a card too.

Bob Uecker looked at me. "I don't have one," he said.

Everyone at the table heard. There was a short silence. Then Yogi said, "Geez, Ueck, get over it. Ya hit .200!"

As the wave of laughter hit, I looked around at the faces. *Wow.* I was having dinner with baseball players I had made cards of in the early years at Pacific, and they were talking about my cards!

Yogi Berra was in the 1988 and 1990 Pacific Baseball Legends sets. Joe Torre, Frank Torre and Bob Gibson were in the 1990 set. Bob Uecker wasn't in the Legends sets, but he was a true baseball legend and was honored by the Baseball Hall of Fame in 2003 with the Ford C. Frick Award.

Later that evening, Frank, Bob Uecker and I asked a waiter to take our picture.

When I told Cheryl all about my dinner, I said, "Don't pinch me—I might be dreaming."

When I told the kids about it, not one of them could understand how my day could have possibly been better than their day at Six Flags.

Crazy thing was, I never thought to ask Bob Gibson to sign the photos I brought. I guess because, for that brief moment in time, I was just one of the boys.

I went to bed that night remembering all the pop bottles I'd gathered and sold as a kid so I could buy and collect baseball cards. And now, I was having dinner with some of the players on those cards.

It was hard to go to sleep that night.

* * *

The next morning, it was back to reality—although, for me, the trading card business was a pretty nice reality. The show had started, and Pacific was busy meeting collectors and dealers.

One of the dealers attending the show was Mike Caffey. He was very enthusiastic about our cards and knew that Pacific was on the cutting edge with some of our breakthrough technologies and card designs.

Mike told me that he had some card design ideas. He wanted to share them with me because, if Pacific could make the cards he had in mind, Mike

Me with Bob Uecker. Bob Uecker once told me I should write a book. That was good advice (Pacific Trading Cards Archives).

10. Growing by Leaps and Bounds

himself could sell more of our products at card shows, and collectors would love them.

I was very interested and always looking for new ideas. So we set up a meeting. I invited Mike to come to Pacific's Lynnwood, Washington, offices.

In our meetings, I found out that Mike did, indeed, have some new and innovative card design ideas. That meeting was the birth of the Cramer's Choice insert set.

Pacific already was making a card insert set called Pacific Picks the Pros, featuring 25 of the top players in the game.

Mike saw a different angle. Because I was shooting players' photos at the games, both baseball and football, he saw that I had an insight to the players. I watched them play on the field; I was close to the action. He also knew I followed the games and players very astutely and studied the players.

He said, "I know you're making Pacific Picks the Pros, but I want you to pick the players: it needs to be your choice."

I said, "You mean, like … 'Cramer's Choice'?"

Wow! A rocket ship went up at that moment. We instantly knew we had a winner.

I grabbed a sheet of paper and started to draw some lines on it to get an idea for the card design. A trophy look—no, not quite … this card had to be something special. We pushed further, bouncing ideas off each other. The trophy lines became obelisk lines. That was it!

I ran downstairs to the graphics department, gave the sketch to Rob Hicks and said, "Here is an idea for a die-cut card,

Jumbo Cramer's Choice Awards acrylic holder. The jumbo-size Cramer's Choice Award cards display wonderfully in the holder (Pacific Trading Cards Archives).

Cramer's Choice Awards. Can you take it further?"

I would pick the players for the Cramer's Choice Awards set, and I would write the card copy for the backs of those cards. After all, I was Cramer.

That same card design and concept we conceptualized that day is still in use some 30 years later by Panini Card Company. It's been called Pacific's Choice and Panini's Choice, but the concept (and the obelisk shape) remain.

Rob did take our idea further. He called me back about an hour later to view the new design on the computer monitor. A couple tweaks later, and the new Pacific Cramer's Choice Awards cards were born.

1996 Pacific Gold Crown Die-Cuts card. This unique card design is a favorite of collectors and is still being produced 30 years after Pacific first made it (Pacific Trading Cards Archives).

When the six-card insert set of 1995 Cramer's Choice Awards was released in Pacific Crown Collection NFL Football later that year, they were an instant hit. Five of the six players in the first Cramer's Choice Award set eventually went into the Football Hall of Fame. I liked them so much that I had our purchasing department order a crystal-clear, acrylic screw-down holder that collectors could display their favorite Cramer's Choice Award in and place on their shelves. The holder was very popular and came in two sizes: one size for the regular-size card and a larger size for the Jumbo Cramer's Choice Award card.

Out of that same meeting, Mike and I came up with several more card design ideas, including Gold Crown Die-Cut insert cards. Mike had seen our new crown logo and asked, "Can you die-cut your logo out of the top of the card?"

10. Growing by Leaps and Bounds

I just loved that. I said, "I'm not sure, but we will figure out how to do it." Then I sketched a card design with the Pacific Crown in gold at the top.

It was an incredible feeling of accomplishment when we printed that card, and I first saw our beautiful new crown design. No other company had any card even remotely close to the Pacific Gold Crown Die-Cut.

That exact card design and concept was also still made by Panini, some 30 years later.

Pacific was literally turning cardboard into gold—in more ways than one!

I liked the Pacific Gold Crown design so much I wanted to use it for an entire card set. And because I was the President/CEO of Pacific Trading Cards…. Yes, I could do that! I could make cards my way.

I got to work developing an entire brand of new Gold Crown Die-Cut trading cards for Pacific.

That new brand was Pacific Crown Royale, first launched by Pacific in 1995. It had 144 different horizontal football players cards, all die-cut with the shape of the Pacific Crown at the top.

It wasn't easy.

We had to handle the Crown cards with kid gloves. We didn't want

1996 Pacific Crown Royale. This card design and brand name has stood the test of time and was still being made 30 years after Pacific first introduced it (Pacific Trading Cards Archives).

any damaged cards going into packs, so our packaging lines had to be revamped to run the card packs.

A regular trading card has four sharp corners, like most pieces of paper. Crown Royale cards had only two crisp corners, both at the bottom of the card; the shape of a crown replaced the two top corners. Still, the cards had to be held in the card hoppers for rotary feeding onto the chain in-feed track.

With a lot of trial and error, we were re-inventing the packaging process.

Our packaging engineers achieved perfection, and the 1995 Pacific Crown Royale Football was up and running. After that first Crown Royale product, the Crown Royale products we produced in following years were a breeze to make.

In recent years, collectors are getting their cards PSA Graded. I saw that many of our Crown Royale Die-Cut cards achieved a grade of 10, gem-mint—a condition that was maintained throughout the packing line.

We did achieve perfection with that card.

Pacific Crown Royale was a huge success, and the trading card industry was paying serious attention to Pacific.

11

Playing with the Big Boys

Pacific and I had come a long way since 1975, when I made a black and white set of Phoenix Giants cards. With our modern, high-speed FMC packaging lines running so well, I only missed those old DF wax wrapper machines for about one second, maybe once a month.

Overseeing our photo library was a favorite job of mine, helping to pull photos and slides to use on our cards. The slides were stored in 20-pocket pages in three-ring binders, sport by sport, team by team.

One day, I was working at the light table, pulling football slides and making my choices when I suddenly realized: we had some of the best NFL football photographers in the business. They were taking incredible action shots that could easily grace the cover of any sports magazine being published.

I didn't own a sports magazine.

I did own a trading card company.

I decided to make a football card set utilizing these great photos.

Out of that thought, Pacific Gridiron Football was born. To show the photos in their true glory, I wanted a larger-size card, three-and-a-half-by-five inches. With a great action player photo on the front of each card, the back would feature a player photo, bio and statistics, and the name of the photographer whose work adorned the card.

I believe this was the very first time a trading card company acknowledged the photographers' excellent work on the card. The Pacific Gridiron cards were new and different, and their larger size made them great cards for collectors to get autographed.

Our bilingual Pacific Crown Collection (Spanish/English Major League Baseball cards) was doing well. We were growing the market and were able to add a Pacific Baseball Prism brand that year. Our insert sub-sets were getting noticed as cutting-edge by card collectors.

Our 1995 Pacific Crown Collection has produced 34 Hall of Fame players' cards as of 2022, and our Pacific Prism baseball brand has 24 Hall of Fame players, not counting insert cards.

* * *

Seattle Mariners fans had an extraordinary year in 1995.

For nearly 20 years, I had two season tickets, just off home plate on the aisle. Some years, when I went to the games, you could literally count the number of fans in the Kingdome.

This year was different: the Mariners had Griffey Jr., Edgar Martinez, Randy Johnson, Alex Rodriguez, Jay Buhner, Joey Cora, Luis Sojo and a host of other talented players. They were winning, and Seattle fans who had been starved for a winning team were flocking to the games like never before.

Seattle won the American League West and played the Yankees in the first-ever AL division series—in my opinion, the greatest AL division series in the history of the game.

The noise and thunder in the Kingdome was deafening. Edgar's walk-off double in the bottom of the 9th inning, the dogpile of Mariners players at home plate after the winning run scored—these were moments no Mariners fan would ever forget.

Cheryl and I were in our seats for that thrilling, decisive Game 5, and my creative juices were flowing. I was thinking! I owned a trading card manufacturing company; I could make a commemorative baseball card set so fans would never forget that Mariner season, the first-ever American League championship in the history of the franchise.

The very next day, I called the Mariners office and got through to the PR director. I explained my idea, and he loved it.

Then I asked him if the team photographer was able to get photos of all the great action during that game. He said yes and Pacific could use those photos in the card set.

The 1995 Seattle Mariners Memories Commemorative trading card set, licensed by the Seattle Mariners and Major League Baseball Properties, was going to happen. I got the *Seattle Times* involved too; their sports writer, Bob Finnigan, wrote the backs for the first cards, and we credited him on the cards. The *Times* did a massive ad campaign, running a full-page ad that promoted the card set several times.

We had the set on the market in no time, and it was an overwhelming success.

That set was one of the most enjoyable and rewarding projects I ever created at Pacific, because it was my team—and also my memories.

* * *

Pacific had always been a good friend of the Seattle Seahawks and, in particular, I was a friend of Seahawks PR director Gary Wright. Gary was a collector. I first met him back in the late 1980s when I put on a very

11. Playing with the Big Boys

successful trading card show in Bellevue, Washington. We remained friends over the years, and Pacific produced the very successful Seattle Seahawks Oroweat bread trading card promotion for six straight years under his guidance.

He also helped me produce the 1989 Pacific Steve Largent set, providing photos from the Seahawks archives.

In the spring of 1995, Gary visited the Pacific headquarters in Lynnwood for a tour of our trading card factory. One of the stops on the tour was our growing graphics department. It was a fascinating place for visitors. You could see firsthand how a trading card set was designed and created on computers. Designing on computers was, at that time, still in its infancy. It was a marvel to see the process, and Gary was very impressed with our graphic capabilities and all the state-of-the-art equipment in the department.

During the next football season, Gary called our PR director to see if Pacific could design and produce some posters and banners for an upcoming Seahawks promotion, using our large-format printer. They needed the materials right away, so the project was brought to my attention.

We would have to devote some considerable graphic time to get the work done on time. I approved the job and the time needed, and Rob Hicks and the Pacific graphic department did a wonderful job. The Seahawks and Gary were very pleased when they picked up the materials we produced for them.

A few weeks later, the Seahawks called our office; they had not received a bill for the work we did. I was notified and asked our accounting people to tell them there was no bill coming. Pacific was happy to do the work for them and happy they liked the job we did. The Seahawks said if there was anything they could do for Pacific to return the favor, just ask.

Now that was a great working relationship.

The 1995 NFL season moved along into November, and every Sunday found me flying out of Sea-Tac airport, crossing the country to shoot on the sidelines of some stadium. As the season wound down, we reviewed our NFL photo files to make sure we had enough pictures of each team's players on file for use on our 1996 Pacific cards.

One of the teams we were short on was the Seahawks. They played home games indoors at the Kingdome, and the high-quality photos we used on cards could not be taken there. The light available was simply not sufficient.

After reviewing the Seahawks schedule, I saw a chance to cover the Seahawks and photograph the team one more time before season's end— but the game was on Christmas Eve, December 24, in Kansas City against the Chiefs.

I could shoot that game, but I dreaded a flight to Kansas City and back to Seattle in the winter, at one of the busiest travel times of the year, plus the challenges of renting a car, getting to Arrowhead Stadium, and getting a hotel. I wasn't sure I wanted to go through all that, plus risk the possibility of weather making me miss Christmas with my family.

Then I remembered: the Seahawks had once said, "If there is anything the Seahawks can ever do for Pacific, just ask."

My wheels were in motion....

We telephoned Seahawks headquarters and asked if I could ride with the Seahawks on their team charter flight to Kansas City, shoot the game, and return with the team on Christmas Eve back to Seattle.

The Seahawks meant what they said: they *were* happy to return Pacific's favor! And so, on Thursday night, December 21, I packed my camera gear, adding my 600mm lens. I always took my 400mm lens but, knowing I would have space on the plane for my 600mm, I took it too. My bags were packed, including my return jacket and tie, packed in my NFL suit bag. I said goodbye to my kids, and Cheryl drove me to the Seahawks headquarters Friday morning. When we arrived, players were milling around, loading their carry-on bags on one of the two team buses.

I said my goodbyes to Cheryl. She said, "You're excited. I can tell."

I said, "A little!"

I got my gear and found my assigned seat on the bus for the trip to the airport. When the buses were loaded with players and team equipment, the door closed and the bus moved out of the Seahawks headquarters gate, where it was met by police cars with lights flashing.

We were being escorted by the police to Sea-Tac Airport. I thought, "How cool is this?" A police escort! We wouldn't be late for our flight.

We moved down the freeway pretty quickly and arrived at a side entrance gate to the airport. The buses went through the gate and straight to our charter plane, which was parked near another gate.

I was up front on the bus. I grabbed my gear and was one of the first people to board the plane. I walked up the boarding steps and was met by a Seahawks representative, who knew I was a guest on board.

He said, "You're with the coaches and staff; your seat is 6A."

I knew what that meant. I had millions of flying miles by this point in my life, and I knew: I was heading to the first-class section of the plane! I went to my seat, stored my gear above in the bin, and sat down in my seat. I got a warm, fuzzy feeling and a big smile. This was too good to be true.

Settling into that padded seat, the plane's engines loud in my ears, I thought back to the winter of 1976, when I was on the deck of a king crab boat in the freezing cold Bering Sea, hauling crab pots. It was so cold, the salty sea spray would freeze on my rain gear and start building up a thin

11. Playing with the Big Boys 129

layer of ice. It was so cold, the deckhands slapped each other's backs and arms to knock off the sheets of ever-thickening ice. The only way to stay warm was to work harder.

I thought to myself, I never want to be that cold again.

Then I remembered back to the early days at Pacific when I was working 18 to 20 hours a day getting my first trading card store up and running ... but it was all worth it.

I was having fun now!

Then I recalled watching the 1978 Seahawks on TV with my dad. He was a Seahawks fan; Zorn to Largent was his favorite play. Steve Largent would catch nearly every pass thrown his way.

I leaned back in my seat and looked up. Then I said to myself, "Look where I am now, Dad, look where I'm at. I'm sitting in first class on the Seahawks charter plane with Cortez Kennedy, Rick Mirer, Chris Warren, Eugene Robinson and all the other Seahawks players. See, Dad? I can make a living selling trading cards!"

And a pretty good living, at that.

The flight attendant served dinner shortly after that and I settled in for the four-hour flight to Kansas City.

There was a man sitting in the aisle seat across from me, and we started talking. He asked who I was because he didn't recognize me. I said, "I'm Mike Cramer, president and CEO of Pacific Trading Cards, Inc."

He asked how I was able to get a seat on the Seahawks charter. I explained to him the great relationship Pacific had with the Seahawks and that the team arranged for me to travel on the flight.

Then I added, "But this trip, I'm just Mike Cramer, Pacific football photographer. I'm going to shoot the game on Sunday."

He said, "Wow, you are one lucky guy! You have two great jobs!" I learned he was a new local sports reporter and this was his first team flight also.

The plane landed at the Kansas City airport, where we were met by two buses and a police escort that would lead the team to the hotel. When we arrived at the hotel, I got my gear off the bus and headed to the lobby.

I did notice it was freezing cold out.

I met the same man in the lobby that had shown me to my seat on the plane. He was handing out envelopes to Seahawks personnel and players. He saw me and pulled out an envelope marked "Mike Cramer" and handed it to me. Inside was my room number and key, food vouchers, and the Seahawks itinerary for the weekend.

I headed to my room and stored my camera gear, then went out and grabbed a quick bite. By then, it was already late, and I was done for the night. I pulled out the itinerary and read it over. My Saturday was marked "open," but the players were scheduled for breakfast followed by two workouts in the hotel ballroom, where they would walk through plays. It was just too cold to go outside (although, in their free time, some of the players did go shop at a nearby mall—after all, it was almost Christmas Eve…).

The next morning I ate breakfast with the Seahawks players. They were big men and consumed mass quantities of food! It was hard for me to believe they were the very same men I would scramble up and down sidelines to take pictures of—the same players I made football cards of. They were just regular people, eating breakfast, talking, laughing, going about their business. Football was just their job.

But to me, they were special. They were NFL football players and, more importantly, they were the Seattle Seahawks—my team!

By early Sunday morning, heading down for breakfast, I was getting excited for the game. I couldn't wait to board the team bus to Arrowhead Stadium!

As the Seahawk players ate, I noticed they were more serious, focused on the game ahead. Guard Kevin Mawae was in line for his breakfast. At 6'4" and 289 pounds, he was a giant next to me as I got in line behind him.

He said good morning to me.

And that made me realize: I was just one of the guys.

Kevin Mawae was ultimately elected to the Pro Football Hall of Fame in 2019. But that Sunday morning, we were just two guys in the breakfast line, trying to get something to eat.

I could even identify with him beyond that: the mass quantities he and his teammates consumed reminded me of the way I ate back in my fishing days!

The bus boarded at 10 a.m., and with a police escort in the lead, we headed to the stadium. When we arrived, I grabbed my gear and headed into the visitor's locker room where that same guy with a clipboard met me—and showed me to my locker.

I stood in front of the locker. *Geez!* I thought. I have a *locker*! Then I looked up and saw my name on the top of that locker, written on a white piece of tape: "Mike Cramer."

I could have quit right then and there and never shot the game. How was I ever going to top that?!

I stored my gear in my locker, took off my jacket and tie, and dressed in the warm clothes that I would shoot the game in. It was going to be sunny but still very cold on the field, with a high of just 31 degrees. But I wasn't worried about being cold. I would be following the plays on the field, running up and down the sidelines to get in position for my next shot.

Seahawk players were getting taped and dressed all around me. Placekicker Todd Peterson and punter Rick Tuten were dressed and ready to go

11. Playing with the Big Boys

out on that cold field and start warming up. I was ready too. That's when the Seahawks equipment manager tossed me a fully-padded, long, blue Seahawks cold-weather coat with a hood.

He said, "You might need this; it's cold out there."

I put it on, grabbed my camera bags, and went out on the field at Arrowhead Stadium. At that moment in time, I was just one of the Seahawks personnel on that frozen field.

It was cold, and I was happy to have that heavy Seahawks coat. I stored my camera bags near the Seahawks bench. Heaters were going, making it a good place for camera gear: my camera batteries wouldn't drain from the cold.

The stadium was huge, and all the seats were a beautiful red, shining in the bright morning sunlight. A few fans were in their seats, and others had come down to the lower seats near the field to watch the Chiefs and Seahawks players warm up. There were four or five Chief fans in the stands behind the Seahawks bench. When they saw me dressed in my blue Seahawks coat, they started to boo me!

I looked over at them and started laughing. I yelled to them, "You guys are wasting your time! I'm nobody!"

That didn't help. They just booed louder!

Seahawks punter Rick Tuten was already practicing punting, and one of the Seahawks coaches asked me if I could help shag the punts in the end zone until the players came out. Yes! Of course I would.

I couldn't believe it! I was going to get on the field and be part of the practice!

I ran into the end zone so excited, I thought I might wet myself. I saw another person at the other side of the end zone, dressed in the same blue Seahawks coat I had on. I watched what he was doing: catching the ball and tossing it back to where the Seahawks long snapper was.

I was ready. Tuten punted the next ball high into the bright morning sky right toward me. I got under it, ready to catch it … but the ball sailed over my head by four feet. The Seahawks guy on the other side of the end zone watched me miss the ball and laughed, shouting to me, "It's not that easy to catch 'em!"

Tuten had a couple more punts before another ball came to my side of the end zone. I thought to myself, "How hard can it be to catch one of these things? NFL players do it with 10 guys running full speed right at them." I told myself, "Just get under it and catch it!"

So I did get under it—and it came down out of that sky like a sack of spinning cement, hitting right in my arms.

It was a good thing I had that big heavy blue coat on, or it would have spun my arms off.

I thought, I don't know how these players make it look so easy catching kickoff returns—it's not that easy! I was happy to realize that I just made trading cards and didn't have to catch footballs for a living!

After a few minutes, I got comfortable and started catching more and more footballs. I found myself thinking, "Give me a uniform and a helmet—I could run one back!" I'd probably get killed, but I would give it a go....

I hadn't expected to get to do this, and I was having the time of my life. Then I saw more Seahawk players coming out on the field, and number 84 was running right toward me. I knew that number and thought to myself, "*Crap!* I hope 84 isn't coming to get my spot!"

I liked my spot; I was getting used to it!

Sure enough, it was Seahawk punt returner Joey Galloway running my way. He got to the end zone and started jumping up and down to warm up. Then he looked over at me. I thought, surely he'll let me catch a few more balls. After all, I was here first!

Tuten punted the next ball. It was coming right towards me. I looked up at the ball and got ready to catch it, but I could see Joey Galloway running over—he looked at me again and waved me off. I realized it was his position, but ... I just wanted to catch one more!

It didn't happen. I was finished. My very short stint as a dream Seahawks punt returner was over.

I watched Joey catch footballs, one after another. He made it look so easy, and he didn't miss any of them. He was a pro.

Back to reality.

I went over to the Seahawks bench and set up my cameras. There were plenty of players out on the field from both teams, and I got to work taking pictures.

When the game started, the Seahawks kicked off, with the Chiefs' Tamarick Vanover settling in to receive the kick from Todd Peterson. The kick sailed high into the air—Vanover quickly settled under it—and it landed softly in his arms.

I focused on him and fired my camera shutter as he started to run with the ball. I thought, "Boy, he made that catch look easy." And I knew it wasn't that easy—I did have a little experience now.

Then, in the next second, Tamarick ran right up the sideline, right past me and all of the Seahawks special team players, rushing 94 yards straight into the end zone for a Chiefs touchdown.

My photos from that touchdown run were used on Tamarick Vanover's 1996 Pacific Football card, number 224, and his 1996 Pacific Gridiron card, number 63.

Halfway through the second quarter, I had to shed my blue Seahawks coat. I was warm from running up and down the sidelines shooting photos!

The game ended with the Chiefs winning, 26–3, over my Seahawks.

All the Seahawks personnel and players went to the locker room to quickly get showered and dressed for the trip back to Seattle. I stored my camera bags in my locker, stripped off my damp, sweaty clothes, and headed to the showers. There were players and personnel scurrying around butt naked all over the place in the locker room and showers, just getting themselves cleaned up after the game.

I found a vacant shower head and got under it. I felt the hot water running over my head, and it warmed up my whole body. I was literally steaming! I finished and headed out of the showers to my locker just as naked as the day I was born.

When I turned the corner out of the shower room there were two women standing right there in front of me. One had a microphone, and the other a pen and notepad. Oh, no! I was butt naked and didn't have a towel—it was still hanging back in my locker!

I wasn't expecting women in the men's locker room! I didn't know what to do. It was about 10 feet to get to my locker. I could see my towel hanging there. I had to get there somehow.

I kind of hunched over and walked the longest 10-foot walk of my life over to my locker, to retrieve my towel and wrap it around my waist. I waited for a minute until the women moved to the other side of the locker room before I toweled off and dressed in my jacket and tie.

The Seahawks player in the locker next to me laughed and said, "You weren't expecting that, were you?"

I said, "Geez, no! I didn't know what to do."

He laughed and said, "You get used to it."

I learned later that having women in the players' locker room was a common occurrence. They were reporters, and reporters had early access so they could get the game's scoop. The players were used to it and had adjusted. Some players quickly dressed, some put towels around their waists, but most just moved around the locker room wearing nothing, like I had done.

But seeing all that for the first time sure was a shock for me!

We boarded the team bus for the trip to the Kansas City airport, escorted again by the local police with lights flashing. On the plane, I was greeted by the same guy with a clipboard who showed me to my seat in the first class section. I stowed my camera gear and my 42 rolls of film. It had been a beautiful, sunny but very cold day. The lighting conditions had indeed been perfect for shooting football card photos.

The Seahawk players boarded. Some carried shopping bags with gifts.

It was their last game of the season and they were, like me, heading home to their families. It was Christmas Eve.

We had a great dinner on the plane, then I walked to the back of the plane to stretch my legs. But really, I wanted to see all the Seahawks players up close one more time before we landed and went our separate ways. For a brief moment in time that weekend, I had the thrill of a lifetime, all because I made trading cards.

When Cheryl picked me up at the Seahawks headquarters in Kirkland, I couldn't stop talking about the experience I had just had.

But, I told her, the biggest gift of all was that I was home for Christmas.

* * *

The new year, 1996, was shaping up to be pivotal for Pacific. Sales for our products were excellent, and the Pacific factory was sometimes running day and night. We were even busier than expected with all the contract work we were getting, designing, printing and packaging everything from trading cards to tattoos to playing card games.

We actively pursued contract work. After all, it was money in the bank, and that financial security allowed us to take chances on our own projects, pushing the creative envelope with new products.

I liked to be a "hands-on" business owner. On my sales trips to Mexico, our representative there would come meet me and we would make sales calls to retail chains. On one of our first sales calls, we secured a nice order for our Pacific Major League Baseball Bi-Lingual (English-Spanish) cards. The OXXO retail chain of convenience stores placed the cards on sale in all of their stores throughout Mexico.

We also secured orders from other retail stores. One of the prospective clients we visited was Bimbo Bakeries.

Bimbo Bakeries was the largest bakery in the world. They were enormous! When I arrived at the plant offices in Mexico City, I was led through a steel gate where a guard gave visitors a pat-down.

In one of our earliest meetings, I told Bimbo management about Pacific and what we did, adding, "We do contract packaging work." I showed them pictures of our packaging lines and our graphics department. They looked interested, but all they said at the time was "We will keep that in mind."

About a month later, I received a call from the purchasing director at Bimbo Bakeries. He had a job for Pacific, if we were interested and could meet their delivery schedule.

They had a promotion scheduled for one of their bread products. They wanted to place one press-on color cartoon tattoo (wrapped in food-grade clear wrap) in each loaf of bread. Could Pacific make and wrap 15 million

11. Playing with the Big Boys

pieces, delivering half of them in six weeks and the remaining amount in four more weeks? Bimbo would send their own trucks to our factory in Lynnwood, Washington, to pick up the finished goods at our factory.

After a quick consultation with Felix, Pacific's plant manager, I called back to Bimbo Bakeries and gave him a price, assuring him we would meet their deadline. He was satisfied, and we got the contract to do the work. Long story short, we delivered the first part of the order in just four weeks. They were as happy as a clam in a bucket of water.

A few weeks later, Bimbo Bakeries launched another promotional program, this time inserting three million Pacific baseball cards into their bread packages.

Pacific was becoming well-known in Mexico, and Bimbo Bakeries was a big part of that. Over the years, we received a lot of contract work from them.

* * *

That winter, Victor, Marty and I attended the Major League Baseball Players Choice Awards in Miami.

The awards have been held every year since 1993 to honor the top players of the past season. Along with the awards ceremony, a golf tournament was held at the Doral Country Club. I signed up to play.

My foursome for the one-day golf outing included Roger Clemens, Terry Steinbach, and Sy Berger of Topps.

Wow.

I would find out that day that Roger Clemens was a great golfer, Terry Steinbach was really good, Sy could play, and I probably spent too much time working and not enough time playing golf. Still, I was able to hold my own and get in a few good shots.

Sy and I rode together in a cart. He drove (it seems, in golf, the older guy always wants to drive the cart). I knew Sy just a little, and he knew who I was. But that day, for the five hours of that round, we got to talk and share experiences of the trading card business. Sy was a great guy and full of stories about Topps. He was with Topps from 1951 until 1997 and was once called "the father of the modern baseball card" by ESPN.

I have always been a big fan of Topps. After all, I had collected their cards since I was a young boy and had nearly every baseball and football card set they ever made. Spending this time with the man so instrumental to Topps was a big thrill for me, and I listened to every word he said with great pleasure. Sy retold the stories about the 1952 Topps baseball cards being dumped into the ocean because Topps couldn't find a buyer for them.

He added, "We really never did that." Then he said, "You helped with that problem by buying up our closeouts in the 1970s and '80s."

(From left) Me, Sy Berger, Terry Steinbach, and Marty Cramer at a golf outing in Florida in 1996 (Pacific Trading Cards Archives).

"You know," I said, "in one sense, Pacific is just a stepchild of Topps." And I told him how Pacific sprang out of sales I made of the Topps closeouts he'd mentioned.

He said he admired what I had accomplished with Pacific Trading Cards and added, "I know it wasn't easy, because I've been there."

He thought for a moment, then said, "Michael—I think we made you a rich man."

What could I say to that? I just said, "Thanks!"

We finished that round of golf. Roger Clemens and Terry Steinbach played great and were two of the nicest players I've ever spent time with. Funny thing was, I didn't even ask for an autograph from them—it didn't even cross my mind. I think I was more excited about playing and talking with Sy Berger.

After all, I was a trading card manufacturer, which made Sy Berger kind of a hero to me.

* * *

In January of 1996, my brother Marty left Pacific to start his own

11. Playing with the Big Boys

retail furniture store business. He had been with me for five years, and I would miss him sorely. I filled in as operations director of Pacific while I searched for a solution.

Actually, it was a good time for me to really review our operations and see if I could make improvements in some areas. Pacific was a real card-producing machine at that time. We had two brands of baseball cards, six of football, and four or five promotional projects.

In February of 1996, I learned that Leaf Co., owned by Huhtamaki Oyi of Finland, was selling off the Donruss Trading Card company. The plant in Memphis that made the Donruss cards was scheduled to be closed.

I was interested. If Pacific bought Leaf, that purchase would include the rights to make baseball, football and hockey trading cards using the Donruss and Leaf brands. I could produce a full line of baseball cards with a good, established collector base and built-in sales driven by brand recognition.

This story is virtually unknown in the trading card world. However, I saved everything (of course). I still have the three-ring binder I marked "Strictly Confidential." It includes the unsigned purchase agreement between Donruss Trading Cards, Inc., and Pacific Trading Cards, Inc.

Unfortunately—or, perhaps, fortunately—unsigned.

In early March 1996, I made a call to Mr. Robert Clouston, President and CEO of Leaf North America. In the call, I explained that I was interested in purchasing Donruss. We talked for a bit and made an appointment for me to visit him at the Leaf headquarters in Lake Forest, Illinois.

I flew to Chicago later that week to meet with Mr. Clouston. I told him I had funds in place to buy Donruss and I would make an offer to do so. He told me that he had a prior offer from Pinnacle and they were already doing their due diligence. I would have to move fast—and I did move fast!

I already had Victor Temkin looking for a capital funds investor to partner with Pacific and he had found one: the investment firm Bastion Capital Corp., whose chairman of the board was Danny Villanueva (former placekicker for the Dallas Cowboys and Los Angeles Rams).

Villanueva's firm agreed to partner with Pacific to buy Donruss. Pacific and Bastion Capital Corp. would make an offer to acquire the Donruss brands and packaging equipment. We would move the equipment to the Pacific plant in Lynnwood, Washington. I would become president/CEO of the combined new (and very large) company. We crunched the numbers, and it all worked for us.

Victor and I, along with the president of Bastion, flew to Chicago to meet with Leaf and Mr. Clouston. Our meeting went well. We made our offer but were told shortly after that, because Leaf wanted to move quickly, they were going to accept the Pinnacle offer. However, if Pinnacle didn't close the sale, Leaf would be ready to accept our offer.

Pinnacle did close the sale and bought the Donruss brands.

However, all was not lost in this venture. Pinnacle bought the Donruss brands, but Pacific went ahead and bought most of the Donruss trading card factory equipment. Pinnacle didn't want it. I did. We came away for pennies on the dollar, acquiring enough equipment to build three new complete packaging lines. Plus, we bought a Rollem Slipstream card-cutting machine.

We had the equipment moved to the Pacific plant in Lynnwood, and it was up and running in less than a month. So, no, Pacific didn't buy the Donruss brands—but Pacific did buy most of the Donruss trading card factory equipment.

Once the equipment was in place and running, I would sometimes go down to our production area to check it out. I'd stand there, watching Donruss equipment package Pacific Trading Cards products ... and smile to myself.

* * *

Right after I returned from Chicago, I met with Phil Roth, the CPA of my outside accounting firm, Perkins & Roth. I told him I needed some strong help at the top to help guide Pacific. We were bursting at the seams.

He already knew the financial condition of Pacific, because he reviewed and prepared our monthly and year-end statements.

I said, "I want you to come to work for Pacific full-time."

Phil said, "I was thinking the same thing."

Phil became vice president and chief financial officer and started at Pacific right away. He was a game changer for Pacific and made an immediate impact on the company.

The addition of Phil allowed me more time to concentrate on card design concepts, produce new products, and work on new licensing possibilities.

We had some great releases during 1996. Our bilingual baseball cards did very well, and we produced a Cramer's Choice 10-card insert set for the Pacific Baseball Crown Collection. At only one card per case, the cards were (and are) very scarce.

To make the set, I picked two pitchers, one left- and one right-handed, and one player each for the other positions. Nine of the 10 players I chose are in the Baseball Hall of Fame. Among those stars, I had the pleasure of including one of my all-time favorite players, Ken Griffey, Jr.

Our 1996 Pacific Crown Collection has 42 total Baseball Hall of Fame players to date.

11. Playing with the Big Boys

The 1996 Pacific Prism Baseball was also as good as gold; it's one of my personal all-time favorite card designs. The set sported a great new foil-etched team color design and a large action photo of the player. As of 2022, that 144-card set has 27 Hall of Fame players.

Also that year, Advil contacted Pacific about putting together a national promotion featuring their spokesman, the great Nolan Ryan. Our 1996 Pacific Nolan Ryan Advil cards would be a mail-in offer premium, featuring some never-seen photos and a new card design. The 27-card set celebrated Nolan's fabulous 27-year career; two of the cards were photos taken the day Nolan retired from baseball.

The mail-in offer was a huge success.

Pacific did the fulfillment for the card set (my mail-order roots were quite useful!). Nolan Ryan was extremely popular and, for six years, Pacific produced various Nolan Ryan card products. We also licensed a line of Nolan Ryan shirts that had our cards printed on them in full color.

The busy year continued. Our 1996 NFL football card line was upscaled that year, and we produced six different football card products, including the new brands Invincible, Litho-Cel, and Dynagon.

At Pacific, two of my most important goals were to create cards that honored the roots of collecting and to point to new hobby horizons with products that had never been seen before.

Creating new designs sometimes involved developing the technology to make it happen, like when we figured out how to print on crystal clear plastic. This "discovery" allowed us to create our Invincible and Litho-Cel cards. Very upscale, cool cards!

Invincible was very successful, and Litho-Cel, too, but we only made that release one year. It was my brain child, but it turned out to be extremely expensive to manufacture. The cards were very laborious for our pre-press graphics department and then required tedious steps to get safely through the packaging line. All in all, it was a fun project for me to create, but it was way out in the stratosphere ahead of its time.

Our 1996 Pacific Power Basketball release was also loaded with absolutely beautiful, eye-popping, advanced-technology insert cards and super-cool parallel cards. (I sketched most of the designs for those cards and still have the original hand-drawn sketches in my library.)

We were in the last year of our Draft Picks Basketball card sub-license from Classic, a product that stood the test of time. By 2022, it had seven NBA Hall of Fame players, including a rookie card of a then–high-school phenom named Kobe Bryant, who went on to NBA greatness.

So far, 1996 had been a rewarding and challenging year. But the best was yet to come.

Victor and I had been in touch, over the years, with the NHL Players

Association and NHL Properties. We wanted to secure a license for Pacific to produce NHL trading cards.

In the fall of 1996, I received a call from Ted Saskin of the NHL Players Association in Toronto, Canada. They had watched the growth of Pacific over the years and were very impressed with our products.

They were awarding a license to Pacific to produce NHL hockey cards for the upcoming 1997–98 season.

Wow! Just like that, we had a new, major card license.

Within a few weeks, we'd signed a three-year license with both the NHL players and NHL Properties. They asked that we let them make the announcement in a week or so.

1996 Pacific Prism Jump Ball Insert Kobe Bryant Rookie Card. This unique card design has a plastic window with the player's image printed on it. We used our crystalline technology to create it (Pacific Trading Cards Archives).

I immediately got to work locating NHL player photos to use on our upcoming cards. The National Hockey League had sent us a couple of sets of media guides, including sheets with all the team logos. We started to design cards and pick players to be in our card sets, turning and burning as only Pacific could.

When the announcement of our license was released, we had a small celebration at Pacific. We were busy, but we had a great, new, fun project and a lot of work ahead. I loved that stuff!

NHL hockey became my new obsession! I knew the big-name players, but we would make cards of 350 different NHL players. I had to learn all about the NHL and all of its players, almost overnight. This was my new baby.

11. Playing with the Big Boys

We hired people with NHL hockey knowledge to help in producing the cards and writing the text for the card backs. We also added a few more personnel in the graphics department to handle the increased design workload.

Our packaging lines were up to the task of producing six more products. (The more products you can produce in your factory, the more cost-efficient it becomes.) The recent additions of the packaging equipment from Donruss, as well as the new addition of pre-press equipment, had been a big expense. But with the new NHL license for Pacific and other new Pacific brands, the expense was all paid for.

Canada is, of course, a huge market for hockey cards, so we beefed up our Canadian sales team. We also added a sales team in Europe, where hockey cards were becoming popular. Many of the NHL players who came to play in the NHL were from the European leagues.

Once we had our 1997–98 NHL hockey sales materials printed and in hand, I took a trip through Canada with the new Pacific Canadian market sales team. We visited wholesalers that would get our new products on the shelves, in both retail and hobby stores in Canada.

Our reception was very warm from the retail distributors. They really liked our new card designs, packaging and pricing. Most of the hobby store distributors welcomed us with open arms: we were a breath of fresh air, with innovative new card ideas. But a couple hobby distributors were skeptical. They said, "How is Pacific even going to make hockey cards? You don't know anything about hockey."

The guys were right in one sense. We were new to the sport. However, we knew how to produce cards and we were extremely good at it.

I told the skeptics, "We are quick learners. Producing NHL hockey cards is not going to be any problem for Pacific. We will deliver our releases on schedule."

I don't think they realized that Pacific had been producing cards for nearly 20 years, on a fairly large scale, and making great hockey cards would not be that big of a challenge. Don't get me wrong: there was a tremendous amount of planning and organization involved but nothing out of the ordinary for Pacific.

We did produce our releases on time that year, and hockey card collectors all over the world got to enjoy our products. Our brands, including Pacific Crown Collection, Crown Royale, Revolution, Paramount, Prism, and others, translated to hockey really well, and we were accepted into the hockey card market.

We signed NHL Dallas Stars player Mike Modano to be our spokesman. He appeared in our advertising and on our packaging, helping to promote our hockey brands. Some hockey dealers and hobby writers felt that we could have picked a better player. Modano was an excellent player, currently in his ninth season, but not universally acclaimed.

But he was my choice to be our spokesman.

Mike Modano went on to play 21 seasons in the NHL and was elected to the Hockey Hall of Fame in 2014. In 2017, he was named one of the NHL's 100 greatest players. He was a good choice!

That was Pacific's introduction to the hockey world. When I visited the hobby distributors in Canada the following year, preparing for the 1998–99 season, we were welcomed again with open arms. One of them said, "Congratulations! I don't know how you did it. What hockey cards do you have for me this year?"

Forty-seven of the players featured in the 1997–98 Pacific Crown Collection Hockey went on to be enshrined in the Hockey Hall of Fame. That includes "the Great One," Wayne Gretzky. One of my greatest pleasures and privileges that year was including Gretzky in my Cramer's Choice Awards insert set. Our 1997–98 Pacific Paramount Hockey was a nice set, too, producing 38 Hall of Fame players cards, including a rookie card (#125) of Hockey Hall of Famer Marian Hossa.

Our 1997 NFL football card brands sold extremely well also. We produced six different products. A new release for us that year was Pacific Philadelphia, a new brand that was different in that it included a tremendous number of players who had never had a card made. I had been looking through our football photo library binders and saw that we had a lot of great player photos that we could make cards out of. These photos featured the kickers, punters, linemen, defensive backs and safeties, all the players whose mothers wished their sons had a football card.

I made cards, and I could make that wish come true—at least for some of them.

Some players only had one photo in the binders, but the photo was a good one. I decided to pull the best of those photos from each team. By adding the star quarterbacks, running backs and receivers from each team, we had enough to make a 330-football card set.

I named the set Philadelphia, which means "brotherly love" in Greek. It's a fitting name for an NFL card set that wanted to show a little love and appreciation for the entire team brotherhood.

It was a fun set to make. The cards had only one photo on them, with a simple, clean design. The back of each card had a little history of the player.

Pacific Philadelphia had insert sets and plenty of Pacific parallels. But, because of lower developmental costs (the photos were from our files), the card pack price was suggested at just $1.99 (a real bargain at a time when most card packs retailed for between $2.99 and $5.99, some even higher). Pacific Philadelphia turned out to be one of my favorite products

11. Playing with the Big Boys 143

ever produced by Pacific. I developed it, named it—and I collected it too.

Pacific Philadelphia had 330 different players, of which 105 were rookie cards. Included in the set is a New England Patriots placekicker named Adam Vinatieri. A little-known player at the time, he would go on to play for 24 seasons in the NFL and become the greatest placekicker in the history of the game. He is also the NFL all-time scoring leader and a sure Hall of Famer.

Nineteen ninety-seven Pacific Philadelphia has the only rookie card ever made of Adam Vinatieri.

That set also has 29 cards (with more coming) of players now enshrined in the NFL Hall of Fame.

Another great product was 1997 Pacific Crown Royale—again. Each box contained a Jumbo Cramer's Choice card. The 10-card set had silver foil. A purple-foil parallel set was limited to only 100 of each card, with 10 serial-numbered purple cards signed by me and issued with a redemption certificate, redeemable for a Jumbo Cramer's Choice holder.

Our two bilingual baseball releases, Pacific Crown and Pacific Prism Invincible, also did very well.

We were on the cutting edge in card designs. We were also still applying for that coveted, full baseball card license, which would allow us to make English-language cards.

* * *

This 1997 Pacific Philadelphia is Adam Vinatieri's only rookie card. Pacific was the only card company to make a rookie card of Vinatieri, a sure Hall of Famer. This card is graded a perfect gem mint 10 (Mike Cramer Collection).

That summer, Frank Torre came out to visit our offices. He had been working for Pacific since 1991. His brother, Joe Torre, was now manager of the New York Yankees, and the Yankees were in town for a series against the Mariners. After our meetings at the office, Frank asked me if my 11-year-old son, Michael, would like to be the Yankees' batboy for the Wednesday night game.

I said, "Yes! I know he would."

Frank said, "Great! We'll get Michael a Yankees uniform, and he can shag balls in the outfield. When the game starts, he will be the Yankees batboy."

This was going to be fun! I had a photographer's season pass to all the Mariners games, so I would be able to shoot the game and watch Michael from the photographers' well.

When Michael and I arrived at the Kingdome with our passes, we went to the visitors' locker room—the Yankees locker room. That felt strange to me. I was not a Yankees fan, I was a Mariners fan and … well, the Yankees were the enemy if you were a Mariners fan!

Frank and I got Michael dressed in his gray New York uniform. This was exciting. Suddenly, all I could think of was Babe Ruth, Joe DiMaggio, Mickey Mantle, Reggie Jackson—and now my son, Michael Cramer, wearing that uniform. I was immediately a Yankees fan … kind of!

Michael was all ready to shag batting practice balls. He grabbed his glove and ran out to the centerfield warning track.

Bernie Williams and Paul O'Neill were out there already, and took Michael under their wings. Michael went after a couple ground balls and threw them back into the infield.

Then a young player named Derek Jeter hit a monster fly ball to center field. Michael took off after it and settled under that ball: he was going to try to catch it! I started yelling, "Get out of there! Get out of there!" from the photographers' well on the third base side, but there was no way he could hear his dad yelling.

At the last second, Bernie Williams came gliding over and the ball landed in his glove. I was a proud papa, watching Michael—but when Bernie caught that ball, I could breathe again!

With Michael in good hands, I went over to the Yankees dugout to greet Joe Torre. We talked a bit; Joe, ever the manager, knew I was a Mariners fan and I studied the players.

He said to me, "Mike, what do you know about Luis Sojo?"

I said, "Well, he's a decent utility player." Then I added, "And he's real lucky."

Luis Sojo was, indeed, lucky: he had always managed to be in the right spot at the right time.

11. Playing with the Big Boys

Within a week, the Yankees had acquired Sojo.

Although Luis Sojo was a good ball player, in this case, his luck brought him to the Yankees. Early in his career, he earned a World Series ring with the Toronto Blue Jays and then four more with the Yankees. A utility player with five rings in a 13-year Major League career? I would say he was pretty lucky. However, like all lucky people, Luis Sojo made his own luck!

There are thousands of major league players who never had a chance to play in a World Series in their careers. The greats Ken Griffey, Jr., and Ernie Banks, along with 18 or so other Hall of Fame players, had long, outstanding Major League careers, but never played in a World Series.

One of my favorite sayings is, "It's better to be lucky than good." I knew I had that kind of luck, to do what I was doing. But people have always reminded me, "Mike, you make your own luck." And that is also true.

During the national anthem that night, the Yankees manager and coaches lined up on the third baseline, hats over their hearts. In the third base lineup that evening was Don Zimmer, Joe Torre, Michael Cramer, Chris Chambliss, and Willie Randolph.

Of course I took a photo of that lineup and had it blown up. It still hangs on our wall at home.

(From left) Don Zimmer, Joe Torre, Michael Cramer, Chris Chambliss, and Willie Randolph in 1997. My son Michael wore the New York Yankees uniform the day he was bat boy (Pacific Trading Cards Archives).

Between innings, I noticed Yankees pitcher Hideki Irabu (who was on the DL) take Michael into the clubhouse for snacks. I also saw Michael bring his ice cream cone out to the bench. Not allowed—and Yankee DH Wade Boggs yelled down at manager Joe Torre, telling him Michael was eating on the bench. Michael was quickly back in the clubhouse to finish his ice cream.

Yankees second baseman Homer Bush befriended Michael, and they tossed a ball back and forth when the Yankees were in the field.

After the game, I asked Michael how he liked being a batboy.

"Best day ever!" he said, eyes wide. "They have so much good stuff to eat in the clubhouse!"

* * *

We wrapped up 1997 with the best sales year in the 17 years since Pacific was incorporated in 1980.

I found out a short time later that this was just the beginning for Pacific.

12

Major League Baseball Players Association License
My Dream Comes True

The Hawaii Trading Card Conference, organized by my good friend Kit Young, was held each February in Honolulu. Many card manufacturers, licensors, dealers and collectors came to attend seminars, meetings and banquets, all sponsored by the card manufacturers and trade publications.

Pacific attended the conference each year to hold sales meetings and events. Of course, it was also a fun time for Cheryl and me and the other Pacific employees that got to go, a perfect time of year to escape the cold, dark, rainy Seattle weather.

Renewing old acquaintances is a welcome part of these events. In 1998, Phil Roth and I were greeted by a representative of the Major League Baseball Players Association we both knew fairly well. As we talked, he suddenly said, "I have a meeting to attend—but can you guys come up to my room for a chat in about an hour?"

We said of course, we would be there—though we weren't sure what the meeting was going to be about....

After an hour passed, we went to his room and knocked on the door. He answered, invited us in, went straight to his briefcase and pulled out a stack of papers.

He handed them to me. "You guys are going to make a lot of money!" he said.

I looked at that stack of papers. In my hand was a full baseball card license for Pacific, the one license I had always dreamed of.

We could begin making Major League Baseball cards starting with the 1998 season! Pacific could now market and sell baseball cards to all baseball card collectors. For the last five years, we had produced and printed only Spanish/English baseball cards, but this new license was the big time: it was a full license, just like Topps, just like Fleer, just like Upper Deck.

This was it! We were in! I had it literally in my hands, my dream since childhood. I was going to get to make baseball cards my way, like no other company ever had! They would be my ideas, my designs, and my choices—Cramer's Choice.

Phil and I were ecstatic. I was floating off the floor!

We gave some big, big, thank yous! Then we were told not to announce this license at the conference. The Players Association would make the announcement to the press and hobby industry in a week or so, once everything was signed.

I said, "Do you have something for me to put this license in? I can't walk out of here just carrying it; someone might see me."

The good gentleman handed me a newspaper, and I wrapped the license agreement in it. Carrying one of my life's most precious dreams all wrapped up like a fish, I went back to my room.

Waiting to announce that Pacific had a baseball card license was not going to be a problem. I had already waited 10 years. During that wait, I had grown Pacific to a level where we could easily manufacture trading cards for three major sports. In 10 years, Pacific had grown from a dream I had into a dream I was now living!

Did I say I was excited? You bet I was! I had, without question, the biggest grin on my face of anyone at that conference—but no one knew why, except Phil and our wives.

The next day, when Phil and I were in meetings with our national sales manager, Bruce Chappelear, he told us he'd heard that "one of the card companies" was telling their hobby distributors that they were getting a baseball card license.

I took Bruce aside and said, "When we are all done with our meetings today about 5 o'clock, let's grab a beer and go for a walk on the beach."

Later, Bruce and I met in the lobby of the Hawaiian Hilton and each grabbed a beer.

I was carrying a bulky, wrapped-up newspaper.

We headed out on that beautiful, white sandy beach on Waikiki, and when we got to a place where no one could see us, I handed Bruce the newspaper. He took it, unwrapped it, and glanced over the first page before finally blurting, "Wow! Congratulations! I thought you were giving me fish!"

It was a fish, the biggest prize fish ever caught in the baseball card business in Hawaii! It was good for Bruce to know what he had ahead of him as Pacific national sales manager. He had a big selling task before him, but he was as excited as Phil and I were.

12. Major League Baseball Players Association License 149

Needless to say, no one else at that 1998 Hawaii conference knew Pacific had a baseball card license. Phil, Bruce, our wives and I just floated on air, grinning our heads off.

My time had finally come.

The 1998 baseball card market would be fairly crowded. Pacific, Topps, Fleer, Upper Deck and Pinnacle all had licenses to make baseball cards. (Pinnacle would not last long; they declared bankruptcy in September of 1998. Their bankruptcy filings online show they had not paid their licensing guarantees.)

When we returned to the Pacific offices from Hawaii, we immediately got things rolling to produce six all-new baseball card brands. Our baseball photo library was already in place, and we had plenty of players' pictures to choose from.

We expanded the pre-press graphics department to nine people. In 1998, Pacific needed to schedule production of 38 different trading card releases across three major sports. We also beefed up the media department, adding two more card copy writers. They would be responsible for gathering and writing the player biographies and stats for the card backs. Once a player's information was compiled, it was placed on the card grids and sent downstairs to the graphics department, where it was converted to the chosen typeface and placed onto the card grids. Writing card backs and compiling player stats was a fun job for the people that got to do it.

With so many products, our packaging lines were going to be right at the max. If we got more contract work for the packaging lines than we had in the forecast, we could possibly have to turn down jobs.

I wasn't going to let that happen.

We still had, stored in our warehouse, two complete MGS suction cup card feeding systems from the Donruss sale. We had the capacity to add another packaging line very efficiently. All we had to do was order a Sabib Packaging Machine for about $250,000, and we had plenty of cash reserves to do so. Delivery was quick, because Sabib already had our machine specs from our previous machine orders, and our plant engineers would do the installation.

Six weeks later, we added our fifth packaging line, and it was a good thing we did: contract work flowed in very steadily for our packaging lines that year.

Everything was in place for Pacific to manufacture our 1998 Major League Baseball cards—everything except a Major League Baseball Properties license to use the team logos on the cards.

We had been a Baseball Properties licensee for more than 10 consecutive years to make our Spanish-language cards; I thought a license from Baseball Properties was a no-brainer.

I was wrong.

It turned out to be a task. But again, I was up for it.

We got the license and full rights to make player cards from the Players Association and immediately applied to Major League Baseball Properties for their side of the license, to use team logos on the cards.

I made several calls to MLB Properties, and none were returned. I had no choice but to charge ahead with designing and producing our first 1998 baseball card products. I really didn't foresee any issues getting MLB Properties to license these new cards—after all, Pacific was already licensed.

A couple weeks went by, and still no word from MLB Properties. So I decided to make our cards without team logos on them. While team logos could sometimes dress up a baseball card, they weren't particularly needed on a card to sell it. The only thing baseball card collectors care about is the player on the card. A baseball card is a photo of the player, not a photo of a team logo.

Pacific was ready to ship Pacific Aurora, our first 1998 baseball card product. In early April, we notified MLB Properties that we were going to do so. We had a license from the Major League Baseball Players Association to make baseball cards of their players, and we were going to fulfill that contract.

Shortly after that, we heard from MLB Properties. They had filed an injunction with the courts in New York City to stop us from shipping our first baseball card product.

That was a shocker. But I was prepared. I had my attorney, Mike Kipling, on board, and he was up to speed. Mike, a Harvard Law School graduate, was a brilliant intellectual properties lawyer. He also was an avid outdoorsman and recreational soccer player. He and his team of lawyers had helped Pacific get through the NFL Properties trouble back in 1990–91. He answered the MLB Properties lawsuit on behalf of Pacific, in the Lower Manhattan district courts.

In early May of 1998, a judge in the district court system heard the case from both sides. The court ruled in favor of Pacific Trading Cards, Inc., denying MLB Properties a preliminary injunction against Pacific Trading Cards. We had won the lawsuit, and Pacific could now release our first baseball card product with players in uniforms that sported team logos. No team logos would be printed anyplace else on the cards, such as borders or other design elements.

But wait.

Mike Kipling had warned me that MLB Properties would likely appeal the case to a higher court. And a few days later, he called to tell me that our case was, indeed, appealed to the United States Court of Appeals, Second Circuit, New York City.

12. Major League Baseball Players Association License

The only higher court in the United States of America is the Supreme Court.

This case was getting some serious attention and moving fast. The judges were scheduled to hear the case on May 19, 1998.

Mike was prepared and ready to argue our case before the judges at the appeals court. Pacific also hired a New York lawyer named Paul Grand, another brilliant attorney. He worked with Mike and also appeared before the judges to argue our case.

Mike and I would fly from Seattle to New York City for the hearing. However, about a week before we were scheduled to leave, I got a call from Mike. The avid recreational soccer player had just broken his leg in a soccer match.

But Mike was a tough guy. He did not want to have this hearing postponed. He strapped on a walking cast, got on his crutches, and we flew to New York City for the hearing.

On May 19, 1998, Mike Kipling, Paul Grand and I went to the U.S. Appeals Court in Lower Manhattan for our hearing before the three appeals court judges. When we entered the courtroom, I was astonished at what I saw.

The courtroom was incredibly beautiful and huge. Wood-paneled walls and plenty of long wooden benches framed both sides of the courtroom. At the front of the room was an elevated, curved wooden bench where all three judges would sit.

There were two desks in the chamber, one on each side of the room. The four or five lawyers from MLB Properties sat on the left; Mike Kipling and Paul Grand sat at the right. The podium where the lawyers would present their cases was in the center of the room.

I sat down on the right side of the courtroom, on one of the long seats just behind my lawyers. Dozens of people entered the courtroom, and they all took seats on the left side of the room, behind the MLB Properties lawyers. Just before the judges entered the courtroom, I looked over my shoulder: the long wooden benches on the left side of the room were filled with people. Then I looked at the seats behind me.

There was no one there.

I was the only one sitting on my side of the courtroom. At that moment, I realized: I was all alone. It was just me, against 30 Major League Baseball billionaires: one guy, up against a powerful group of people with all the money in the world.

I saw Mike and Paul in front of me, arranging and rearranging their papers, leaning sideways to confer with each other, Mike standing on one foot, supported by his crutches.

For a brief moment, I flashed back to my crab fishing days, standing on the deck of the *North Sea*, looking out over miles of the cold, rough Bering Sea, and realizing I was alone. One big, rogue wave could sweep me overboard at any second.

And now, I sat alone on a cold, hard, wooden courtroom bench.

Except I wasn't completely alone. My attorneys were in front of me, battling to keep me and Pacific from being swept overboard.

The judges came into the courtroom, and the hearing began.

Each lawyer would have a limited amount of time to present their case. The lead attorney for MLB Properties presented his arguments to the judges first. His arguments were interesting to the judges, and they took notes. At one point, the judges seemed to agree with his arguments. (Major League Baseball was very well known to all of the judges.) He finished with his case presentation, and it must have been a good one, because the judges looked enlightened.

Then it was Mike Kipling's turn to argue the case for Pacific. He got up to the podium with the help of his crutches and basically balanced himself on one foot. Paul Grand joined him, standing at his side, notes in hand. Mike began to present our case to the judges. He was formidable and answered one question after another from the judges while Paul Grand passed him notes. At one point, the judges were grilling Mike, asking why Pacific should be allowed to infringe on MLB Properties logos. At that point, the lead Major League Baseball Properties attorney turned back to smile at me, as if to say, "Gotcha!"

I was not sure where this hearing was going. Mike was still talking to the judges. Paul was still passing notes as fast as he could. I was still listening as close as I could. Then Mike made a couple of arguments, and the judges took notes of what he said.

This was all going very quickly, and I was, at this point, feeling like a spectator at a sparring match, sitting there listening to every word being said in that courtroom. The judges knew I was in the courtroom, and I'm sure they could see I was sitting there all by myself. I wasn't the head of a giant corporation: it was just me, a baseball card collector turned card manufacturer, trying to realize my dream of making baseball cards for all collectors.

I remembered Mike saying that, once you get in a courtroom before the judges, anything can happen.

It did.

Suddenly, the chief judge said that they were going to take a short recess and come back with their decision. Mike looked back at me and whispered, "This is it."

After a short break, the three appeals court judges returned to the courtroom and took their seats on the bench.

Chief Judge Winters then made a statement, but all I heard him say was "Would Pacific Trading Cards be willing to put up a bond so they can ship baseball cards now, and then we can decide this court case at a later date?"

I knew right then: we had won this lawsuit.

MLB Properties had been seeking an injunction to stop us from shipping. With the decision of the judges, we were going to be able to ship our cards. Mike Kipling looked back at me and I was already nodding yes. I was no longer a spectator in that courtroom: I was actually involved.

All the people in the long wooden seats on the other side of the courtroom looked stunned. They were gaping over at me like "Who is this guy?" At that stage, I wasn't sure, but I did know this: I was going to be making my baseball cards. I truly wanted to make Major League Baseball cards. It had been my dream for as long as I could remember, and I had persevered.

I remembered Joe DiMaggio telling me: "You never know where fate will take you."

My fate was to be able to manufacture baseball cards, but it took the United States Court of Appeals to seal it.

It was over, one of the most interesting and hair-raising ordeals I have ever been a part of. The lead attorney for Baseball Properties then came over to Mike Kipling, and we went to find a room to settle our issues.

Pacific Trading Cards was issued a Major League Baseball license to go with our baseball player license right there in those meetings.

The case, *Major League Baseball Properties v. Pacific Trading Cards, Inc.*, was extremely important to Pacific in the fact that we prevailed. We were proof that the little guy can beat the odds, if he perseveres. But in some sense, it was also important to the people of the United States, in that the case wrote law. It is public record and available online. Our case can be (and has been) cited as a precedent in similar court cases.

I called Cheryl and told her we had won.

And I was coming home.

13

Turning and Burning

Pacific had seen trials and tribulations—literally—but we prevailed and were licensed by Major League Baseball Properties.

With that license, plus the Major League Baseball Players Association license we already had in place, Pacific produced our first fully-licensed mainstream baseball cards for all collectors, no matter where they lived. Ever since I was a kid, I had collected, bought, and sold baseball cards, and now I would make the baseball cards that fulfilled other kids' dreams. My dream of making baseball cards for all the collectors was no longer a dream: it had come true.

To help market our Pacific baseball cards, we signed a three-year endorsement deal with Major League hitting superstar Tony Gwynn. One of the purest hitters the game of baseball has ever seen, Gwynn was also an old Pacific friend from the candy bar days. In his new capacity, Gwynn would appear on Pacific baseball card packaging and in advertising, make personal appearances, and sign autographs for Pacific. He was a joy to work with.

The first baseball product we launched was Pacific Aurora Baseball, a 200-card set featuring nine insert sets including parallel sets. Pacific Aurora was printed on a very thick card stock, twice as thick as regular cards, with an action photo and headshot on the fronts of the cards. The backs of the cards included a headshot and player biography with stats. The insert cards were laser cut, die cut, embossed and foiled.

It was a complicated but nice-looking card. I liked it. And 24 of the players featured in Pacific Aurora's 200-card set became Baseball Hall of Famers, including Hideo Nomo, who is in the Japanese Baseball Hall of Fame.

We released eight baseball products that year, including two Spanish/English releases. My favorite was Pacific Crown Royale Baseball. With all die-cut cards, the set was beautiful but very complicated to make. Baseball card collectors loved this set.

Our 1998 Pacific Baseball included a 10-card insert set of Cramer's

13. Turning and Burning

Choice Awards, the first mainstream baseball Cramer's Choice Awards cards we made. This was very rewarding for me, as I had the honor of picking the top player at each position, plus two pitchers. Ken Griffey, Jr., Cal Ripken, Jr., Tony Gwynn, Greg Maddux, Larry Walker, Mike Piazza, and Roberto Alomar became Hall of Famers. Nomar Garciaparra, Roger Clemens, and Mark McGwire all had incredible Major League careers and are all in that set.

In 1998, Pacific Trading Cards developed, designed and produced a Major League Baseball Card Collectors Kit for Scholastic. The kit consisted of a 500-count box to hold cards, a 24-page collecting guide, and packs of baseball cards representing two of our brands, Pacific and Omega. More than 700,000 Pacific Baseball kits were sold in 1998. We were now marketing and selling baseball cards to all the school kids in America.

The Scholastic program was so popular with students that, the following year, we added a Pacific NFL Football Card Kit to the Scholastic program. More than two million of those kits sold at the Scholastic School Book Fairs.

But in 1998, a year of baseball milestones, Pacific got a major home run with a boxed set called "Home Run History: The Mark McGwire and Sammy Sosa Home Run Race of 1998." The set included a Gold Crown die-cut card of Cal Ripken, Jr., highlighting his Ironman streak of 2,632 games, which the great shortstop voluntarily ended in 1998.

This card set was the brainchild of Ken Goldin. Pacific had first worked with Goldin five years before, when the former head of Classic card company had sublicensed Pacific for a basketball card set. Goldin was outstanding at marketing trading cards. The idea and concept for Home Run History was his, but he left it to Pacific to design the cards and print and box the sets.

This was a really fun set to make. There was huge fan interest in the home run race, and Ken knew there would be collector interest in a commemorative set. He called Pacific because he knew we had a trading card factory and we designed beautiful cards. He also knew we could manufacture the sets of cards in a very short amount of time and be ready to ship in just four weeks. He himself would present the Home Run History set, live, on the nationally-broadcast home shopping network QVC.

Ken thought we could get orders for at least 20,000 sets. So Pacific designed the cards and sent Ken oversized promotional cards to use on TV to help sell the set.

We started printing the actual-size cards, made the 20,000 sets of 72 cards each, and began to box and overwrap the sets, all within a few weeks. Pacific, the card factory, could turn and burn when we needed to. Our people were so good that the more work we had, the better they performed.

The QVC broadcast was September 28, 1998. Ken did the Home Run History presentation himself; back home, we were all hoping we would sell the 20,000 sets we had in production.

Cheryl and I had gone to my daughter Angela's volleyball game at her high school. When we got home, I turned on the TV to QVC, to see if I could catch the sale broadcast. It was still on—and I could not believe what I saw.

They had a ticker bar running with the number of sets sold. *It was up to 72,000 sets!* Every baseball card collector in America must want a set of these cards!

All I could think was, "We are going to need to get some more sets made."

I watched Ken's presentation. He was a master, but the set also sold itself. The 1998 home run race was, at that very moment, captivating American sports fans and baseball card collectors. I tuned in to QVC for a little longer and, just before I went to bed, the QVC presentation had generated orders for more than 90,000 Home Run History sets. This was unbelievable—unprecedented.

All I could think was "Tomorrow's going to be a busy day."

I went in to work early to get a handle on things and had a message from Ken on my voicemail. I called him right away.

"Mike! Did you see the number?" he said.

"Yes! Looks like you sold about 90,000 sets," I said. "That's way more than we planned."

He said, "Way more! But, Mike ... orders are still coming in. The cut-off for ordering the set was extended, and it's still two hours away!"

Orders were still coming in? I loved this set—after all, it was one of my company's "kids." But even I couldn't believe how much interest there was!

Ken called back a couple of hours later. The final number of sets ordered was 142,500 sets.

We had hoped for 20,000.

This was gigantic! Pacific would need to turn and burn like tires at the Indy 500.

Because the numbers had caught everybody off guard, I asked if there could be any leniency in the delivery date.

"Not much," Ken said. "QVC has a delivery window, and we need to meet that window."

I said, "We will get it done."

The printing and cutting of the cards actually didn't take that long: that was mostly automated. The slower obstacle was boxing up the set, which was all done by hand. We expanded to three shifts a day to get

13. *Turning and Burning*

the work done and deliver on schedule. Happily for everyone, it all went smoothly, and we proved to ourselves once again that, if put to the task, the crews at Pacific could get the job done.

Home Run History is a beautiful card set, and collectors love it.

* * *

Our six 1998 NFL football card brands were fueled by two can't-miss rookies, Peyton Manning and Randy Moss. True to expectations, both went on to Hall of Fame careers. I liked Peyton Manning so well, I picked him for one of my Cramer's Choice Awards that year.

Our football products were full of parallel cards. If you were a football card collector, our football insert cards were just outstanding to collect, featuring intricate laser- and die-cut designs. And the parallels gave collectors a big challenge, as the cards were inserted in packs at various ratios.

Pacific Revolution is another football brand we made. The card design was meant to be revolutionary, with an action photo set against a boldly designed foil background. I loved it, and lots of collectors liked it too. In fact, nowadays a lot of the cards being made look like Pacific Revolution.

Including the Peyton Manning rookie card, Pacific Revolution has 33 Hall of Famers. The number is even more astonishing for 1998 Pacific NFL Football, which has 52 Hall of Fame cards.

Football and baseball made great showings for Pacific in 1998. So did hockey. Our second year of NHL hockey cards was defined by the use of our own player photos. Because a trading card is, in essence, a photo, we wanted only the very best player photos on our cards. We hired the best photographers available to shoot NHL games just for Pacific, and it paid off. We had many dazzling photographs to choose from.

Our 1998–99 Pacific Revolution Hockey set was my favorite hockey set of that year. The card design was perfectly laid out for a hockey card, hinting at both the boards circling the rink and the speed of skaters circling the ice. That set produced 36 NHL Hall of Famers, including a beautiful Wayne Gretzky card.

Pacific NHL Hockey cards were selling very well, and collectors loved our creative new designs. And it probably didn't hurt that our new Pacific hockey spokesman that year was goalie great Martín Brodeur, my personal favorite NHL player of all time.

While the sets we made that year are loaded with Hall of Famers, one player stood out: an undrafted rookie named Martin St. Louis, who went on to a stellar NHL career, became a Hall of Famer in 2018.

Also that year, we made Jumbo Cramer's Choice Award cards with seven different parallels. *That* was fun! The cards were large and showed off the players' photos really nicely. One purple parallel set was serial numbered 1 of 1; another purple set was not serial numbered but was personally signed by me. So each parallel was a unique one of one set. There was also one unsigned purple set numbered 1/1, made as replacement cards if needed (for example, if a customer got a pack with a damaged card inside). The unsigned replacement cards were kept in safe storage, and I'm glad to say were never needed.

The purple parallels were numbered 1/1, and I personally signed the backs of the cards—this helped make the cards authentic 1/1s.

As the 1998 NHL season got underway, I decided I wanted to shoot a few hockey games myself. I was still shooting a full schedule of baseball and football games on the weekends and got the itch to give NHL hockey a try.

The closest NHL games to me were a three-hour drive north; Vancouver, Canada, was home of the Canucks. The Pacific photo department booked me to shoot the October 21 game, Canucks vs. Capitals.

Cheryl and I drove up from Edmonds. This would be my first NHL game, so we arrived early at General Motors Arena to meet the Canucks team photographer and get me set up.

Shooting hockey is totally different from baseball or football, where you are shooting photos outdoors. In the elements, lighting can change by the second. But NHL hockey is indoors, shooting with primarily a 28–70mm, 200mm or 400mm lens. The indoor lighting at the hockey rink is a bit too dark to light up the player.

That's why, if you are at an NHL game, you might notice flashes of light going off above the ice. That is a photographer taking player photographs: a remote control connected to the camera fires the strobe lights in the arena's rafters. The strobe lights up the players, and beautiful, well-balanced color shots can be achieved.

In baseball or football, I could shoot up to 10 photos a second. In hockey, I had to pause three seconds between shots, to let the strobes recycle. When I fired my shutter, the lights flashed, illuminating the player while I took the photo. That made it very easy to get great results with nearly every shot.

There are three 20-minute periods in a hockey game. I was scheduled to shoot one period from the first level mezzanine above the stands (that's where I used the 400mm lens). I was also scheduled to shoot one period through a cutout hole in the glass, in the corner turn down by the goalie. Finally, I would have one period right down on the ice in the photographers' well between the players' bench and penalty box.

An NHL game moves very fast. Players skate fast, shoot the puck fast, and change fast. From the first level on the mezzanine, I was able to

13. Turning and Burning

focus on a player and get great shots. (Every player on the team played, so it didn't matter what player I focused on—though I did recognize when I had Mark Messier in my lens.)

I was also able to aim right down the bench shooting headshots, as the players were always looking up, out onto the ice. But the game just moves so quickly. I couldn't believe when the period ended and it was my turn to shoot from the photographers' well on the ice.

I got down there, and the first thing I heard from the Canuck team photographer was, "Mike, have you shot on the ice before?"

"No, this is my first time," I said. "But I've shot seven years of NFL on the sidelines, so I'm up for it."

He said, "Keep your eyes focused, and watch for pucks. *And* sticks—and they come quick."

I got my 28–70mm lens and stepped into the photographers' well. I was ready. The players came out on the ice and the period began.

I quickly found out that NHL hockey players are giants, standing in their skates on the ice. They moved fast, and they were zooming by me, left and right. I had to pick out a player, focus on him through my lens and shoot, player after player, all the while watching out to make sure I didn't get a puck or a stick in my face. But my Canon camera was so high-speed that I rarely missed a shot. Every once in a while, another player would skate right into the player I was shooting and blur my photo. About 20 percent of my photos were not sharp and tossed in the trash at editing time—not bad, considering the velocity of every moment.

Shooting from the box was incredibly exhilarating! But when my 20-minute period ended, I thanked God I was able to walk out of that box with no damage. I also knew that I had taken some great player shots.

My last period was shooting through the hole in the glass. Sounds easy—I figured there was a one-in-a-million chance a puck could go through that hole, so this was going to be fun! And I was right at ice level, with players from both teams skating right by me. This would be easy pickings!

The period started. I rested my body right on the glass, with my camera lens in the hole, and I got off a couple shots. Then I focused on Mark Messier, Canucks captain and future Hall of Famer. He was skating right at me with the puck. I took a photo, waited three seconds for the strobe, fired the shutter again—and then there was an earthquake.

The entire place erupted. The glass in front of me shook violently back and forth, players from both teams piled all over the ice just outside the window, and in that second I learned not to get that close to the glass—just shoot through the hole. Because when a player gets checked into the boards, the glass above is no longer stationary. It billows and heaves, your own private earthquake.

I loved shooting hockey! I felt like I was part of the game!

The game ended in a victory for the Canucks and a victory for me: I had shot my first NHL game and survived! Not quite like surviving a king crab fishing season, but surviving, nonetheless. I couldn't wait to get my slides developed and see my results.

With baseball, football, and hockey, too, Pacific photographers were shooting so many games that we installed a Fuji slide film processor machine at Pacific. It automatically processed the film, mounted the slide photos in plastic jackets, and printed the game, date and photographer's name on each plastic jacket.

I turned in my 21 rolls of film the next morning and asked the photo department to get them moved up in the photo processing line so I could see my results. Around an hour later, I went into the photo library and laid out my slides on the light table. It was a bigger thrill to me to see my great, card-making player photos than it was actually shooting the game. I had nice stuff, and the lighting in the slides was always perfect because of the strobe lights. That's why Pacific hockey cards always had great, consistent, beautifully-lit photos.

I thought, "If I hadn't been a king crab fisherman or owned a trading card manufacturing company, I could have made a living as a sports photographer and it would have been a fun job."

* * *

In the fall of 1998, my secretary dropped a trade fax on my desk. The big headline read "Pinnacle Cards files for bankruptcy," citing $68 million in assets and more than $100 million in debt. This was huge in the trading card industry, as Pinnacle would no longer make cards.

It was immense for Pacific, as I thought we would capture a fair share of the card market left by the Pinnacle void.

Our 1998 baseball card sales started out as we projected and we were running on all cylinders. With the Pinnacle bankruptcy, we immediately thought sales would come in better for the year than originally expected. Unfortunately, that didn't quite happen as it should have.

The Pinnacle debacle is well documented in their bankruptcy statements, which can be found online. Pinnacle owed millions of dollars, including money owed on the Donruss purchase. Moreover, Pinnacle had produced baseball cards under a license for which they hadn't paid the full guarantee and were sitting on more than $2.5 million in card products at the time of bankruptcy.

Unfortunately for the card market, the courts allowed this product to be sold off. Turned over at deeply discounted prices, Pinnacle merchandise truly disrupted the supply and demand in the card market. Discounted

Pinnacle items continued to sell for years, even though these products were no longer new. Collectors viewed the marked-down products as good, affordable investments—after all, collectibles often increase in value as they age.

The cut-price Pinnacle baseball card product affected Pacific and most likely the other card manufacturers. Sales for our new baseball products were greatly affected, as was our sell-through at retail stores for new baseball products, and we received more product returns from our distributors than we had projected. Our leftover cards had to be sold at a deep discount in an effort to clear inventory and to recoup money to pay our big licensing fees. The cycle seemed never-ending because the market was clogged with cheap product for a very long time.

A chain reaction begins with a single event. In this case, the bankruptcy of Pinnacle and the sell-off of their unsold product most likely led to the demise of Fleer, Upper Deck and Pacific a few years later.

Sales for new baseball cards never recovered enough to earn out the baseball license guarantees. (Guarantees are royalties that card makers pay to the licensing entity. For example, Pacific would pay a fee to MLB based on the projected number of unit sales. If fewer units sold, Pacific lost money. If more units sold, Pacific simply paid more royalties—but now had fresh capital to do so.)

In an attempt to make up for low unit sales and earn back the guarantee dollars, manufacturers released more and more baseball products. This led to an oversaturated market, which resulted in fewer sales per product, which meant that new product development costs could not be recouped. This, in turn, made development cost per product seem higher. It was a vicious cycle.

Even with this blow to the market, Pacific was able to sustain and move forward, paying our way with our NFL and NHL products and our contract packaging work. Our Major League Baseball card sales were, at this time, good—but they needed to be better. Unfortunately, no hot baseball rookies emerged in 1998, making the market even tougher.

It was a storm we had to weather.

But the dumping of Pinnacle products was to have a greater effect on the overall trading card market than even I could have imagined. The downturn would last nearly 20 years before making a worthwhile recovery, when quarterback Tom Brady (the GOAT, the "Greatest of All Time") and his rookie card surged in popularity—and price—a surge upheld with the influx of free pandemic money.

There was a silver lining in all of this for turn-of-the-century sports card collectors. Fewer case runs created very short print runs for some of the inserts as well as some of the base cards. The competition among card manufacturers created some of the best ideas in card designs ever produced in the history of baseball cards, with Pacific continuing to lead the way.

Pacific's foiled, embossed, laser-cut and die-cut cards outpaced all others. We also continued mastering parallel cards, using every new foil color we could muster up. This drove card collectors nuts, as they scrambled to find all of the parallel cards of their favorite players or to collect the full sets of parallels we made. Most of these cards had very limited production runs and were quite rare in most cases. This created enormous challenges for the collectors and helped drive case sales.

As crazy as parallel cards seemed to collectors in 1998, these cards led the way to the future of card collecting. It has become mainstream for card manufacturers to make an abundance of parallel cards in their products.

Pacific was once again 20 years ahead of its time.

* * *

I spent a lot of time traveling in 1998, most importantly with monthly sales trips to our sales offices in Monterrey and Mexico City. I hoped to gain sales and distribution for the Pacific English/Spanish baseball cards and loved to visit our friends at Bimbo Bakeries. I also made several trips to Europe to visit distributors of our NHL hockey cards. We had sales offices and distributors in Stockholm, Sweden; Prague, Czech Republic; Cologne, Germany; and Brussels, Belgium.

On one of my trips to Sweden, I discovered a new hobby.

I have always been a collector and had, at that time, one of the largest (if

1999 Pacific Revolution Icons. We made this beautiful die-cut card design for baseball, football and hockey players (Pacific Trading Cards Archives).

13. Turning and Burning

not the largest) collection of baseball card sets ever accumulated in private hands.

While in Stockholm for sales and marketing meetings, I visited the Swedish Army Museum. I have been interested in military history since I was a boy, and at the museum I discovered a fascinating collection of Swedish army uniforms displayed on mannequins. The uniforms, dating from the early 1500s up to pre–World War I years, were complete with elaborate headgear all the way down to boots and spurs. Most had beautiful belts, pouches, and swords from a bygone era, when kings and queens ruled countries and their armies were a show of power and wealth.

On my way out after touring this incredible museum, I passed a large, open hall and saw that there was an auction in progress. Lined up in the back of the room were mannequins in Swedish army uniforms, all complete, with swords and magnificent helmets.

My collector's instincts vibrated. More than a little.

I asked the lady at the desk what was going on. She replied that the museum was auctioning some duplicate uniforms from the museum collection.

I immediately signed up to bid. The uniforms in that hall stood out, shining in the light with all of their gold lace and beautiful blue and yellow trimmings, the Swedish national colors.

By the time the auction ended, I had purchased three beautiful historical uniforms.

I then realized: I had to figure out how to get these things home on the airplane.

But back then, there was no problem taking swords and guns in your luggage! My treasures made it home safe with me, along with some nice orders for Pacific hockey cards.

I showed Cheryl my new acquisitions.

She said, "Oh, boy! What have you done now? What are you going to do with those uniforms?"

"Well...," I said, "get three mannequins so I can display them?"

We had our Thanksgiving dinner that year with three Swedish soldiers in the dining room. I do believe I saw smiles on those mannequins' faces as we ate our dinner with them.

Within a few years, I had amassed one of the largest private collections of antique military uniforms in the world, covering 17 different countries including the United States, dating from the early 1800s to 1916.

* * *

In spite of all the turmoil in the trading card market, Pacific still had a very profitable year in 1998. Our sales at retail stores were strong, and we always knew where we stood financially because our CFO, Phil Roth, did monthly sales and expense projections that were extremely reliable. We also had a very loyal customer base that loved and bought our cards, and that was the most important thing.

We had a steady stream of card releases for the new year, led by our hockey card brands, Pacific Crown Royale and Pacific Prism. Our eight different NHL card brands were doing fantastic and being acquired by hockey card collectors all over the globe.

There were also baseball and football card brands to design and produce, all on a scheduled time frame to meet a release date—a date that had to be met, period! The system was never allowed to break down, our people were so good.

I helped choose the photos/slides for our first football card release that year, 1999 Pacific Football. We had a great supply of current player photos, and our base set was going to be large: 450 different players' cards. But I wanted to get even more players in the set, so I decided to put two players together on 36 of the cards in the set. That would allow us to add a few football players who didn't have a card yet.

I chose the photos for the set in February and March. When I was picking St. Louis Rams players from the Rams photo binder, I saw just two slides (enough to make a card) of an unknown player that didn't have a card: Kurt Warner. He was a quarterback and had played in the Arena Football League for a few seasons. In 1998, he was the Rams' third string quarterback and played in only one game that season.

Still, Warner's photos were good, and I needed to finish selecting photos, so I chose his two photos and added them to the set.

It was a great choice. For, even though Warner was 28 years old, his long, phenomenal career was just beginning.

Our national sales manager, Bruce Chappalear, had booked sales for most of our 1999 Pacific Football cases. We shipped the product in May of 1999 and were hopeful we would sell the remaining cases on reorders.

Then came the twist of fate for Kurt Warner and his Pacific rookie card.

Before the season began, Rams quarterback Steve Bono left for free agency, and the Rams signed Trent Green to be the starter. When the team traded back-up quarterback Tony Banks to the Ravens, Warner found himself second on the Rams quarterback depth chart. And after Green suffered a torn ACL in a preseason game, Rams coach Dick Vermeil named Warner as the Rams' starter.

Vermeil hadn't even seen Warner work with the first-string offense.

But with the support of running back Marshall Faulk and wide receivers Isaac Bruce, Ricky Proehl and rookie Torry Holt, Warner put together

13. Turning and Burning

In 1999, Pacific made the first-ever Kurt Warner card. This card won us an award for NFL Rookie Card of the year (Pacific Trading Cards Archives).

one of the top seasons by a quarterback in NFL history, throwing for 4,353 yards with 41 touchdown passes and a completion rate of 65.1 percent.

Because Pacific had the first 1999 NFL football cards on the market (released in May), Kurt Warner's first ever, true rookie card was in that football card set, #343. Pacific had the only NFL football card of Kurt Warner for most of the 1999 season, and the demand for the product went through the roof. Needless to say, we sold through every case we made.

When Warner started the season on fire, I lobbied the hobby press writers to give him and his Pacific rookie card recognition. They blew it off, claiming the 28-year-old Warner was too old. He was just having a good year, they said, but he wasn't a potentially great player.

But by this time, I had shot a 1999 Rams game. I had actually seen Kurt Warner play early in the season, and I recognized his great potential. Not all NFL quarterbacks have that look of poise and control, arm delivery and stature. Warner had it, and I saw it firsthand. I had watched Montana, Marino, Favre, Elway, Young, Manning, and Aikman, and they all had the *look*. I was on the NFL sidelines shooting games and had seen them play—I knew that look.

The beauty of it was, he was already in our 1999 Pacific football card set when I realized how good he was. I knew we had an unknown, hot rookie card in that set, and it wasn't long before some astute football card collectors realized it too.

However, it wasn't until *USA Today* acknowledged Kurt Warner's 1999 Pacific card as a rookie card that the hobby publications followed suit, in an overwhelmingly positive way.

And at the annual NFL Properties licensing meetings that year, the NFL finally gave our 1999 Pacific Kurt Warner rookie card the recognition it deserved. Pacific received the 1999 NFL Rookie Card of the Year Award. I still have that beautiful wooden NFL football trophy in my library.

Kurt Warner would go on to play in the NFL for 12 seasons, primarily with the St. Louis Rams and the Arizona Cardinals. He is regarded as one of the greatest stories in NFL history, ascending from an undrafted free agent (the greatest undrafted free agent to ever play in the NFL) to a two-time Most Valuable Player and Super Bowl MVP.

Kurt Warner was elected to the Pro Football Hall of Fame in 2017.

Warner had a truly great career and proved me right, just like Ken Griffey, Jr., did in 1989, when Pacific made his candy bar.

* * *

Some of the hobby publication writers ignored us until very late in the season. Fortunately, the collectors did not. Our 1999 Pacific Football cards sold out 100 percent. Sales for the set were driven by rookie cards of Warner and two other future Hall of Famers, cornerback Champ Bailey (card #422) and the great running back Edgerrin James (card #437).

So far, 1999 Pacific Football has yielded 52 Hall of Fame players.

Pacific made a total of seven NFL football card products in 1999, including a really hot one, Pacific Crown Royale Football. The year also included my favorite football design ever made for Pacific Gold Crown, the 36-player Gold Crown Die-Cut set. The design showed off the player so perfectly, it is one of the reasons the Gold Crown Die-Cut design is still being made more than 20 years later.

My 1999 Pacific Football Cramer's Choice Awards set has seven Hall of Famers, with the potential for a couple more. Kurt Warner is one of the 10 players I picked for the Jumbo Cramer's Choice Awards, sets that were serial numbered 1 to 299.

Trying to make up for sluggish baseball card sales, we released 10 baseball card brands in 1999. We added a new brand we named Pacific Private Stock. We transcended this brand across our three major sports trading card lines. Pacific Private Stock cards were printed on thick card stock, and the product was loaded with really cool insert cards, including a new concept I based on the old 1910 T-206 Tobacco cards (which I now had a complete set of).

13. Turning and Burning

These new homage cards were the same small size as the T-206 cards, with a beautiful color photo on the front and a one-color printed back, designed in the 1910 baseball card style. I read that Topps later tried to take credit for reintroducing the T-206–style cards to the card market, but our 1999 cards exist to prove that Pacific did it first. We named our new card PS-206. I loved them, and we made them for our MLB, NFL, and NHL Private Stock brands.

I always collected all the card sets we made: they were my favorite cards. I had all of the Pacific cards, except for a few of the really short, serial-numbered prints. The little PS-206 cards are among my favorite cards that we ever made.

* * *

The 1999 Major League Baseball All-Star Game was held that year in Boston, and Pacific Trading Cards, Inc., was a sponsor of the John Hancock All-Star FanFest held at the Hynes Convention Center, July 9–13. We made a card of Boston Red Sox Hall of Famer Carl Yastrzemski, one of my boyhood favorite players (and now I could pronounce his name!). We gave the card to fans who came to our booth at the FanFest.

Pacific Trading Cards, Inc., had grown from a personal hobby of mine into one of the major players in the trading card hobby industry. At the FanFest that year, I knew we had arrived. With three major sports trading card licenses, Pacific was at the top of the game. My dream was real, and I was living it night and day.

What most people really didn't understand is that the other major card manufactures were owned by big money investors and groups of very rich people. Pacific Trading Cards, Inc., was owned by me, built out of love for my hobby: collecting trading cards. Some days, I had to pinch myself to bring myself back to reality. I couldn't believe I was getting to make trading cards on this scale! Of course, collecting cards was still a hobby for me. But more than that, it was now my "business," an extremely fun business for a guy who started out as a card-collecting kid and was once a crusty old king crab fisherman out of Dutch Harbor, Alaska.

* * *

In the fall of 1999, we learned from the NHL Players Association that McDonald's of Canada would be taking presentations from each of the NHL trading card companies. Pacific was invited to make a presentation for the upcoming 2000–01 McDonald's card promotion.

This was a huge promotion. Every McDonald's restaurant in Canada would be involved. During the promotional weeks, each Canadian McDonald's would give away and also sell packs of NHL hockey cards, with point-of-purchase signage and displays promoting the cards—and the card manufacturer.

This would be great exposure for Pacific. Every collector in Canada would know of us and have our cards.

Prior to our presentation, Ted Saskin, director of licensing for the NHL Players Association, let Pacific know that we had little chance of getting this huge promotion as Upper Deck had won it for the last couple of years. But McDonald's had invited Pacific to make a pitch at their headquarters in Toronto, Canada.

We had just two weeks to develop our proposal before our presentation.

I took the lead on this project and started to develop ideas for the card set we would propose.

A 1999 Pacific Prism baseball card. The Prism brand was our hottest trading card brand. Twenty years later, the brand was still being made, with a new spelling: Prizm (Pacific Trading Cards Archives).

I knew collectors liked our Pacific Prism cards best of all the cards we made. I decided this would be one of the three different Pacific hockey card brands we would offer to McDonald's for their upcoming promotion, along with a variety of our best die-cut insert cards.

Then we put together a presentation booklet with the most pertinent facts about Pacific and our trading card production capabilities. I also got our Canadian national sales manager, Oliver Lea, on board, absorbing his advice on the Canadian hockey market and which Pacific hockey insert cards were most popular in Canada.

My team was ready to give the Pacific presentation to the McDonald's of Canada marketing people.

Our materials were ready, and we had gone over our presentation many times and were well prepared. I flew to Toronto where Oliver met me at our hotel and we did some more prep work. I would lead the

13. Turning and Burning

presentation to the McDonald's staff, presenting our proposed trading card designs; Oliver would field any questions about the hockey card market in Canada. We were a well-oiled machine and we knew the trading card market like no one else.

When we gave our presentation, I could tell the McDonald's people were thrilled with the beautiful cards we proposed for their upcoming hockey season promotion. Our price to produce the cards was excellent and in line for the quality we proposed. McDonald's had many questions, which we answered with ease. They were most intrigued that we had our own production and packaging facilities. We would not be relying on someone else to produce the cards: all cards would be produced in-house at Pacific, and our people would be watching over every phase of the most important promotional product Pacific had ever been a part of.

We left that meeting with a good feeling, but we knew we had plenty of competition from the other hockey card companies.

We were seasoned creators of trading card promotions. Over the years, Cramer Sports Promotions and Pacific Trading Cards, Inc., had produced dozens of different trading card promotions with some very important clients, including Circle K, Motorola, Coca-Cola, 7-Eleven, King-B Quality Meat Products, Bimbo Bakeries, Oroweat Bread, Franz Bakery,

Packing Room #2 at the Pacific factory wrapping football cards, 1999. Card feeders on the left; Shanklin shrink-wrap machine, center; card wrapper machine #3 on the right (Pacific Trading Cards Archives).

Hasbro Starting Lineup, Dairy Queen, Canada Post, Pepsi, Meadow Gold Dairy, Advil, McCormick & Company, NationsBank, Nestlé, Scholastic, Backyard Sports for baseball, football, and hockey computer games—and others.

But we had never had the chance to be involved with a promotion of this magnitude.

We would have to wait for their answer. Oliver and I went back to our regular duties at Pacific, knowing we had given it everything we had.

A couple of weeks later, I got a call from the head of the NHL Players Association. He said McDonald's had selected Pacific Trading Cards, Inc., to produce the cards for their 2000–01 NHL card promotion. McDonald's of Canada would be sending us a contract, and they would send out a press release announcing the promotion in short order.

1999 Pacific Revolution Hockey, one of my favorite card designs. We made this design concept for baseball, football, and hockey cards (Pacific Trading Cards Archives).

This was huge for Pacific. We had won the biggest prize in the hockey card market!

I was doing back flips all day. This job would be about six months of solid work for Pacific. It would require our packaging department to run some of our packaging machines two and sometimes three shifts a day on McDonald's alone, while still producing our other, regular card products.

Thanks to this opportunity, Pacific Trading Cards hockey card brands would become the most widely-known hockey cards in Canada during that promotional period. And Oliver, our Canadian national sales manager, had a great new selling tool.

From December 18, 2000, through January 11, 2001, a 36-card 2000–01 Pacific Prism hockey set and inserts were available through McDonald's of

Canada with the purchase of a large French fries or hash browns. The card backs were in both English and French. A pack of five Pacific hockey cards could be purchased at McDonald's for 89 cents.

Pacific had one of its best years ever in 1999 because we were making a lot of different products and we were able to sell our cards in both local hobby shops and national retail outlets. We were on a very strict production schedule, but there were virtually no problems that we couldn't overcome. All phases of Pacific were running as smoothly as clockwork, and 1999 was a good year for us financially. That was very important too: we loved our work, but we always watched the bottom line.

14

What a Way to Start a Century!

I started the year 2000 the way I'd started the previous several years: shooting football photos at the January East-West Shrine game at Stanford Stadium. The Shrine Bowl has been played annually since 1925 to raise money for Shriners Children's Hospitals. Notable past participants include Eddie LeBaron, Hugh McElhenny, Joe Greene, Gale Sayers, and Brett Favre, among others. The Shrine Bowl is the last college all-star game for senior players coming out of college. Most seniors playing in it hope to get more exposure, be seen by an NFL scout, and get drafted.

It was a good game for Pacific to shoot because of the number of potential NFL draft picks that played. We could immediately make rookie cards of these players if they signed with an NFL team.

I took an early flight from Seattle to San Francisco and rented a car for the drive south to Stanford. I arrived at about 10 for the noon game start; the players were just coming out onto the field for the morning workout.

I set up my 400mm lens and started shooting head shots of some of the players. I had the roster and checked off a few players with high draft potential. But I shot photos of all the players I could get. You just didn't know for sure what players would get drafted into the NFL or signed by a team.

Once the game started and the players were on the field, I captured action photos of every player I could point my lens at. It was a bit overcast, so the lighting was soft and excellent for football pictures.

The East started the game with a quarterback from Michigan named Tom Brady. He wore his Michigan helmet. He'd had a really good college career, despite struggling for playing time.

In the two seasons that Brady started at Michigan, he posted a 20–5 record, which included wins at the 1999 Citrus Bowl and the 2000 Orange Bowl.

When he took the snap center and rolled back to pass, I focused in on him and fired my camera shutter. I knew I was getting great photos.

14. What a Way to Start a Century! 173

After a few plays, I realized Tom Brady was something special. He had the quarterback *look*—the look I had seen in Favre and Montana and other NFL quarterback greats I had photographed over the years.

Brady could deliver the ball with smooth precision. He was tall and poised in the pocket. My camera focused on him all the time he was in the game at quarterback. He did throw an interception, got sacked and threw a wobbly pass deep downfield, but there was off-and-on rain and the ball was wet at times.

He also threw a touchdown pass to Michigan receiver Marcus Knight and one to receiver Jerry Porter.

Tom Brady was etched in my mind. He had great potential, and I saw it during that game.

I flew home knowing I had done a good job. I couldn't wait to get my film developed and see my slides. When I did a few days later, I was happy with my work. I probably over-shot Tom Brady, but that just meant Pacific would have plenty of photos of him to make cards for the upcoming 2000 NFL season.

That spring, the NFL Players Association (through their trading card licensing arm, Players Inc.) held a photo session with all the top 2000 NFL draft prospects. This is where card companies could get pictures of the players for upcoming rookie cards.

Tom Brady was not expected to make it in the NFL and was not at the rookie shoot.

This surprised me. I'd seen strange things happen in professional sports, and this was one of them.

Even so, I was confident that the football world had not seen the last of Tom Brady. And Pacific was ready: we had plenty of photos of him, because I had taken them at the Shrine Bowl.

Years later, when Pacific Tom Brady rookie cards started selling for unheard-of prices, I found that shooting that game proved to be one of the most critical choices I made in the history of Pacific Trading Cards, Inc.

* * *

I watched the 2000 NFL draft on April 15 and 16 on ESPN. It was important to Pacific, because we would learn which players would be our best choices for 2000 Pacific rookie cards. I watched players being picked all day. The Seahawks' first pick was running back Shaun Alexander (as a Seahawks fan, I was happy about that).

I watched Chad Pennington become the first quarterback taken in the draft. I thought Tom Brady would be next, but then five more quarterbacks were drafted. During all this waiting, I thought, "What's going on? Somebody pick Tom Brady! I know he will be as good as I think he is."

But it became obvious to me that, at that point in time, Tom Brady was not high on anyone's list but mine.

Finally, in the sixth round, with the 199th pick, the New England Patriots took quarterback Tom Brady.

At least he got drafted—but sixth rounders rarely had a chance to even make an NFL team. No matter. I still liked him and saw his great potential.

In February, our Pacific football people picked rookie players for our 2000 Pacific NFL Football card set. Tom Brady was on the list of players we had rights to, a list provided by the NFL Players Association, but he was not on the Pacific list of players to be included in our set.

I always reviewed our player choices before we began to pull photos and write the copy for the card backs. Going over the list, I saw Brady's name was missing and called a meeting with my football people.

"Where is Tom Brady?" I asked. "He's not in our set."

They said, "New England has Brady, but they also have quarterback Drew Bledsoe. Brady has no chance. And Brady's a sixth-round pick—we'll get him in the next set."

I said right then and there, "Put Tom Brady in our sets and make sure he is in every 2000 Pacific football card product we can put him in. He's a rookie and a quarterback, and I saw him play. I think he has great potential."

There was some head-shaking, but I was the boss. My people made the changes to add Brady. We included him in all nine Pacific NFL card products made that year, including many insert sets.

No other football card manufacturer made as many different Tom Brady rookie cards as Pacific.

This is why, when collectors look back at our 2000 Pacific Football sets, they can see Tom Brady in all of them. I picked him early as a great one, even though he was a sixth-round pick. I insisted we include him in all of our Pacific football sets.

Along with the Ken Griffey, Jr., Candy Bar and Kurt Warner's Pacific Rookie card, Tom Brady in the year 2000 was my other great choice.

Pacific also signed Tom Brady to an autograph deal that year. He signed 200 of his Pacific Football cards (#403) and 500 Crown Royale Football cards (#110), and we randomly inserted the autographed cards into packages of cards that were available on store shelves. I wish I would have kept one of each in the Pacific card sets I collected, but all of them went into the products.

When the season started, Brady was the fourth-string Patriots quarterback. By the end of the season, he had worked his way up to Drew Bledsoe's back-up. But he appeared in only one game, completing just one pass

14. What a Way to Start a Century! 175

that season. So 2000 Pacific Brady rookie cards didn't exactly drive our football sales that year.

Then, early in the 2001 season, Drew Bledsoe went down with an injury. Tom Brady became the New England Patriots starter, and the rest of his story is history.

But my pick, my choice, and my insistence to put Tom Brady in all of our 2000 Pacific Football products would, nearly 20 years later, help a struggling trading card market recover as collectors scrambled to get a rookie card of the GOAT.

When Tom Brady led the Tampa Bay Bucs to Super Bowl victory in 2020, I cheered him on. I'm one of his biggest fans. Tom Brady was still playing with the Bucs in 2023, continuing to prove himself the greatest quarterback to ever play in the NFL.

Released in late May 2000, Pacific NFL Football was the first NFL football card set to hit the market that year. And without question, if you have card #403, you have the first NFL card ever made of Tom Brady.

That set has 42 cards of players elected to the Pro Football Hall of Fame, with more to come in the future—including the GOAT, Tom Brady.

In February of 2000, we again went to the annual trading card conference in Hawaii, put on by my good friend Kit Young. Pacific Trading Cards, Inc., was again one of a host of sponsors. In meetings with our card distributors, dealers, and friends, we learned that Pacific could gain a larger trading card market share if we made cards that incorporated bits of game-used jerseys and other memorabilia.

I wasn't a fan of this type of card. I couldn't see why a collector like me would want to cut up a perfectly good, historical, game-worn player's jersey (or bat or hockey stick). I was a collector, and this went against every bone in my body.

But Pacific was a business, and I had a business to run. I listened to what people were telling me. This type of card, sometimes called a "memorabilia card" or "relic card," was very popular and collectors craved them.

Later that week at the conference, Pacific announced we would start to include cards autographed by players in our products as well as game-worn uniform cards with pieces of MLB and NFL player jerseys and NHL hockey sweaters.

This was an instant hit. Collectors, dealers, and distributors that we talked to all said we had the best card inserts, and this would give collectors everything they were looking for in a product.

Many people congratulated us on the decision, and it did make a difference in our sales and market share. But, though adding those cards gave Pacific a market share boost in 2001, we had to add additional releases to our card lines. Case sales per product were still declining, and cost of goods was going up. Acquiring authentic game-used jerseys, sweaters, bats, and hockey sticks was a new expense—and it was expensive.

Obtaining autographed cards from players was laborious, requiring large amounts of pre-planning. Pacific did have some experience with autographed cards. In 1993, Nolan Ryan, Tom Seaver, Steve Largent and Bob Griese each signed cards for Pacific products. However, they were all retired players, and it was much easier to arrange a signing session with them. Now we were dealing with currently active players. Scheduling an autograph session with each of them was a whole new ball game.

To reach the players we wanted to sign for us, we contacted their agents (with help from the MLB, NHL and NFL players associations). Once we reached an agreement, the cards had to be printed, then sent to the player; the player would sign the cards and have them sent back to Pacific.

2000 Pacific Football Tom Brady rookie card, his first ever NFL card. 2000 Pacific was the first NFL football card product to hit the market in 2000. This card is graded a perfect gem mint 10 (Mike Cramer Collection).

We found the players' agents to be extremely helpful with getting this autograph card process completed. And, since many agents represented several different players, we could make deals with many players at once. The whole process of getting baseball, football and hockey players' autographs on our cards was a logistical nightmare, but the Pacific staff coordinated it all with a sure and steady hand.

Acquiring authentic, game-worn sweaters and hockey sticks for our 2000–01 Pacific NHL brand was a struggle that first season, but we were finally able to get through to the NHL teams themselves (after all, they had the game-used hockey sweaters we wanted!). We made a deal with each team, and the teams sold us the sweaters. We amassed well over 100 different NHL game-used sweaters to use in our 2001–02 Pacific Hockey products. In the years after that, most of the hockey sticks we cut up for our game-used cards came directly from the players themselves.

For what we paid for a single used sweater, each team could have bought a number of new ones! Fortunately for us, NHL hockey sweaters were very large and yielded a tremendous number of game-used sweater patch pieces small enough to include in a trading card.

In our first game-used sweater cards, the sweater swatch pieces were three-quarter-inch squares. When we reduced the size of the sweater swatches to half-inch squares, the total number of pieces we were able to cut from a player's sweater increased by more than one-third. We were then able to make more game-used sweater cards, using each sweater in several products. Each tiny patch was glued in place onto a card.

Most NHL teams would sell us game-used hockey sweaters. One team that would not was the Los Angeles Kings. They flat-out refused, so no Kings game-used sweater cards are in our 2000–01 hockey products. We did acquire two game-used Kings sweaters later in the season from a well-known, reputable collector; we cut up and used those sweaters in our 2001–02 products. For items to use on other teams' cards, we were able to find some game-used hockey sweaters and sticks on the open market from reputable dealers.

Our game-used baseball jerseys mainly came from California Sports Investments and from Gray Flannel, two well-known dealers of sports memorabilia. We also obtained a fair number of game-used baseball jerseys directly from players, including Tony Gwynn and Cal Ripken, Jr.

I absolutely hated the fact that we were cutting up these jerseys! But it was what it was....

Our NFL game-worn jerseys came from the NFL in New York City. We made a deal, and the NFL got the uniforms for us directly from the teams. We paid a lot of money for each jersey, but we could get a game-used jersey from almost any player on our list.

We had a great pipeline for NFL game-used jerseys for a couple of years. A few came directly from players. Our autograph deal with Kurt Warner included two game-used jerseys and, because the deal read "autographs and game-used uniform," when the package from Kurt Warner arrived at Pacific it contained a game-used jersey ... and pants!

So Pacific made Kurt Warner game-used jersey and game-used pants cards!

That gave us the idea for more game-used pants cards. We tried to get more NFL game-used pants but only had a little success. It was easy for a player to strip off his jersey at halftime during a game and put on a new one, so players focused on jerseys.

Years after Pacific ceased to be, I was watching a Seahawks vs. Cardinals game on television. At halftime, the Cardinals players were headed to the locker room, and I saw quarterback Kyler Murray stripping off his jersey on the way in. That brought back memories. Most likely that jersey was headed to the chopping line of a card company.

* * *

In December of 1999, 2000 Pacific Baseball was released. It fared pretty well in the market. Our other baseball brands, including our bilingual English/Spanish brands, held their own, and sales for baseball were good—not excellent, just good.

But good was fine. In 2000, our baseball card sales were receding a bit, with case sales per product dropping slightly. To make up for this shortfall, we produced 11 different brands of baseball cards. They included Pacific, Aurora, Pacific Crown Collection, Crown Royale, Invincible, Omega, Paramount, Private Stock, Revolution, Vanguard and our steady flagship brand, Prism.

Prism was the only baseball card brand we had for which sales were actually up. We had first introduced Prism trading cards in 1993, with both football and baseball. It was our most popular brand of trading cards.

In early 2000, we had planned our Prism baseball brand to have 150 different players in the base set and three different parallel foil versions of the base set, serial-numbered, along with six insert sets. Our sales brochure was already printed, and our sales force was selling and taking orders for the product when I made a significant change to the product.

A few weeks before we were ready to go to press, our foil vender called and said he had sent us a FedEx package with 14 brand-new foils that they had developed for us. This was exciting, as we always wanted to be out in front of the competition with beautiful new cards—and we always were.

The box arrived and was delivered to Rob Hicks, the head of our graphics department. He came to my office right away with the samples, and we pored over the sample foil swatches, examining each one over and over. They were all new prismatic patterns, different from any trading card foil we had seen. Rob and I had a conference call with our supplier to see if the foils were ready now, and if we could use them for our upcoming 2000 Prism baseball cards.

Our foil supplier said yes, they had foil ready for each of the 14 designs—but not in equal amounts. This meant that, depending on which foil Pacific chose, we would get a different number of sets of that prism parallel. Then our supplier said, "So which foil would you like to use for your new parallel in Prism baseball?"

I said, "All 14 of them! We want to print 15 different parallel card sets, including the base set, and an embossed, numbered Premiere Date card."

He said, "Fifteen different parallels of each card? Wow! That's a lot of parallel cards and a mountain of work."

Rob and I looked at each other, speechless, as the ramifications of what I had just said sank in.

We were about to do what no card manufacturer had ever done.

And we were going to have to reconfigure our entire card packaging sequence so we could get all the parallel cards properly into the 2000 Prism baseball product.

We got busy. We printed the base set cards for 2000 Prism baseball: 50 different player cards on a sheet, with three different sheets for a total of 150 different players in the set. At Pacific, these printing sheets were called "forms." (Our suppliers called them "forms," so we did too.) A different form indicated a different, specific sequence of 50 players' numbered cards.

Once the base cards were printed, the forms had to receive their foils. When the foiling process began, everything was going fine quality-wise—but we were not getting an equal number of sheets for each form. We had known this was going to happen, because we had been able to buy more of some foil colors than we could buy of others. So we printed what we had, and we simply had more of some colors than others.

Because the 2000 Prism set and these parallel cards are of great interest nowadays, here is the breakdown of the foil colors for the 15 different parallel sets issued in the product:

Comet Shower, used on the base set.
Comet Shower, Premiere Date Embossed, 61 numbered sets.
Holo Gold, 480 numbered sets.
Holo Mirror, 160 numbered sets.
Holo Purple, 99 numbered sets.
Holo Blue, 80 numbered sets.
Woodgrain Silver, 331 sets, only issued in retail products.
Texture Silver, 448 sets, only issued in retail products.
Tinsel Silver, 331 sets, only issued in hobby products.
Rapture Silver, 916 sets, only issued in hobby products.
Rapture Gold, 565 sets, only issued in retail products.
Sliders Silver, 117 sets, plus 214 sets of Form #1; 331 sets of Form #2; 448 sets of Form #3. Cards issued in both retail and hobby products.

Drops Sliver, 799 sets, only issued in hobby products. Form #3, 117 sets, issued in both hobby and retail products.

Sheen Sliver, 565 sets of Form #1; 448 sets of Form #2. (The end of the roll of Sheen Silver had a flaw in it and, for quality purposes, was not used for form #3. No cards exist for Sheen Silver form #3.) Cards issued in both retail and hobby products.

Pebbly Dots Silver, 448 sets, issued in hobby products. Plus 243 sets of Form #1 and 243 sets of Form #2 were issued in both hobby and retail products.

The complicated mixing of the cards was done in a separate room, on a long card-collating machine. Using a preset formula, we could mix a stack of cards that, when placed in the packaging machine hoppers, would allow the machine to pick and place the right number of the right type of cards onto the packing line.

Workers loaded cards into as many as 30 different hoppers on that machine, mixing base cards and parallel cards in a sequence that had been determined in pre-production. The sorted and mixed stacks of base and parallel cards were then loaded onto trays and moved to another packing room. There, they were again loaded by hand, this time into the packaging machine hoppers, to be wrapped in a printed foil package.

Packs of five cards were made to sell at hobby stores; retail packs contained three cards. The outer packaging would tell the buyer the minimum number of parallel cards contained in that pack (the rest of the cards would be base cards). But sometimes, an unexpected parallel was added to a pack, an extra above and beyond what the wrapper promised.

I am a collector. I know that collectors love the surprise of opening a pack, never knowing what exactly is inside, which is why, when we released 2000 Pacific Prism Baseball, the Prism parallel cards with their amazing, new, innovative foils were unannounced.

Collectors went nuts! "What are these cards?" they wanted to know. Our customer service department phone lines were swamped.

But Shannon Johnson, our head of customer service, and her team were ready. All the 2000 Pacific Prism product details had been compiled by Shannon and were in her office in "The Shannon Books." These are the binders that contained not only samples of each card in our products (along with insert ratios for insert cards) but also actual printing production spreadsheets and sales brochures for products back to around 1997.

Of course, some collectors complained about having to collect 15 different parallels in the set. If they were an Alex Rodriquez card collector, how could they possibly get all of his 15 different cards for their collection? It was, in their eyes, going to be impossible.

14. What a Way to Start a Century! 181

The issue was brought to my attention. And, as a collector myself, I totally understood what they were facing.

It would be similar to me collecting the 1910 T-206 baseball card back variations—which I had been doing since the 1960s. The process was an ongoing challenge. But every so often, a card would surface, and I would snap it up for my collection.

I didn't know what to tell them, other than yes, we made those cards, and if you want to collect them, yes, you were in for a big challenge. Over time, I think collectors accepted the Pacific Prism challenge and found it truly rewarding when they discovered a parallel card they wanted to add to their collection. It was the same satisfaction I found when I uncovered a 1910 T-206 back variation I didn't have.

I suppose some people might say that baseball card collecting is a little like life: it's really about the journey, even more than the destination. (Hey, I came of age in the 1960s—people said stuff like that!)

I am told nowadays, by collectors and hobby writers, that Pacific pioneered the parallel card concept back then. The idea is still in use a quarter of a century later by the current card manufacturers—and they make more parallels in their sets than we ever did.

* * *

In May 2000, Phil Roth, my trusted CFO, met with me for our monthly discussion of our products, production numbers, and projections for the month. Pacific had, at the time, 11 combined baseball and football products and eight hockey products.

But our costs to create each product were still rising, and our sales per product were not keeping up. This was eating into our bottom line. We were still turning a profit each month, but it was a small enough profit that the long-term projections were starting to look like we had a thin road ahead of us.

The domino effect of the Pinnacle product dumping was still haunting us.

I had the rising question: Was it just Pacific, or were all of the trading card industry manufacturers being affected by that dumping of product? Were their sales on the same decline ours had been experiencing since 1998?

I made some calls to vendors that did card production work for some of the other card manufacturers. And I called some of our trading card distributors who also distributed for the other manufacturers and asked where Pacific stood in the trading card industry.

I found our case runs per product were within a few cases, give or take, of the other card manufacturers and our retail orders per product were no different, either. This wasn't just a Pacific problem.

There was a declining market for new trading cards.

Baseball had no superstar rookies emerge in 2000, making it a tough year for baseball. NFL football had a few rookies helping drive sales: Ron Dayne, Chad Pennington and Peter Warrick were hot. Of course, Tom Brady would have a breakout year in 2001 but, in 2000, he was still an unknown commodity to most football card collectors.

In June of 2000, Pacific released one of our bilingual baseball card brands, 2000 Pacific Invincible. It shipped to the trading card market just as it had for the last three years—except this was different.

Our Invincible game-used gear insert set of 32 cards included a game-used bat card of Manny Ramirez, card #16, serial-numbered 1 to 200. (There were a total of three Manny Ramirez game-used gear cards in the set. The other two were card #6, serial numbered 1 to 975 with a piece of his jersey on the card, and card #12, serial numbered 1 to 145 with a game-used jersey piece and a game-used bat piece on the same card.)

But card #16 caused a stir when one of those cards was found to have pieces of both wood and cork on it.

Here is the story of the cork bat.

We purchased three Manny Ramirez game-used bats from a local, well-known sports memorabilia dealer. I'd known this dealer since he was a kid coming to my Pacific Trading Cards store back in the 1980s. All three bats came with a certificate of authenticity, stating that they were game-used by Manny Ramirez.

We sent two of the bats to the vendor that made the memorabilia cards for Pacific.

Our vendor's employees' first laborious task was cutting the bats into small, thin pieces for use on the cards (or trimming uniforms down into tiny fabric swatches). Next the vendor glued the pieces of wood or fabric to Pacific's printed cards. Once the tiny relics were glued to the cards, the cards were laminated.

This labor-intensive process was repeated every day with hundreds of relics, piece by piece, card by card, over and over, all day long, day after day.

The people cutting up bats and placing pieces of wood on the cards were just workers, doing their jobs. They didn't know what a bat was made of: their job was to put little pieces of wood on the cards.

When we received the shipment of laminated trading cards back from our vendor, the cards went into the packaging room. The game-used gear cards were gathered in big handfuls and placed into the card hoppers on the packaging machine feeders. No Pacific employees looked at the cards individually; they only handled stacks of cards. It was all in a day's work.

Pacific Invincible Baseball was produced on schedule and the first cases shipped to market. Shortly after the cards hit the market, Pacific received a call from a dealer saying a customer had pulled a Manny Ramirez bat card in his pack, and it looked to have cork on it instead of wood.

Yikes.

I knew this was not good. Pacific was a trusted licensee of the Major League Baseball Players Association. This simply could not happen.

We weren't finished packing Invincible Baseball, so we immediately inspected the game-used cards being readied for the packing lines.

We found a few more Manny Ramirez cards with cork on them. Of course, they were removed.

I called the vendor that assembled our game-used cards and asked what was going on. He said he was sorry, but how could his people know there was cork in a bat? They would never even be looking for it.

He went out into his production shop and inspected the leftover Ramirez bat pieces that were scheduled to be used in our upcoming baseball product. He found and removed several more pieces of bat with cork in them.

He had already started to cut the second Ramirez bat and found there was no cork in that one. He also inspected other players' bat pieces that were ready for the next job. Sure enough, he found cork pieces in a couple more players' bats. All the cork pieces that were found were destroyed, and none of those cork pieces were ever used on our cards.

We had one more game-used Manny Ramirez bat still at Pacific. I had one of our employees get it X-rayed to see if it had cork in it: it did. We didn't use that bat; I still have it, along with its certificate of authenticity. Two out of three game-used Manny Ramirez bats that we bought had cork in them. What was up with that? How could we have ever thought a major leaguer would cork his bat? Geez! That was against the rules!

But the damage was done. A story came out in *Trade Fax*, and we had to defend ourselves over a cork bat. We didn't cork the bat! I didn't like it. Pacific didn't make that bat; we just cut it up for a trading card. But a mistake had been made, and we didn't have safeguards in place to look for cork bats. Why would we, though? Until this issue surfaced, who would have ever thought we would need it?!

However, Pacific was my company, and I took any responsibility there was to take.

After that, every game-used card we received from our vendor for future products was hand inspected by Shannon and her crew to avoid any more mistakes. We made and shipped the rest of our 2000 baseball card releases that year with no issues.

I read a later hobby article claiming that Pacific put those cork bat cards in Pacific Invincible for publicity. This was most definitely not so.

Pacific didn't need or want that kind of publicity. Pacific was—and I was—a friend of the baseball players. I admired all of them. They had been my heroes since I was a kid. I was devastated and heartbroken that the card got out on my watch.

But there was basically nothing I could do. I made no further comments about it and just hoped it would all go away.

I read stories later that said Pacific lost its baseball license because of that card. But the corked bat card was not the reason Pacific sold our brands and left the card market. After the cork bat incident, we produced five more baseball card products, including 2000 Pacific Private Stock, released in late December.

A few years later, after Pacific was gone from the trading card industry and our brands were being produced by Panini, I read in the newspaper that players were being banned from baseball for using steroids and cork bats. This didn't give me any satisfaction. I was still disappointed that a cork bat card had gotten out into the market on my watch. Twenty years later, I think the players involved have had to pay the price for using steroids and cork bats. Some who would surely have been inducted into the Baseball Hall of Fame have been excluded. But they made their choices. I can only join in the fans' lament: "Say it ain't so, Joe."

* * *

The 2000 Major League Baseball All-Star Game was scheduled for July 11 in Atlanta, Georgia, at Turner Field. Pacific again would be a sponsor of the annual Baseball All-Star Game FanFest.

Hall of Fame great Hank Aaron was slated to throw the ceremonial first pitch. Each of the licensed baseball card manufacturers, including Pacific, made a commemorative Hank Aaron baseball card for the FanFest. I chose, for the second year in a row, to use our most popular card design, Pacific Prism.

It was an honor for Pacific, and for me personally, to make a card of Hank Aaron. He had held a special place in my heart since the day he signed 41 cards for me, just some kid who collected cards, as we stood around a parking lot at Arizona spring training. Hank Aaron's greatness, like Joe DiMaggio's, was equal parts athletic ability and generosity of spirit.

The Prism Hank Aaron card was given out to collectors that came to visit our Pacific booth at the 2000 Atlanta FanFest.

One of the people that visited our booth at FanFest was from a video game company named Backyard Baseball. He was there to bring us great news: Backyard Baseball had chosen Pacific Trading Cards to make baseball cards to include in their new Major League Baseball kids' video game! We would design, print and package thousands of custom-made baseball

14. What a Way to Start a Century!

cards for them—with the Pacific logo on the cards. This was a great opportunity for Pacific! Our cards would be in tens of thousands of video games that kids would buy.

As sponsors of the FanFest, we represented Pacific at our trade booth and also received several tickets to the All-Star Game. Those tickets included a voucher that let one person from Pacific participate in a baseball workout at Turner Field.

I picked me to participate.

Each participant got the opportunity to hit (or miss) eight batting practice pitches and to field balls while others batted. Also included was a glove and an All-Star Game jersey to wear (mine was a National League jersey).

We rode to the stadium on the bus and on the way were briefed on the day's agenda. We arrived at the stadium, and it was really cool walking into Turner Field and then right out onto the infield grass. When batting practice started, I ran directly out to shortstop, a position I was playing on my church softball team.

Turner infield was so smooth compared to our church infield! I got to field several balls hit my way and felt really comfortable at shortstop. I thought it was easier to field a hardball than a softball: I was back further in the infield, and the ball was smaller.

Then it was my turn to bat. There were metal and wood bats to choose from. I picked up a wood bat and started taking a few practice swings. I was next in the batting cage.

2000 Pacific Baseball FanFest Hank Aaron card, given to collectors that came to the Pacific booth at FanFest. It was an honor to make this Prism card of the great Hank Aaron. This graded 10 card is in my collection.

I got in the batter's box, settling in to hit right-handed. The practice pitcher was a pro, and he threw nearly every pitch right down the middle at about 70 mph. I swung at the first pitch and missed; I needed to settle down more. The next pitch came in right over the heart of the plate, and I hit that one on the ground to the shortstop. The next three pitches I hit on the ground at the third baseman. I had only three pitches left. My turn was going fast! I dug in, and the pitcher delivered—and I hit that pitch off of the base of the left field wall. I thought to myself, "I hit that ball as hard as I could!" I don't know how those guys could hit one over the wall at Turner Field. A couple fly balls later, and my batting turn was over. I went out to the outfield to shag balls.

I was having one of the most fun experiences of my baseball card career! I got to keep the glove and National League jersey as souvenirs of the day.

* * *

Just a few days later, I was back in my office at Pacific headquarters in Lynnwood. Everyone was busy. I loved hearing the constant rumble of the packaging rooms below the offices at Pacific Trading Cards. It was music to my ears.

One morning Felix, our chief engineer, came up to my office. My door was always open, and he gave a little knock as he came in. I looked up from the stack of work on my desk, and he waved at me to come with him downstairs to the card-packing rooms. I followed him, and we entered the first production room, where two card-wrapping machines were spitting out packs of Omega Baseball Cards.

2000 Pacific Aurora Tony Gwynn autographed and numbered card. Tony Gwynn was one of the purest hitters to ever play the game. We made a candy bar of him too (Pacific Trading Cards Archives).

14. What a Way to Start a Century!

Some of our people were loading the card hoppers with raw cards (bulk, unpackaged cards). Some were packing off the machines, putting 36 packs in a box, then sending that box down the line to the big automatic Shanklin Shrink Wrap Tunnel, where the box of cards was shrink-wrapped. Twenty shrink-wrapped boxes went into the shipping carton, which moved on a conveyor to the carton-sealing machine, and was automatically taped both bottom and top. The case of cards next slid down a roller conveyor where it was "palletized." When the pallet was full, it was wrapped and moved to the warehouse (by forklift) and placed on a pallet rack bay, ready for shipping to stores.

The same thing was going on in packing room #2. Here, football cards were running on one machine; the other machine had McDonald's hockey cards running on it. The whole place was buzzing. Felix turned to me and said, "Every machine you have in this card factory is running."

I smiled, watching as packs of cards streamed steadily off the end of each machine and workers scurried about doing their jobs. I had a factory, a trading card factory! And it was running at full capacity! Long gone were the early days of wrapping packs by hand.

Felix was usually so busy in production that I'm not sure he'd noticed me taking that same walk about twice a day. I would get up from my desk to get some exercise and walk a route through the Pacific building, going down the back stairs into the warehouse, watching and talking to our shipping people who were loading the trucks at one of our docks with pallets of Pacific products. At the other docks, they were unloading raw materials to place on the pallet racks in the warehouse. I would walk through the warehouse, looking at all the raw materials: rolls of wrappers, display boxes, shipping cartons, and pallets of boxes each holding 8,900 bulk cards packed in paper trays, ready to load into the packaging machine card feeders. All the things used to make Pacific Trading Cards products were sitting there on the pallet racks, waiting for their turn to be taken into the production rooms and be turned into a collectible.

My route then took me into the collating room, where a long machine with 30 card hoppers ran nonstop, placing a single card from each hopper onto a chain with lugs. The cards continued on the chain to where a worker at the end gathered the stack of 30 cards and placed it into a tray, all in a matter of seconds. With my help, our engineers designed and built this machine to give us more card collating flexibility. I would stand there and watch as collated stacks of 30 cards came off the line every couple seconds. I remembered back to the early 1980s when I had a crew of workers walking around a long table, picking up one Baseball Legends card at a time, until they had a stack of 30.

Wow, times had changed.

Then I went through our pre-press graphics department for a look at our latest designs. Work was in progress on every computer. New card designs filled some of the screens. I'd stop and look and sometimes make a suggestion. Next, I walked up the stairs into the main offices of Pacific and back through the accounting department, which was always nonstop busy. There was one office room at Pacific just devoted to auditors, and there was always someone in it, doing an audit of Pacific.

When I checked in with the six people who worked in the photo library, they were always consumed in thought, selecting slides and photos for the next card set in line. The library slides were categorized by sport, alphabetically by team, in three-ring binders that covered a whole wall. We had three big light tables that were always covered in slides and photos. I always checked over our photo selection progress, to see what photos we were using to make our next cards.

Then I would head back to my office to answer calls and get ready for the next staff meeting in one of the conference rooms.

Our hockey products were doing the best of the three major licenses we had. Hockey cards were unique in the sense that we had global markets with the United States, Canada, and Europe. The McDonald's promotion was a huge advertising and promotional campaign for Pacific in Canada.

We had captured the lion's share of the hockey trading card market because of this. This meant that guaranteeing money for the NHL and NHL Players Association licenses was manageable for us.

In July of 2000, we released our first hockey product of the new year, Pacific NHL Hockey. We added a totally new insert idea to this release: actual metal printing plates.

Card makers like Pacific need four different metal printing plates to print the front of each card and four more metal plates to print each back. Each plate is a different color: black, cyan, magenta or yellow. Master plates were large metal sheets used on the printing press. These sheets held the images of 100 different cards. The same group of 100 cards had four master plates, one for each color.

Each of the four metal master plates was cut down to individual card size by hand in the Pacific machine shop. This created a tremendous amount of new work for our engineers that did the cutting, but it yielded a beautiful new trading card collectible.

Each individual metal plate card was stamped "Pacific Press Plate" in black ink on the blank back side. A black circle held the name of the plate's color (for example, "CYAN"). All of the Pacific press plates we released have this mark.

Twenty-five years later, I saw a seller of 1988 Pacific press plates on eBay. These plates were *not* made by Pacific. We didn't start releasing the press plates to collectors until 2000, and all plates used before that were melted down or, in a couple of cases, blown up at the Pacific headquarters in Lynnwood for a publicity photo. I wouldn't recommend buying any plates that are not stamped by Pacific on the back, certainly none purporting to be from before the year 2000.

We were happy with our new press plate adventure. Ready for more fresh ideas, we hired Jeff Morris as our marketing director in October of 2000. He was a hobby veteran and had previously worked for Pinnacle. Jeff was a go-getter and full of great new ideas to help grow the Pacific product lines. We incorporated many of his ideas into our card designs and configurations. He was a breath of fresh air.

One day, I overheard Jeff tell a co-worker that Shannon, our customer service director, had heard from "her stalker" again.

"This guy calls me like three times a week!" she said. "He wants this card replaced and that card replaced, and he is always asking questions about serial numbers on rookies and different parallels."

We were all collectors, so we understood that.

"Oh, and get this," she said. "He says he's famous."

Now, this was getting interesting.

"His name is B.J. Thomas or something," she continued. "He lives in Dallas. He says he's a singer and he sings the anthem at Dallas Stars games."

Clearly, Shannon was not yet born when B.J. Thomas was getting major airplay and winning Grammy awards. She may have been annoyed with her "stalker," but Jeff was star-struck.

As the hockey season went on, B.J. Thomas kept calling, and Shannon always took care of him. He was a hardcore hockey card collector. He examined each card thoroughly. He put base sets and parallel sets together and loved our insert cards, and he always asked lots of questions.

I learned a few months later that a package arrived for Shannon from Dallas. Jeff was more excited than she was when she opened it.

It was a complete set of B.J. Thomas CDs.

Autographed.

That, I thought, is a great Pacific customer.

* * *

By October, we knew we were not going to renew our Major League Baseball Players license. The guarantee to MLB and MLBPA was simply too high, and sales for baseball were still slipping below the earn-out level.

My baseball card manufacturing dream was going to end when our baseball license expired in 2001.

Not what I wanted.

However, I came to the realization that at least my dream had been fulfilled. I had spent nine years making Major League Baseball cards and, for three of those years, Pacific had a full license.

What a great job—my great job! My dream job! How many people in the world get to live their dream? I knew I was a very rare person that did!

Since the late 1800s, various companies have tried their hand at making baseball cards. I knew the names of all these companies, because I collected the cards they made over the years. No one company or person ever made baseball cards forever. They simply had their moment recorded in time, and the cards and brands they made lived on to tell their story.

Pacific would release just two baseball card products in 2001, Pacific Baseball and Pacific Private Stock Baseball. Knowing these would be the last baseball cards I would get to make, I took the reins for the card designs and product content.

I had fun with those two baseball products. I added three parallel card sets to the Cramer's Choice Awards cards released in Pacific Baseball. We started with a base set of 150 players, and I loaded up Pacific Private Stock with plenty of PS-206 cards, with beautiful color photos on the front and only blue ink on the back. We made a parallel to this set, using only red ink on the backs. We also made four more PS-206 sets for the product, named Action (60 different players), Rookies (20 different players), Stars (20 different players), and New Wave (20 different players, serial numbered 1 to 199).

The base set of 2001 Pacific Baseball has 27 Hall of Fame players, including two players, Hideo Nomo and Kazuhiro Sasaki, who are in the Japanese Baseball Hall of Fame. Oddly, the set of 500 different players only has one rookie card, that of Alfonzo Soriano.

Like Pacific Baseball, the PS-206 Pacific Private Stock was loaded up with parallel and insert cards.

It was the last Pacific Baseball card set I ever produced. That Pacific Private Stock set has 27 players in the Hall of Fame. I take great pride in this set, as it contains the last baseball cards I made for Ken Griffey, Jr., Tony Gwynn and Edgar Martinez, three of my favorite players. Two were Seattle Mariners players I had followed and watched through the best years the Mariners have had so far.

The dream I had when I was a kid had come true, my dream of producing Major League Baseball trading cards. I relished the fact that not many people in the world get to live out their dream job, but I did.

Pacific came out of 2000 in pretty good shape, still turning a profit, as we always did. Yes, the company had a little flesh wound, but it was really my flesh wound.

I would survive.

15

Pacific After Baseball

Pacific still had NFL and NHL card licenses, and we concentrated all our efforts on making great trading cards for football and hockey. We still had plenty of card products to produce. Not producing baseball cards—a third line of products—took the extra sharp edge off our employees: they were able to be more relaxed instead of running at 110 percent all the time.

The biggest news we had at that time was that Pacific was awarded the 2001–02 McDonald's of Canada NHL card promotion, our second straight year. This was huge, and it lifted the spirits of all our employees—and especially for me. In business, like in baseball, you win some and you lose some, and this was a big win at just the right time.

We also had high hopes for our Pacific NFL card line. The 2001 draft class was extremely promising, with several can't-miss rookies. These included quarterbacks Drew Brees and Michael Vick and running back LaDainian Tomlinson. Pacific signed autograph contracts with all three, and each signed a limited number of their Pacific cards that we randomly inserted into our products.

When we were choosing rookie players to include in 2001 Pacific Football, the hot quarterbacks, running backs and receivers were quite obvious. The next step was to choose a few linemen and defensive backs. I looked into the rookie photo binder we had on hand and began to choose a few players to fill in the set.

Who makes it onto a trading card is really up to each manufacturer. To sell cards, we had to make cards of high-demand players; that's why rookies were always something of a gamble.

One player's name that stood out was "Pork Chop Womack," a guard from Mississippi State. I thought that anyone with a name like that has got to have a football card! So I pulled the photos and included him in our football set.

Turns out, Pork Chop was a fourth-round draft pick by the Seattle Seahawks and ended up playing 10 seasons in the NFL. His 2001 Pacific Football rookie card, #476, is his only NFL card.

2001 Pacific Prism Atomic football card. We were always developing new card designs. Collectors comment that Atomic was one of our best ever (Pacific Trading Cards Archives).

Guards like Pork Chop were not in high demand as collectors go. But … I liked fun stuff. I did make cards of some obscure players because it was fun and, for me, not all about money.

The great thing was that the rookie players we selected that year didn't miss and our 2001 Pacific Football card products were hot. Sales were excellent, even though we had to produce 10 brands to meet the sales levels we needed to make the minimum royalty guarantees.

Cramer's Choice Awards was a great insert set for 2001 Pacific Football. My picks for that set included rookie LaDainian Tomlinson and quarterback Kurt Warner. (That year, Warner led the St. Louis Rams to the Super Bowl, becoming the NFL's MVP.) Future greats Brett Favre, Marshall Faulk, Randy Moss, Emmitt Smith, Eddie George, and Super Bowl quarterback Trent Dilfer were also among my picks, along with running back Jamal Lewis, a probable Hall of Famer.

As of 2022, 2001 Pacific NFL Football yielded 37 NFL Hall of Fame players, with more sure to come.

Of course, partnering with McDonald's of Canada again gave us a huge boost in the Canadian market, and all our 2001 Pacific NHL Hockey card brands did great.

15. Pacific After Baseball

The 2001 NHL All-Star Game was played February 4 in the Denver Pepsi Center (later renamed Ball Arena), home of the Colorado Avalanche. Pacific was a sponsor of the NHL FanFest event and collectors visited our booth in droves, complimenting us on our hockey cards.

Back in June of 2000 at the NHL Draft, Pacific created and sponsored the first-ever trading card show to be held in conjunction with the draft. The card show we started was still being held at the annual draft more than 20 years later.

But the biggest news of the 2000–01 NHL hockey season was the return of one of the game's greatest players: Mario Lemieux. He resumed his career after a three-and-a-half-year hiatus spent battling lymphoma.

In our 1997–98 Pacific NHL Hockey card set, we had honored Lemieux (who wore #66 on his Penguin sweater) by retiring card #66 in that set. That year, both Lemieux and card #66 were absent from the Pacific hockey set.

Upon his 1997 retirement, Mario Lemieux was immediately elected to the Hockey Hall of Fame. When he made his spectacular and unprecedented return to the ice in December 2000, Pacific choose to honor Lemieux again, this time by introducing the Hall of Famer's missing 1997–98 Pacific NHL Hockey card, #66. That card was issued as an update card in 2001–02 Pacific Hockey.

* * *

We added an all-new NHL hockey card product to the growing Pacific line of trading cards in 2001. Our creative team, led by Jeff Morris, was always looking for new, innovative ideas, and our Heads Up brand was developed in a brainstorming session.

Pacific produced the very first trading card product that included an NHL bobbing head doll in a hobby box. (A "hobby box" is a group of card packs in a factory-sealed box. Sometimes, hobby boxes offer a premium in the box as an incentive to buy.)

Bobbing head dolls were a perfect premium. They have always been very popular with collectors. I collected "bobbers" as a kid and sold them back in 1976 when I had an exclusive deal to sell souvenirs at the San Francisco Giants spring training games in Phoenix.

So in 2001, Pacific designed 12 NHL player dolls, including veterans like Mario Lemieux and Mark Messier and rookies like hot Oiler draft pick Mike Comrie (who went on to play 10 NHL seasons).

We learned that China was literally the only place we could get the bobbing head dolls made. So we made the necessary arrangements, sending over our list of players, photos, and designs with an order for 1,000 dolls per player.

Soon after, we heard back from the factory representative, who said that if we added one more doll to the 12 we'd ordered, we would qualify for a price break that would almost pay for the extra doll.

However, adding a new player—and getting the player's approval for a doll—was going to take time. The process could hold up our order. We couldn't let that happen! But we had the opportunity to make an additional bobbing head doll for nearly free—we had to do that!

We kicked it around … and the idea came up to make a bobbing head doll of me. We had a photo and could meet the manufacturing time frame needed.

Why did Pacific produce a bobbing head doll of Mike Cramer? For fun, and, well, why not? It would be a great conversation piece, a great marketing tool, and something to show my grandkids someday.

The Mike Cramer doll was added to the line, and production for the dolls of 12 NHL players plus one of me was underway in China.

About two months later, Pacific received the shipment of bobbing head dolls from China. Our head of purchasing inventoried the Pacific Heads Up dolls so the packaging of the Heads Up product could get underway. Mario Lemieux, Martin Brodeur, Patrick Roy, Joe Salic, Jaromir Jagr, Paul Kariya, Dominik Hasek, Steve Yzerman, Mark Messier, Johan Hedberg, Curtis Joseph, and Mike Cramer were all accounted for … but no Mike Comrie. His doll was missing.

Our head of purchasing called the representative at the doll factory in China and said we were short one doll.

Our contact person said, "No, you're not short one doll. We made Mike Cramer; that's the same as Mike Comrie, right?"

They got the two dolls mixed up, and we were now without a Mike Comrie doll!

The 2001 Pacific Heads Up Hockey cards were ready to be shipped, so we quickly printed a redemption card to randomly insert in card packs.

A collector who found a redemption card could redeem it for a free Mike Comrie doll by simply filling out the card with their name and address and mailing it (along with a specified shipping and handling fee) to Pacific.

Redemption cards were also added to the hobby and retail boxes. Each hobby box contained one of the existing 11 hockey player dolls, while retail boxes held randomly inserted redemption cards, a different card for each of the 12 different dolls.

Oh, and we put some Mike Cramer dolls in the product too.

The Mike Cramer dolls issued in the hobby boxes contained a redemption sweepstakes card for a complete set of all 12 Heads Up hockey dolls. So when collectors found a Mike Cramer doll in their box, they were

15. Pacific After Baseball

immediately happy as the card read, "Congratulations! You have won a complete set of all 12 hockey dolls, courtesy of Mike Cramer, President/CEO of Pacific Trading Cards, Inc."

We always had my doll on display at shows, and many collectors asked how they could get one. So we told them to buy three packs of any Pacific product and come back to our booth with the wrappers. We would give them a doll.

I signed a lot of my dolls at shows.

It was a fun idea, and it worked out even better than expected.

* * *

Pacific turned out to be having a pretty good year in 2001. Both our NFL and NHL trading card products were doing well, so Cheryl and my mother and I planned a much-needed vacation. We decided to go to Europe for two weeks.

On the evening of September 10, 2001, we boarded a flight from Seattle to London. When we landed at Heathrow on the morning of September 11, we rounded up our luggage and hired a cab to take us to the Le Meridien Grosvenor House on Park Lane in London. The ride in the black London cab was supposed to take about 45 minutes. We settled back, talking and enjoying the sights we could see on the drive into London, when the cab driver suddenly turned up his radio so loud we couldn't talk among ourselves. I thought he was listening to some kind of *War of the Worlds* program on the radio.

Since we couldn't talk, I tuned myself into the broadcast to see what he had on the radio. I could hear the broadcaster talking about the World Trade Center in New York and airplanes and bombings—and the United States being attacked.

I finally asked, "This isn't real—is it?"

He said, "Yes, it is. New York City is under attack."

We weren't sure what was going on, but we knew it wasn't good.

The cab arrived at our hotel, and we went to the registration desk to check in. The desk clerk knew right away we were Americans and offered her condolences.

That really wasn't good. Something was up, and we needed to find out what it was.

We had arrived early, so our rooms weren't quite ready. We decided to store our bags and go visit a friend who owned a military collectibles shop near the hotel.

It didn't take long for us to get to his shop. When we walked through the front door, he immediately greeted us and said, "I am so sorry for what is happening to your country."

I said, "We don't know what's going on! We just arrived in London and heard there has been an attack on New York City. What is going on? Do you know?"

He said, "Yes. A plane has hit the World Trade Center in New York City. The news says it could be a terrorist attack."

We were shattered.

We walked back to our hotel, went to our rooms, and turned on the TV.

We saw our first images of the devastating attacks on a great American city. Cheryl tried to call home to let the kids know we were all right, but no calls were getting through to the United States from Europe. She tried to email, but that was down too.

We felt isolated and helpless. There was nothing we could do.

That evening, we went out to eat, and we couldn't help noticing that everything in London seemed to be … normal.

When we were back in our room, we repeated our useless attempts at phone calls and emails to home.

The next day, we decided to just go visit and tour the places on our itinerary. They were open, and there was nothing we could do to get through to home.

The day after that, Cheryl called British Airways to see if we could get an earlier flight back to Seattle. She found out all flights to the United States were canceled until further notice.

That was eerie. Even if we wanted to go home, we couldn't.

We were stuck in Europe until further notice.

Our trip was scheduled for two weeks. The itinerary: London, Paris, Vienna, and back to London before flying home. With no phone calls getting through to home and no way to *get* home, we decided to just continue on with our trip and fly to Paris the next day as scheduled. We arrived at Heathrow Airport early in the morning on September 13 and encountered the most bizarre situation I've ever experienced.

I had been through Heathrow dozens of times in my life. It is one of the busiest airports in the world: millions of people use it every day. Not on that day—not on September 13, 2001.

Heathrow Airport was empty, except for Mike Cramer, Cheryl Cramer, Dorothy Cramer, and just a handful of other people.

No one was traveling that day.

We checked in for our flight to Paris and headed to the gate. As we walked, we looked up at the flight monitors and were astonished by what we saw: every fight from London to the United States was canceled.

A shiver ran down my spine.

Our flight to Paris had only a few people on it, including us.

15. Pacific After Baseball

We toured Paris for a couple days, seeing all the sights. My favorite, of course, was Les Invalides, home of Napoleon's tomb and the great French military museum.

On Sunday, September 16, we were finally able to phone home. Everything was fine in Washington State; the family was well but still trying to process the horrific headlines.

On Monday, I was able to call Pacific and talk to Phil Roth.

He said, "We are all here, but not much is going on." Business had come to a standstill. A couple of our products would be late in shipping, and we were using our cash reserves to make payroll.

"We're doing the best we can under the circumstances," Phil said. "Just go on with your trip; there's nothing you can do here, anyway."

Phil was right. It would take time to get back to normal business.

We finished our trip in Europe on September 23 and boarded our British Airways flight from Heathrow to Seattle.

We were just a bit nervous flying back to the United States, as flights had only just resumed, but we landed with no issues in Seattle.

The next day, I was back to work at Pacific.

*   *   *

Our 2001 Pacific Crown Royale Football was delayed, but we had good lines of communication with our distributors and managed to work through the issues.

But a small domino effect was happening in the trading card market. A chunk of sales were lost forever, and we also had a disruption in the game-used jersey pipeline we had perfected so well: two weeks of NFL games had been postponed and rescheduled, therefore our jerseys were not getting worn and therefore not shipped to us.

One breath of good news was that our McDonald's hockey card promotion would not be affected. This was simply because the timing was right; we were even a bit ahead of schedule in that production process.

Despite 9/11, Pacific managed to build back cash reserves and turn a profit for the year. I also started to get inquiries from other card companies, asking if I was interested in selling our trading card brands.

That sort of thing happened a lot in the trading card industry. I said, "Sure; make me an offer," just to see what would happen. I knew these other companies were mostly trying to learn how we were doing financially, to get a grasp on what was going on in the market. I even had talks with Fleer and Upper Deck. They actually sent a guy to do due diligence, which let him examine our finances so they could make a serious offer.

We were doing well, so we didn't mind them taking a look at our books.

As the 2001 NFL season resumed, things got back to normal, and Pacific started making plans to attend the Super Bowl and Super Bowl Experience in New Orleans on February 3, 2002.

I followed the NFL playoffs, and when they ended, I couldn't believe my two favorite quarterbacks—Tom Brady and Kurt Warner, my choices for Cramer's Choice—were both going to the Super Bowl. Tom Brady had stepped in as starting quarterback and led the New England Patriots to their first-ever Super Bowl. Meanwhile, Kurt Warner had guided the St. Louis Rams to the Super Bowl, where he would become the NFL MVP for the second time.

Before the game, the 11–5 Patriots were not given much of a chance to win against the powerful 14–2 Rams, who were dubbed "the Greatest Show on Turf."

When the game started, I wasn't sure who I should root for. I liked both quarterbacks and figured I would be happy with the game's outcome no matter what. However, Warner and the Rams had won the Super Bowl in 1999, so … I was just a little in favor of the Patriots and my guy, Tom Brady.

In fact, at this moment, I was a gigantic Patriots fan.

With one minute and 30 seconds remaining in the fourth quarter, and without any timeouts, Brady led his team down the field to set up kicker Adam Vinatieri's field goal try. (Vinatieri was another Pacific hero, although not many at the time knew Pacific had made his only rookie card.) The 48-yard kick sailed through the uprights as time expired, giving the Patriots their first ever Super Bowl victory in what has been considered by many to be a Cinderella season. Tom Brady was named Super Bowl XXXVI MVP, and the Patriots' dynasty began.

I high-fived myself a few times!

Our first release of the upcoming season was the 2002 Pacific NFL Football. As always, it contained our very popular insert, the Cramer's Choice Awards. We decided to serial number the cards that year, 1 of 120. Only 120 of each card was made, along with nine unnumbered sets to be used as replacement cards if needed. We also made a set numbered 1 of 1.

I had the pleasure that year of choosing Kurt Warner, Emmitt Smith, Marshall Faulk, Terrell Owens, Shaun Alexander, Brett Favre, Priest Holmes, David Boston, Anthony Thomas and my guy, my choice, Tom Brady. Yes, he had only one good season under his belt thus far, but Brady was my choice for Cramer's Choice Awards. He was starting to prove me right for making so many different Pacific rookie football cards of him in 2000.

Based on the success of our Heads Up hockey cards, we created a new

15. Pacific After Baseball

2002 Pacific Cramer's Choice Tom Brady, 30 of 120. This very rare card is graded mint 9 (Mike Cramer Collection).

brand as one of our eight different NFL football card products. We named it 2002 Pacific Heads Up NFL Football. It was a great new card design, and we added, for the first time in NFL trading card history, an NFL player bobbing head doll to each hobby box. Collectors bought the box with the doll inside, not knowing which doll was in the box—just like they never knew which players were in a pack of cards.

Pacific was again leading the trading card industry in new, creative ideas.

The Pacific NFL dolls were an immediate hit with collectors. We made 14 different players, including Jerry Rice, Emmitt Smith, Brett Favre, Kurt Warner, Randy Moss and my choice (and at my insistence) Tom Brady, who was at the time in only his second NFL season. We also included some Mike Cramer dolls in the product, with a bonus certificate for the entire set of 14 NFL player dolls.

* * *

Our 2002 hockey cards were doing excellently. We would produce 11 different NHL brands that year. The 2002–03 Pacific NHL Hockey cards proved to have a bumper crop of Hall of Famers, with 39 NHL Hall of Famers by the end of 20 years. Our new brand, Pacific Atomic, was an instant hit with collectors, who raved about the new sleek, all die-cut card design. And we again produced the very important McDonald's NHL Hockey card promotion in Canada, the third straight year McDonald's awarded us that contract.

Our Pacific Complete NHL Hockey cards debuted for the 2002–03 season. The set contained 600 NHL players issued 100 cards at a time over six different Pacific hockey products. We also made 99 Limited Edition boxed red parallel sets, 600 cards in each set; each card in the first set was numbered 1 of 99, each card in the second set was numbered 2 of 99, and so on. Set number 1 of 99 of the red-parallel is in my personal collection. After all, I am a collector, and collectors covet these rare and unique sets.

With the success of our new NFL card brands (Exclusive, Pacific Private Stock Reserve, and Private Stock Titanium) we had a total of eight football card releases. Our new 2002–03 NHL trading brands (Pacific Calder, Pacific Quest for the Cup, and Pacific Vanguard) gave Pacific a total of 11 different hockey trading card releases.

2002 Pacific Cramer's Choice Martin Brodeur. Brodeur was my favorite hockey player. His likeness was featured on our card packs, display boxes and advertising (Pacific Trading Cards Archives).

We were set to have one of our best years ever at Pacific. We were a state-of-the-art trading card factory.

At the 2002 National Sports Card Convention in Chicago, Pacific created a promo card to give attendees that visited our booth. Numbered 1 to 500, the card had second-year football player Tom Brady on the front and hockey star Joe Thornton on the back. Of all the players in the NFL and NHL to choose from, we picked these two players to be on our card.

The incredible thing about this card is that, 20 years after its release, Tom Brady was still playing in the NFL and Joe Thornton was still playing in the NHL.

15. Pacific After Baseball

That card has definitely stood the test of time.

In the fall of 2002, Phil Roth, Victor Temkin, Jeff Morris and I flew to Washington, D.C., for our annual meeting with the NFL Players Association. After our meetings, we had a dinner scheduled at the Palm Restaurant in Washington, D.C., where NFLPA principals met us for a relaxing evening. We all sat down, ordered drinks, and began sharing and enjoying stories.

Jeff Morris was just finishing telling a pretty funny story, when suddenly almost all of the people in the Palm Restaurant stood up and started clapping. (Jeff thought they were clapping at his story!) Then he saw: walking into the restaurant to be seated for dinner was none other than Elizabeth Taylor. As she passed by our table, I saw just how beautiful her violet eyes were. She was one of the great actresses of all time and still commanded a presence.

We went into the new year of 2003 knowing we were leading the trading card industry in card designs and in the innovation of new trading card ideas. Topps, Fleer and Upper Deck were definitely noticing that we were on the cutting edge. To keep up, they began to incorporate our ideas into their cards. Parallel cards, die-cut cards, laser-cut cards, limited serial numbered cards, prism foils—we saw all of our ideas being used on their cards.

Those same innovative Pacific Trading Card ideas were still being used 20 years later.

With the new year, we settled into a busy but comfortably familiar schedule. In late January, Pacific attended the 2003 Super Bowl Experience with a big trade show booth. Our marketing and

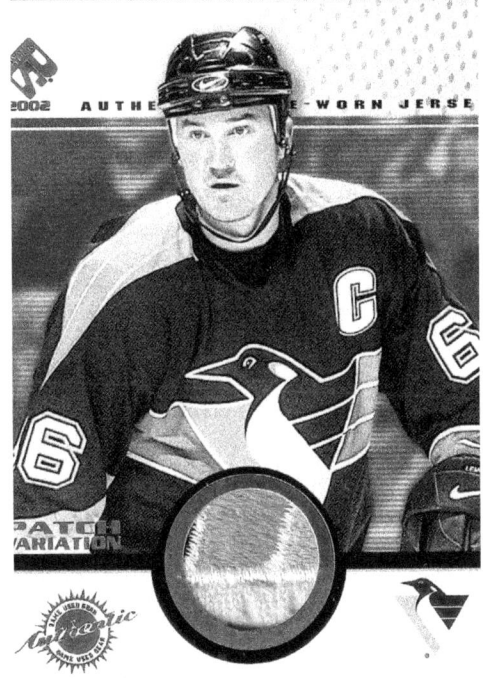

2002 Pacific Private Stock Game-Used Jersey Patch Card. It was one of only 20 made, according to the Pacific production records (Pacific Trading Cards Archives).

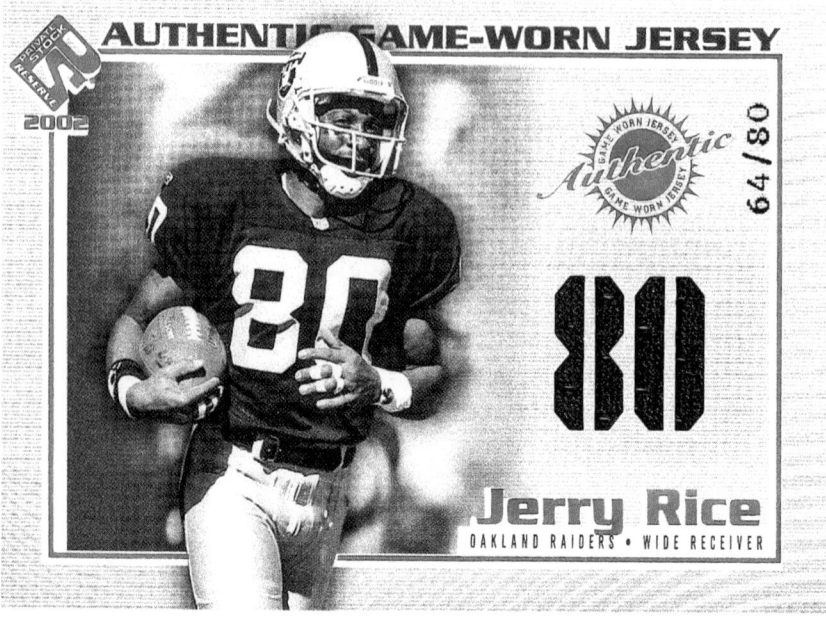

2002 Pacific Private Stock Reserve. The player's jersey number determined how many of that player's cards would be made and serial numbered in this set (Pacific Trading Cards Archives).

sales crews were on hand, promoting our upcoming 2003 Pacific NFL Football card products.

In February, we sent our top NFL photographer, Jack Wallin, to Hawaii to photograph NFL Pro Bowl players in their Pro Bowl uniforms. These photos were for our very popular upcoming 2003 Pacific NFL Football cards die-cut insert set. (Since 1995, Pacific had included an annual NFL Pro Bowl die-cut insert set in one of our football card products.)

In late February, our football card staff began to compile our player choices and write card copy for both the 2003 Pacific NFL Football set and the 2003 Pacific Private Stock Football cards. We then pulled slides or photos from our photo library for each of the 380 different players to be included in 2003 Pacific NFL (including player photos for the six insert sets) and for the 100-card set of 2002 Pacific Private Stock Football.

We were comfortably busy, preparing to produce these sets on schedule with our upcoming 2003 NFL Football card releases. Then, in March, the manager of our accounting department came to me with a letter she had just received from the NFL Players Association.

She handed the envelope to me. "You're not going to like it," she said.

15. Pacific After Baseball

She was right.

The letter from the NFL Players Association informed Pacific Trading Cards, Inc., that our NFL football card license was not being renewed for the 2003 season.

That was it. A letter in the mail. No phone call, no discussion—nothing but a letter.

This was hard for me to believe. I thought we had a strong relationship with the NFL Players Association. Pacific made football cards for all NFL players, not just the star players. We had been a licensee for 12 years and had paid the NFL Players Association and NFL Properties each millions of dollars in royalties.

But, just like that, Pacific was out of the NFL football card business.

I heard, years later, that the head of the NFL Players Association, Gene Upshaw, was led to believe that the football card market was slipping because of too many card companies and too many football card products. So he decided to eliminate one football card manufacturer, thinking that would fix the market and make the distributors happy.

That manufacturer was Pacific. Why? Years later, I heard that he just picked us out of the air. The way it came down, with just an impersonal business letter—I believe that story was fairly accurate.

I called the NFLPA. The representative I spoke to told me that the PA was, indeed, making a change, that the market was crowded and Pacific was out.

They were right in that it was a crowded market. Football card manufacturers were each making more and more different card brands to get sales in a shrinking market.

I knew they were right, but I also knew that, for 12 years, Pacific had designed, produced, printed, cut, collated, packaged, sold and shipped football cards. And now ... it was over.

The last NFL football card product Pacific would ever make had already been released: 2002 Pacific Private Stock Titanium appeared in January 2003.

I still have the binders with the original slides/photos that would have been used to make 2003 Pacific Football and Pacific Private Stock. On the outside of the binder are the words "NEVER USED."

It was a shocker for Pacific, and we had to let several people go, people that helped produce our football cards.

Looking back at that time, it's clear the decision to eliminate Pacific did nothing to rectify the football market. In fact, more and more football cards products kept being produced.

NFL football card collectors would live on, keeping interest in the hobby alive, including interest in the Pacific brands. But most of the card manufacturing companies that existed in 2003—and the people behind them—wouldn't be there 20 years later.

Maybe it's true, the old saying that "hindsight is 20/20." Looking back, I can't thank Gene Upshaw enough for giving me some of the best 20 years of my life. The same kind of crazy licensing snafu happened to Topps in 2021 when they were told their baseball license was over and they were out of the baseball card market. I believe their brands were bought up, like Pacific brands were purchased by Panini.

But the fact that even Topps could lose their baseball license—Topps, the granddaddy of the modern baseball card era—proves that the trading card market is brutal for manufacturers. I was very thankful to have survived in it for as long a period as I did.

With football gone, Pacific was left with just one major license: NHL hockey cards. Luckily for us, we were the top hockey card manufacturer at the time. Hockey cards were different, in the fact that there were three markets to sell to, the United States, Canada and Europe. There was always a good crop of rookie players we could count on. And we were in our fourth year with McDonald's of Canada, ensuring that Pacific NHL Hockey cards would be promoted and sold in every McDonald's in Canada.

As CFO, Phil Roth was already working on new budget and sales projections. Right away, I knew that Pacific would be fine, and we could make a profit with just our NHL hockey card license (and the contract packaging work we continued to get). We charged ahead, intent on making the best and most collectible NHL hockey cards of the 2003–04 season.

We were also looking for new trading card products we could make. We ventured out and signed a two-year license agreement with the Canadian Football League to produce trading cards of Canadian football league players. (Canadians use the same words for "football" and "soccer" as U.S. citizens do, so Pacific was very much in our comfort zone working with Canadian football.)

Our inaugural issue of 120 different players has 21 cards of players elected to the Canadian Football Hall of Fame.

We produced a hockey set to be sold at Canadian post offices: the 2003 Pacific NHL All-Stars set featured 24 NHL All-Time Greats. The cards were so popular, we produced six new players in 2004 and 2005, making a total set of 36 different NHL players. All 36 players are in the Hockey Hall of Fame.

Our first NHL hockey card product of 2003–04 was Pacific NHL Hockey. The base set was released in July of 2003, before the NHL season began, and contained 368 different NHL players, with two parallel variations (red or blue foil). The 2003–04 Cramer's Choice Awards 10-card insert set was serial numbered, each card numbered 1 through 99. My choice of players for the set included Mario Lemieux, Martin Brodeur, Mike Modano, Patrick Roy, and a new sensational rookie named Henrik Zetterberg.

Twenty years later, the Pacific NHL Hockey set had 30 Hall of Fame players; more players will certainly be inducted in the future.

We also added to the base set an unannounced rookie update set, cards numbered 351–368. These rookie cards were serial numbered 1–999 and inserted one card per pack. Two of the rookie cards in this set are of Marc-Andre Fleury and Eric Staal. Both went on to have great NHL careers and as of 2022 were still playing in the NHL. As an added collector bonus, we offered a 10-card rookie update set available from Pacific through the mail. Customers learned about the offer from a printed order card that was inserted in packs of Pacific 2003–04.

We also brought back our most popular brand, Pacific Prism, after using it exclusively for the McDonald's promotion the previous couple years. After two years of being heavily promoted, Pacific Prism was even more popular with hockey card collectors. One little twist we added to Pacific Prism was to make blue parallel cards for the base set issued only in the United States and red parallel cards of the base set only issued in Canada.

A rookie named Patrice Bergeron debuted that year with the Boston Bruins. His rookie cards are in several of the 2003–04 Pacific hockey cards brands, including Pacific Prism. He was still playing with the Bruins 20 years later and seemed certain to be picked for the Hockey Hall of Fame.

Our new 2003–04 Pacific brands that season were Pacific Exhibit, Pacific Luxury Suite and Pacific Supreme. All three new brands did very well in the hockey card market. The Pacific Luxury Suite cards were thick cards, 64 points thick as opposed to a regular 10-point trading card.

We also made a major change with our Pacific Heads Up hockey brand that season. The hockey player bobbing head dolls we had put in the product were great and sold well. But our marketing director, Jeff Morris, had come up with an all-new idea to replace the dolls: NHL hockey player mini sweaters, another first for Pacific and the hockey market.

These were miniature replica sweaters just like the players wore. We choose nine players' sweaters to replicate, including those of Marc-Andre Fleury, Martin Brodeur, Steve Yzerman, Peter Forsberg, Joe Thornton, Ilya Kovalchuk, Ed Belfour, Todd Bertuzzi and Marian Gaborik. We had the sweaters (and mannequin-like torsos to display them on) made in China. When the all-new 2003–04 Pacific Heads Up Hockey was released to the market in late February of 2004, collectors raved about the cards and the new mini sweaters.

In the meantime, we acquired two more licenses to produce trading cards, *Garfield: The Movie* and TNA Wrestling.

In April 2004, we came out with Pacific TNA Wrestling cards. The 75-card set sold well and featured a couple of wrestling legends, Dusty Rhodes and "Rowdy" Roddy Piper. The set became extremely popular a few years later when the rookie cards of A.J. Styles got hot. He is universally recognized as one of the greatest in-ring performers of his generation. His Pacific TNA rookie cards are now highly sought-after and command big bucks.

In May, after we released Pacific Calder Collection (our last hockey card product of the 2003–04 season), we started to hear statements from the NHL and NHL Players Association that a player lockout was looming for the 2004–05 NHL season. The upcoming season was an uncertainty. However, no one knew for sure at that time, so we were hopeful an agreement would be reached and the 2004–05 NHL season would be played.

Our relationship with McDonald's of Canada continued for the fifth straight season, and we had already begun to produce the NHL hockey card promotion for the upcoming 2004–05 season. All card designs were completed and approved, and the players were chosen for the set. The card design for the main 55-card set was to be Pacific Atomic. The insert sets were to be a six-card set of Atomic Invincible, a 10-card set of Atomic Provincial Collection, a six-card set of Canadian Captains, a six-card set of Atomic Rise to Stardom, a six-card set of Atomic Trophy Die-Cuts, and a 25-card set of Atomic Authentic Game-Used Gear, along with checklist cards.

This very important promotion was moving along right on schedule.

We also had our first NHL hockey card release of the upcoming 2004–05 NHL season in production, to be shipped in July of 2004.

Little did I realize that 2004–05 Pacific NHL Hockey would be the last sports trading card set ever produced and shipped by me and Pacific Trading Cards, Inc.

It was a beautiful set, 300 different hockey players plus a score of insert cards, including my two favorites, Cramer's Choice Awards and Gold Crown Die-Cuts.

The Cramer's Choice Awards was a 10-card set serial numbered 1 of 99. It featured, among others, Mario Lemieux, Martin Brodeur, Joe Sakic, Joe Thornton, and a new addition, Martin St. Louis, who would go on to have a Hall of Fame career.

The Gold Crown die-cuts had been one of my favorite card designs ever since Pacific first introduced the cards in 1995. We had been making that crown card design for 10 straight years.

The 2004–05 Pacific NHL Hockey set had 30 Hockey Hall of Fame players as of 2022. But several players in the set were still playing in 2022, including Joe Thornton and Marc-Andre Fleury, giving the set more Hall of Fame potential.

15. Pacific After Baseball

That May, we also released Pacific *Garfield: The Movie* trading cards to a good response in the trading card market. It was our first non-sport card product since *Saved by the Bell* in 1993.

It was also the last product Pacific Trading Cards made.

The looming player lockout for the 2004–05 NHL season was beginning to look like it was going to be a reality. In late July, I had a phone call from Ted Saskin, the senior director of licensing for the NHL Players Association. He was coming to visit Pacific Trading Cards at our offices in Lynnwood. Ted was a good friend of Pacific, and we always had a great working relationship with the NHLPA.

Ted arrived at our offices. I think he wanted to tell me, in person, how severe the situation was. The worst news he brought was that the 2004–05 NHL season would most likely be canceled and the lockout could last a year—or longer.

When Ted left the Pacific headquarters, I went to my office and closed my door. I sat down and weighed my options for what they were. It only took me a few minutes.

I went in to meet with Phil Roth, my CFO, to discuss our options. The first option was to hibernate Pacific for a year, shutting everything down and just waiting it out. This would be a bit tricky, although we had the cash reserves to do so. However, holding our key people together would pose a risk: we were not sure what the hockey card market would be like when the lockout ended.

The second option was to take an offer to sell the Pacific Trading Cards, Inc., brands, all 17 brands that we had developed over the past 30 years.

It wasn't a long meeting. We had set our minds: our option was to hibernate and wait the market out.

However, that afternoon I received a call from Ann at Playoff. She made an offer to buy the Pacific Trading Cards, Inc., brands and card designs.

The sale would include Pacific, Prism, Crown Royale, Invincible, Heads Up, Vanguard, Private Stock, Titanium, Supreme, Luxury Suite, Crown Collection and others. Card designs that collectors favored, like Cramer's Choice Awards, Gold Crown die-cuts and Crown Royale, were also part of the projected sale.

The offer to buy the Pacific brands came as a shock to me as I realized—really realized—that if I sold Pacific I would be out of the trading card manufacturing business after some 31 years.

It meant I would be closing down Pacific.

It's not what I had planned. It's just what happened.

I just said yes to the offer. Then I realized: that was it.

I was done.

* * *

Looking back, after having crunched the numbers and really seeing the costs to wait out the NHL lockout with no guarantee for what the hockey card market would be like when the lockout ended, I definitely believe I made the right choice to sell. It was also the hard choice.

I'm happy, though, that the legacy Pacific built in the trading market would live on in our brand names and card designs.

It was my choice to sell Pacific. All I had ever done my whole life was work, and I really enjoyed working. But now I had put myself out of a job for the first time since I collected pop bottles to sell as a kid.

Having made a deal to sell the Pacific brands, my next step was to tell my people and friends that Pacific was sold and we were closing. That was hard: we had without question the best people and creative minds in the trading card business working at Pacific.

I sat each of the department managers down and explained that we were closing and that I had sold the Pacific brands to Playoff.

We all knew we had had a great run, some of us for more than 30 years, and we all had much to be thankful for.

My next step was to list and sell the Pacific corporate office building and manufacturing plant in Lynnwood. Cheryl and I had built and owned the building since 1989. We put the building on the market and got our price right away.

This was moving quickly. I only had six weeks to clean out the building so the new owner could move in.

All of a sudden, that was my new job: closing down Pacific and clearing out the building. It was actually an easier job than I thought.

I was still a collector, and there were a few Pacific items I just couldn't sell off. I wanted to keep them, and I did. Nearly every slide and photo published on our Pacific cards I kept for my personal library. The original photos used to make most of our entertainment cards, several cases of Cramer's Choice Awards acrylic card display holders and, most importantly, "the Shannon Books" (the samples and production records for Pacific) I took home. These items, along with much more, were stored away in my attic. I just couldn't get rid of them. My collecting instincts just took over.

Pacific Trading Cards, Inc., had no debt whatsoever and plenty of receivables. Every single bill we had was paid. Our accounting department was kept on to close out books and collect our receivables. The Pacific customer service department was also kept open, and Shannon took care of customers right up until the very last day.

In the interim, we sold much of our card manufacturing equipment, including our Rollem Slipstream card-cutting machines and the Industrial High-Die fabric cutting machine we used to cut game-used jerseys and sweaters. Much of our high-end furniture was sold to the new buyer of the Pacific building. I was on a tight schedule, so I called an auction house to sell off our remaining card packaging lines and office furniture.

Our surplus photo library of unpublished photos was also sold at the auction. Virtually all of the photos published on Pacific trading cards remain in my library. Over time, a few—very few—got removed from the binders and collectors have them.

When the auction was held, I was there. Among the people who came to buy were collectors who asked me, "Where are all the cards?" I told them there were no cards for sale. I repeat: there were *no* Pacific cards sold at the auction—none.

For the last three to four years of its life, Pacific produced and printed only products that we had orders for. We had no cards left in-house, therefore we had nothing to sell. The auction inventory list has no Pacific cards on it.

I see card dealers advertising that they are offering Pacific cards they bought at the Pacific auction. These cards were *not* bought at the Pacific auction.

The auction ended, and nearly everything we put up for sale was sold, except for a few office desks.

On the days when the buyers of our packaging equipment sent in trucks to pick up their machines, I stayed away. That way, when I came back into Pacific, I only saw the empty packing rooms that had once turned plain white board stock paper into gold.

The nice thing was, the buyer of the Pacific building had bought my office desk, several other desks, and the two conference rooms complete with all their furnishings. So I still had my desk to use right up until the end.

My wife, Cheryl, my daughters, Rachael and Angela, Angela's husband Adam, and my sons, Cory and Michael, came to work for several days to help me clean up the building so it could be presentable to the new owner. The Pacific building was a lot of square feet. We had a lot of work to do and, with their help, in just a week or so, all the work of closing down Pacific was completed.

Phil, Shannon and I also completed our work. The Pacific online cyber store was closed and the last orders were shipped to collectors. Then we took the Pacific website offline.

The payment for the sale of the Pacific brands and the payment for the Pacific headquarters building had arrived, both on the same day. The new owner of the building arranged to pick up the keys to the building the next day.

(From left) Rachael, Cory, Cheryl, me, Michael, and Angela: my family saying goodbye to Pacific Trading Cards in 2004 (Pacific Trading Cards Archives).

We left work, having finished our last full day as employees of Pacific Trading Cards, Inc.

We decided to return on the morning of September 25 and finish cleaning out our desks together and then leave Pacific for the last time together.

That morning, we all arrived about 8:30 and carried the last items from our desks out to our cars. Then we had the phones turned off for the last time and said our goodbyes to each other. When the new owner arrived to pick up the keys, we realized it was time for us to leave Pacific.

It was just Phil Roth, CFO, Shannon Johnson, director of customer service, and Mike Cramer, president and CEO. We all left the building at the same time. I was very surprised that I wasn't emotional. Actually, I was excited for what might lay ahead for me.

Shannon did shed a tear, and I saw that. I said my last goodbyes to her. She had given 100 percent to Pacific and had the honor of walking out the door with us.

16

Life After Pacific

The new owner met us, and I handed him the keys to the building. This place had been built by selling trading cards; it had been the home of Pacific for more than 16 years. All the trading cards Pacific ever made since 1990 had passed through this building.

The new owner took the keys from me, and Phil, Shannon and I walked to our cars and left Pacific for the last time.

On my 15-minute drive home, I was kind of comatose, not sure of what I had just done. But I knew that, whatever it was, it was permanent. And on that drive home, I began to have a feeling I'd never had before:

I began to feel that elephants were climbing off my shoulders.

Then I began to realize I didn't have a job anymore. And a few more elephants climbed off.

When I got home, Cheryl was waiting. The first thing I said to her was "I don't have a job."

She gave me a big hug. "Mike," she said, "you don't need a job!"

I hugged her more. "I'm free," I said. "And I don't need a job!"

And some more elephants climbed off my shoulders.

I sat down and thought for a moment. It became apparent to me that I had been on call and available to Pacific Trading Cards, 24 hours a day, seven days a week, every day for the last 30 years.

I had gone to my office nearly every day. Even when I had a day off, if something came up and I was needed, I was always ready to stop whatever I was doing and go in to work or advise in endless telephone calls.

Now I was no longer the president and CEO of Pacific.

Wow. That was a new feeling for me.

I went to sleep that night and actually slept.

I had nothing to worry about. No deadlines. I didn't have to create any new trading card product. I just felt relaxed and ... relieved. My wheels had been spinning at high speed forever and, for the first time in my life, I could tell they were beginning to slow down.

When I woke up the next morning I had the strangest feeling that I have ever had: I didn't have to go to work. It was a shocker, because all I had ever done was go to work.

I was most definitely a workaholic. People had told me that many times, but I never felt like one because I had the best job a human could ever want. I made trading cards! That wasn't work (although, obviously, it was; I'd just never felt like it was…).

That morning, I went out on my back deck and looked out over Puget Sound and the mountains beyond. I saw a whole new world out there, and I could now be part of it.

More elephants climbed off my shoulders—by the thousands! I couldn't believe this new relief I felt.

I remembered a similar feeling I had, back when I fished king crab in the Bering Sea. Once, our boat's lights, power generator and main engines suddenly shut down in the middle of the night when we were hauling gear. For just a few minutes, it was so peaceful … quiet and dark, with no noise from the engines … it was like the entire world had just stopped, dead silent.

Of course, the chief engineer quickly got the engines back online; it was just an air gap in the fuel line. The engines and noisy hydraulics roared back to life, and we got back to hauling gear. Incredibly, though, just for a few moments, it felt like the world had stopped.

But I knew this new feeling I had was different. My own engines, my workaholic instincts, had been running 24 hours a day, non-stop, for such a long time, but were finally taking a break. Shutting down a bit. I felt like my brain actually took a break from the non-stop thinking about business all the time. I saw the world around me in a different light: it all used to just pass by—I was in such a hurry all the time. It sounds like the biggest cliche in the world, but when I got home I did, literally, stop and smell the roses in our garden. They had been there for 20 years. But now, I had time.

I just started to enjoy the day.

It was hard to believe I could do whatever I wanted.

And I did do what I wanted.

The very next day, I joined Inglewood Golf Club (Phil Roth was already a member there). I started to play golf three to four days a week. This was new for me. I didn't go to work; I went to play golf.

But I also found other activities to keep me busy.

For example, I had built a museum hall onto our home to house my growing antique militaria collection. I wanted to finish it out in gold ornamentation, like some of the great palaces I had seen in Europe. So I got a book and learned how to gild. It was my new labor of love and I got really good at it.

Shortly after I retired, Cheryl and I decided to travel. We booked a month-long trip to Europe. My great friend and consultant, Victor

16. Life After Pacific

Temkin, had said the best thing I could do after Pacific was to have fun. That fun began on this trip to Europe.

It was after we got home from that great trip that it really hit me: Pacific was gone. I didn't have a job. No one was expecting me at work or anywhere. Cheryl just kept reminding me that I didn't need a job, that I could do whatever I wanted to do.

By summer of 2004 I was immersed in my new hobby: collecting antique military helmets, medals, uniforms, swords, paintings and guns. My enormous trading card collection sat idle, and I didn't look at my sets of trading cards very often. I started to have thoughts of selling my cards, including my baseball cards. These were the same cards I had collected as a kid, the cards my mother and father had not thrown away when I left home to go fishing crab in the Bering Sea. Some of these card sets were in the trunks that Cheryl and I loaded onto the processor ship *Mokihana* on our wedding night in Dutch Harbor back in 1973.

I wasn't sure I could part with my cards but finally made the choice to do so. I would sell my complete sets of cigarette cards, my T-3s, T-206s, and T-205s including my Honus Wagner, and all the rest of my card collection—except my Pacific cards.

Sotheby's auction house in New York City printed catalogs and sold my collection. The catalogs show the scope and volume of my collection. I didn't attend the sale, but Cheryl, our son Michael and I were able to follow the sale live on the internet.

Most of my sets achieved record prices for that time.

But I didn't sell all of my cards. Some, I just stored away in a room in my house, forgetting all about them for some 20 years. I also kept my entire collection of Pacific card sets, the cards I made—I couldn't part with them.

I had always kept a complete set of each card product we made, storing the cards in plastic sheets and a binder. These card sets were extremely helpful for me during the Pacific days, as I would study each card in the set and see how we could improve the next card set we made. I still have one each of almost every card Pacific made, except for some of the very low serial-numbered cards: those went into the product cases, and even I didn't get them.

Pacific did produce a lot of serial-numbered cards. The sets I have in my collection are unnumbered, for the most part. Unnumbered cards were printed to be used as replacement cards; very few were printed, making them quite scarce today. A distinguishing feature is that these cards have the foil swatch where the serial number would go, but it is left blank.

My Pacific cards were stored away on the shelves in my library for nearly 20 years before I began to look at them again. I am still amazed by the quality and the creativity of our cards. (I confess, I have thought this before....)

* * *

In spring 2006, Cheryl and I visited her parents in Phoenix, timing it so I could also attend the Orders Medals Society of America Convention. That's where I met Shep Paine, a collector and dealer of militaria including uniforms, helmets, and swords. He was friendly, talkative, and knowledgeable. He told me that the Napoleonic Historical Society was holding its annual conference in Seattle later that fall and asked if I was interested in attending. When I shared some photos of my home museum, he asked if conference attendees could take a tour of my museum!

The conference attendees that year did have a tour of "the Cramer Museum" and most said it was the highlight of the conference. For me, a true highlight was meeting Shep. We often found ourselves on the same European tours after that and could talk non-stop on the long bus rides about history, battlefields, military uniforms, orders, medals, baseball—and more history.

I also learned that Shep was a model builder—that is, he sculpted and painted military dioramas, complete with detailed, life-like figures, most only one to three inches tall. He also painted miniature busts of military people or historical personalities. Painters like Shep sold these figures to collectors worldwide and even had competitions. This was all very interesting to me. I told Shep I would like to try my hand at painting historical miniatures.

I discovered I really liked this new hobby. I wanted to paint more, and I wanted to have even more choices in what I painted. I decided to commission sculptors to create figures based on the uniforms, medals and paintings in my home Cramer Museum. Then it occurred to me ... once I commissioned a bust, I would own the work outright. I could reproduce it and sell copies for other hobbyists to paint. I could have a mail-order catalog! (That sounded familiar....) Yes, it could be "Michael Miniatures," a small business—a "miniature" business!

"You never do anything lightly, do you?" Cheryl said.

As I continued to immerse myself in my new hobby, perhaps the most amazing thing I learned was that my Napoleonic friend, the fellow militaria collector who had introduced me to dioramas was, literally, a legend. Shep Paine was the most well-known miniature figure artist in the world. He had never let on to me about that in our long talks on the bus through Poland.

* * *

I was busy enjoying life after Pacific. I rarely thought about the trading card business any longer. My world had moved on in the same way it had back in 1979, after I quit fishing king crab and devoted myself full-time to Pacific Trading Cards.

Sometimes, though, my current world had unexpected reminders of the other worlds I had known.

In 2005, more than 20 years after I stopped fishing, a television program called *Deadliest Catch* debuted on cable television. The reality series became a long-running hit and is still in production 18 years after its launch. About 10 episodes premiered each year. In each installment, camera crews follow crab boat crews like the ones I worked on, capturing the hard work and the dangers of crab fishing in the rough, cold Bering Sea. Dutch Harbor is a frequent setting.

The program's premise is that crab fishing is the most dangerous job on the planet. And it is true that, in the race to get a share of the king crab jackpot, crews take risks, boats sink, and injuries and death are chillingly regular.

Because of those dangers, the three-man crews of my days have been generally expanded to crews of six, with a rotating shift of one or two crewmen in the bunks getting some sleep. This has greatly reduced injuries on the crab boats.

But it's still compelling enough to keep people watching, including me.

As I was watching an episode, I suddenly realized this might be a revelation to Cheryl. I called her to come watch too. They were hauling gear in rough seas, and the boat was tossing all around. I said, "Look! This is what I did."

Cheryl watched for about a minute, barely moving. "That's what you did out there?" After a moment, she whispered, "I'm sure glad you don't do that now!"

I asked Cheryl if she had ever worried about me when I fished.

She said, "I never worried about you; fishing was just what you did. But ... I was not aware, at that young age, how dangerous it really was."

Not once, in all the time I fished king crab, was I ever worried myself, even when I was on the *Scotty*. My instincts told me to get off that boat, and I did—but I wasn't afraid.

My brother, Marty, said he was never afraid either. "I think we were just too young and too dumb to know better."

I guess, if you were afraid, you didn't become a crab fisherman. I knew dozens of men that had quit after just one trip. The Bering Sea crab grounds were just too rough for the timid.

But my dad's legacy will live on in that show. Kris and Anji's son, my nephew Edward Poulsen, is part of the Cramer family that still fishes crab. He is part owner of two crab boats. One of them, the *Patricia Lee*, will be part of *Deadliest Catch*'s 2022–23 season.

And my son Michael works for Keyport, a company based in

Edmonds. Keyport wholesales a good share of the crab caught in the Bering Sea to stores all over the country. These two young men continue the legacy started by my father's family migration to Dutch Harbor.

* * *

I am a Seattle Seahawks fan and have been since the team's inception in 1976. In 2013, a mesmerizing Seahawks season took the team to the 2013 Super Bowl, playing the Denver Broncos.

No team I followed had ever won a championship. I didn't know what it was like for my team to win the big one.

Until that game ended, 43–8: Seattle had won.

Seattle had won! *Seattle had won!*

I had been with them for 38 years, through the fun years of Zorn, to Largent and the Shaun Alexander years, when we got so close but didn't win it.

I wasn't making football cards any longer. I was just a football fan. But I now knew what it was like to have my team win, and it was *incredible!*

The next year, the Seahawks went back to the Super Bowl, this time with a gut-wrenching, last-second loss to the New England Patriots. But, oddly, there was a silver lining for me.

New England Patriots quarterback Tom Brady had won, and was named the game's MVP.

Brady was still my guy, my choice, so at least some good came out of that game for me.

* * *

In August of 2016 I made the ultimate golf trip of a lifetime to Scotland, with seven golfer friends from the Seattle area.

I played some really good golf on the trip and actually had some moments of brilliance. Other times, I was just happy my caddy could find my ball.

In April, I was off on another golf outing to Georgia and Florida, playing courses ranked in the top 100. And Florida is where the unforgettable happened.

At Streamsong's Red course, on hole number 8, I teed off first. And as soon as I hit the ball, my caddy yelled, "Go in the hole!"

The ball landed on the green and rolled into the hole ... as simple as that. *Eureka!* My first-ever hole in one! It was a long time coming!

* * *

For the next few years, I honed my painting skills, entering my painted figures at different shows across the United States. I got a lot of

16. Life After Pacific

silver medals for my work but never gold. I was determined to get a gold medal and be among the best artists in the world.

I worked harder than ever at my painting, and the more I painted, the better I got. I could see my skills improving. My painted faces started to look more like human faces, and I painted the clothes with highlights and shadows that made the clothes come to life.

In the summer of 2017, Cheryl and I drove to Chicago for the World Model Expo Show from our home near Seattle.

I chose what I thought were my best four figures: three military busts and a 54 mm Viking diorama that I had designed and built.

At the award ceremony, when the names of the silver medal award winners were being called, I got really nervous. A lot of incredibly good artists' names were being called out, and they were walking up to pick up their silver medals. I listened for my name, but it wasn't being announced.

The awards for gold medal winners were next, and just like that, a photo appeared on the big screen of my diorama "Vikings: Two Generations," and I heard my name.

"Mike Cramer."

I thought, "Incredible! *I got gold!*"

My gold medal figure at the World Expo Figure Show in 2017, "Vikings: Two Generations." I modeled and painted this miniature diorama. The seated Viking is two inches tall. A very proud moment for me (photograph by Mike Cramer).

I looked at Cheryl, and she had the biggest grin on her face. I whispered to her, "I've done it! I got gold! I'm an artist!"

I jumped up and walked to the presentation area to receive my gold medal. Euphoria had set in. I believe I may have skipped on the way back to my seat! This was a great moment for me, and it was my first gold medal ever in miniature painting. My determination and perseverance to paint miniature figures at the level of the best in the world had won out. I won a gold medal at the 2017 World Expo of Model Painters.

Now I knew the feeling a player gets when he wins the World Series, the Super Bowl, or the Stanley Cup. It's the best feeling of achievement ever.

I had great satisfaction in all of the years of achievements and accomplishments at Pacific Trading Cards. But they didn't match the level of satisfaction I felt winning a gold medal at the World Model Expo in 2017.

17

The Comeback Kid

My world had changed since my days at Pacific Trading Cards, and I had changed with it.

I painted and played golf, and Cheryl and I traveled. Over the years, we visited most of the national parks and battlefield sites in the United States. More than anything, we were enjoying our grandchildren. We eventually had 12, and they all got our devoted attention.

I was very active and busy, and I always walked the golf course when I played. Around 2017, I began to notice I was feeling different—a little sluggish after I played golf. I was just plain worn out when I finished my round.

Over the next three years, I just did what I could, but I did notice everything I did was making me tired. Even getting out of my chair was a struggle.

By the spring of 2020, I couldn't do the things I wanted to do. I was just exhausted all the time. Finally in the late summer, I was able to see my doctor for a physical, which included routine blood tests.

I started taking a prescribed iron supplement to help bring up my low red blood counts and figured that would end my fatigue. So I signed up for a golf outing with the same foursome I had been going on golf trips with for more than 30 years.

My brother Marty, Don O'Neal (my trusted financial adviser for the last 40 years), Phil Roth and I all drove over to Gamble Sands in Brewster, Washington. (Remember the little town where I was born? It is also home to Gamble Sands, my favorite golf course in the world.) We looked forward to four days of golf.

But it didn't work out that way for me.

I was exhausted—just drained. And while I was playing really well, I could barely walk from the golf cart to hit my ball.

On the last day we played, I knew something was really wrong with me.

I couldn't even drive home. Phil had to drive my car. I was too exhausted. I just laid down in the back seat wondering, *What the heck is wrong with me?*

I got home and went to bed. The next morning, I was finally ready to admit that, whatever was wrong, it might be big.

The emergency room doctors at the hospital did all the tests they could—scans, blood work, everything. They found nothing, only that I was severely anemic: borderline blood-transfusion anemic. The emergency room doctor told me to get in to see my regular doctor right away.

More appointments led to referrals with more doctors, more tests that led nowhere until, finally, I was scheduled for cancer tests. That is not a good thing to hear, but I was feeling so horrible, I just wanted to get to the bottom of it and deal with it, no matter what it was.

At last the answer came.

It was cancer.

I was, oddly, horribly, relieved to know. At last, I knew what was happening, why I was in such bad shape that even my vision was starting to get blurry.

But the doctors still didn't know enough. What kind of cancer was I facing?

I was able to get an appointment with Dr. Edward Libby, a renowned hematology and oncology specialist.

The two weeks before I could get in were the toughest two weeks of my life. I was progressively getting worse, and the anticipation of what lay before me was grueling.

I'd always been able to learn how to deal with new challenges, to find people to help and to teach me, then to apply that knowledge.

I'd learned to haul and bait crab pots. I learned to reconfigure a card-packing machine.

I learned to manage a factory. I learned how to deal with the court system of the United States. I learned to paint artistically, for world-class competition.

But I couldn't learn how to do this.

So I did what I could: I prayed. I prayed and prayed and asked Jesus to help me get through this ordeal, to fix me. I still had things I wanted to do. I wasn't ready to meet my maker. I wouldn't be happy in heaven just yet—I wasn't done living.

This was a scary time for me and my family. I was so weak that I needed help to do just about everything, including walking and even sitting down in a chair. I had lost 40 pounds when I didn't have 40 to lose. I was skin and bones.

Finally, in September, Cheryl drove me to Seattle for my appointment.

After talking with me for 10 minutes, Dr. Libby said, "Mike, you have Waldenstrom's macroglobulinemia."

Waldenstrom's macroglobulinemia (WM) is a rare form of cancer that causes large amounts of abnormal protein to build up in the blood and crowd out the red blood cells. Dr. Libby told me it's a form of cancer so rare that a person's chances of getting struck by lightning are better than the chances of getting Waldenstrom's.

Then Dr. Libby said, "Mike, if you got to choose, you'd want Waldenstrom's." He told me I would die *from* many other forms of cancer. "But you will die *with* Waldenstrom's," he said. "We can treat Waldenstrom's with chemotherapy."

Dr. Libby's words were the answers to my prayers, and Cheryl's prayers, and all the people that were praying for me. God answers prayers, and I am living proof of that!

Dr. Libby scheduled me for a biopsy that confirmed that I have this very rare cancer.

My treatment started right away. But I was so far out of whack, my earliest treatments concentrated on making me strong enough for the actual cancer treatment, chemotherapy. My first chemo infusion began the first week of October 2020. It wasn't so bad—but the doctor said the more chemo I got, the worse the treatments would get.

He was 100 percent accurate on that. After the third round, I struggled just to sit upright in my chair. During the fifth round of chemo, I managed to sit in a chair and watch the NFL playoffs on TV.

Tom Brady was now playing for the Tampa Bay Buccaneers and, since my Seahawks had been eliminated, I was rooting for the Bucs and Brady to win Super Bowl LV. They did! That lifted my spirits. Tom Brady was my guy, my choice, and he had done it again, with a new team.

Wow, he was making me look good for making so many rookie cards of him.

* * *

In late February of 2021, I got my last chemo infusion. It was a good thing it was my last: at that stage, I figured if the cancer didn't kill me, the chemo surely would. I thought back to my crab fishing days when I was young and strong and could work through anything. Even though I was much older, I still had the same determination and drive. I thought about Mario Lemieux and his struggles to beat a similar cancer and how he came back to play in the NHL.

With Cheryl's and my children's help and encouragement, and the prayers I received, I started to gradually recover.

In mid-February, my son Michael and his family came over to see how I was doing.

We were talking and he said, "Dad, do you know what the card market is doing?"

I said, "No, I haven't been paying attention."

Michael said, "Dad, it's on fire! Some Pacific Tom Brady rookie graded cards are selling for tens of thousands of dollars." He barely paused before asking, "Do you still have your Pacific cards?"

We went into the library, and Michael pulled down my 2000 Pacific Paramount football card binder. Sure enough, I had the complete set. I turned pages in the binder until I saw my 2000 Pacific Paramount Tom Brady rookie card, number 138.

I remembered the photos on the front and back of the card.

I told Michael, "I think I took those photos. I have binders with the photos we made cards from." We located that binder of 2000 Pacific Paramount football slides. I turned pages in the binder until I found slides numbered 138, Tom Brady. Sure enough, the slide jacket read "Tom Brady, photo by Michael J. Cramer." I started to remember the day I shot that game at Stanford Stadium and how impressed I was by that young quarterback from Michigan.

Michael and I looked at my other 2000 Pacific football binders, and I realized I had taken almost all of the photos of Tom Brady that Pacific had used on his rookie cards that year.

I really enjoyed looking at my collection of Pacific cards. Baseball, football, hockey and non-sports: the cards are absolutely stunning. I am probably the biggest collector and fan of my own work. When I was making Pacific cards, I always said, "I am making these cards knowing that the first set is for me." I made them, and I did collect them, with a passion.

Seeing my life's work all over again gave me a big uplift, and I wanted more than ever to recover from the cancer and chemo. For the first time in some 20 years, I wanted to look at all of my cards over and over, the cards I made, my Pacific cards.

I started to eat. Nothing tasted good, and I had no appetite, but I had dwindled down to nothing, so I forced myself to eat. I needed some strength and to gain back some of the weight I had lost. Gradually, day by day, I began to improve.

I was not going to let this cancer beat me.

During that time, my son Michael told me about a blogger who was searching for me for an interview.

The fan's blog stated, "Mike Cramer, the man behind Pacific, has become a recluse, and has done zero interviews or made any public appearances in the world of sports cards for the last 20 years."

I thought, "What is this all about?"

I have to say, I wasn't that hard to find. I had been living in the same house and had the same phone number and email address for more than

17. The Comeback Kid

25 years. I for sure wasn't a recluse; I was just busy doing new things. The trading card world had gone on without me.

I started to feel better and remembered my attic, where 20 or so years earlier I had put most of my boxes from Pacific. (Yes, it is a big attic!)

I came across a few cases of Cramer's Choice Awards jumbo acrylic holders I brought home some 20 years earlier. I wanted to keep about 60 of them, so I could display a few Jumbo Cramer's Choice Awards in my library. I decided to sell the rest of them on eBay.

I was amazed how quickly they sold out. Collectors messaged me, asking for more, but I had no more.

When I mailed out one of the holders, I wrote a note to the collector that bought it.

My note read, "Will Spence, you bought a Cramer's Choice Award holder from Cramer." I wrote that note for fun. When he received the package with the holder and read my note, he sent me a message asking if I was Mike Cramer of Pacific Trading Cards. I wrote back and said, yes, that's me.

A few days later, I got another note. It came from a collector who said he was a friend of Will Spence; his name was Matt Burrows.

Matt told me that many collectors wished to talk to me and ask questions about Pacific. He said, "You have just disappeared for the last 20 years, and collectors love the cards you made. They were so innovative," he said, adding, "I'm a big collector of the cards you made."

2000 Pacific Paramount Tom Brady rookie card. I shot the front and back photographs for this card. I still have the original slides used to make the card. This card is graded a perfect gem mint 10 (Mike Cramer Collection).

Then he asked, "Do you know you started it all?"

I said, "Started what?"

He told me, "The card companies that make trading cards now, in 2022, are making cards the same way you did back then. You were way ahead of your time. It's all Pacific's ideas, just rehashed a bit. Parallels cards, die-cuts cards, laser-cut cards, prism cards, serial-numbered cards, and foil cards—these are all ideas Pacific pioneered back when you were making cards. They are still making the card designs that Pacific first introduced 30 years ago: Cramer's Choice Award, Crown Royale, Gold Crown Die-Cuts, and others."

I said, "*Wow!* Those were all great ideas and designs. I'm happy collectors are still enjoying collecting the card designs Pacific created."

Matt then said he would like to come and meet me so he could ask questions about "long-lost Mike Cramer" and Pacific, the brand he and many others call their favorite. I thought, "Well, how can you turn that down?" I wasn't a recluse or in hiding; I had just found other interests and become absorbed in them, the same way I'd once been absorbed in creating trading cards.

I said, "Sure. I would love to answer your questions."

About a month later, Matt and a friend of his did come to my house. They asked me many questions about the days when Pacific was the most creative and innovative card manufacturing company in America.

Later, Matt texted me and said that more collectors would love to hear about Pacific. Would I do a podcast? I did that podcast and have participated in several since. I wasn't a recluse, and I'm still not!

I was still recovering from chemo but definitely feeling better. My energy level came back a bit, so Cheryl and I went back into the attic. After moving a few more boxes, we discovered "the Shannon Books." This was an incredible find! Those books contained sample cards and the printing and production records for Pacific Trading Cards, Inc. I could now answer with confidence several more of the questions collectors had. The records were right in front of me.

I was most happy to learn that Panini Trading Cards had acquired the Pacific Trading Cards brands and that all of my Pacific brands and card designs were still being made on new cards by Panini.

Most satisfying was hearing that Prism, a brand Pacific first introduced in 1993, had become Panini's flagship brand. They changed the spelling to Prizm, but it is still Prism, the same great-looking cards. It had also been the flagship brand of Pacific, and collectors still loved it nearly 30 years later.

I began to explore the different cards being produced by Panini. I saw Crown Royale, Aurora, Gold Crown die-cuts and Cramer's Choice Awards, cards still made exactly the way Pacific first made them 30 years ago. A small but necessary adjustment was that Cramer's Choice Awards were now being called Panini's Choice, and Panini chose the current, featured players. But they used card brands and designs I had created—those were still my choices.

I wasn't making cards anymore, but I didn't need to be: the card brands and card designs I had created were strong enough to live on.

Like Mr. Hershey's candy bar.

The great Pacific card designs stood the test of time and, over the first 20 years after Pacific closed, Panini made cards for every brand name Pacific created.

Pacific never had an NBA license to make cards, but I got the satisfaction of seeing my brands and card designs being used for Panini's NBA cards.

One night not long after I learned about Panini, I dreamed I had a license to produce NBA basketball cards. It was just a dream, but when I woke up from the dream, it was more than a dream.

The cards really did exist! They were real! My brands, my card designs, were all real…. Wow! What a dream!

Sometimes dreams do come true. This one did.

Epilogue

The trading card market in 2022 included Pacific. Collectors were still collecting the cards I had created. This is exactly what I wanted when I sold the Pacific brands to Playoff in 2004: I wanted Pacific to live on.

My dreams had lived on.

It's most rewarding for me to see that the mission has been accomplished.

I have been able, in the course of my life thus far, to somehow take an idea or concept I had in my mind and bring it to fruition—and I have had many ideas.

How did I do that? How did I actually make things happen? This is the question I am most asked by people. So many people have an idea or concept, but very, very few ever see their ideas make the light of day.

I am a very free thinker, always thinking outside of the box. I only had a high-school diploma, no college education. I was very fortunate to be able to turn my card collecting hobby into a thriving business. I probably would not have accomplished that if I had a college education, because I probably would have never taken some of the risks that I did. If I had gone to college and learned to think like all the other students, I probably would have known better. (But I still do recommend getting a college education for all who can. I think that only a handful of humans can achieve their goals without a college education.)

I always thought I could do anything I set my mind on. I didn't know any better. I didn't know I couldn't do something just because someone said I couldn't.

If I was told no, I just figured out a way to do what I wanted to accomplish in spite of what I was told. That's truly a different mindset, but I had it: I was bound and determined to get done whatever I was trying to accomplish. My determination and perseverance were the biggest factors in succeeding with my desires. I just wouldn't quit until I figured it out and made it work.

One time in 1999, we had a Pacific celebration dinner at a nice restaurant with some of our close people: Victor Temkin, Phil Roth, Jim Fowler, Mike Kipling and me. These were very smart, well-educated, great guys, and they were all attorneys. We were talking, and they were each naming the university they had gone to: Victor went to Wisconsin, Phil went to Gonzaga, Jim went to Michigan and Mike Kipling went to Harvard. We were talking away, and it was very interesting to hear their stories. When the conversation came to me, I could only say, "I never went to college, but I'm thrilled to be sitting at this dinner, surrounded by a great bunch of attorneys that work for Pacific."

Mike Kipling then paid me one of the best compliments ever. He said, "We might all be lawyers, but, Cramer, we would rather have your job!"

I said, "Why? You're all attorneys!"

He said, "Yes... but you are the one making all the money!"

I say there are three ingredients to success: hard work, brains, and luck. The three are of equal importance. Success is 33 percent hard work, 33 percent using your brains and 33 percent plain old luck.

There is 1 percent left over. And that 1 percent can make the crucial difference in getting your missions accomplished.

Just work 1 percent harder or just think 1 percent harder—or, sometimes, just get 1 percent luckier. Luck is a big factor. Whichever way the extra 1 percent tips can determine your fate.

People often tell me that I was so lucky. Then they ask, how did you get so lucky? It's a real simple answer: you make your own luck. Seeing an opportunity and wrapping your mind, body, and soul around it is not luck. When I saw an opportunity, I put myself out there and persevered. That tipped the scales in my favor, making my dreams come true.

Pacific Trading Cards was built on new ideas and innovation and was often criticized for pushing our card designs outside the box. But 20 and 30 years later, those same exact card designs and concepts are still being used and have stood the test of time. My hope is that the people that criticized Pacific back then see that the card innovations Pacific created are driving today's card market.

Pacific was, and still is, a factor in the trading card world. We weren't the biggest card manufacturer out there, but we were bigger than most will ever realize. Pacific was not owned by billionaire investors: it was just owned by me. I turned cardboard into gold! My dreams did come true!

I loved and lived every minute of my day when I was president and CEO of Pacific Trading Cards, Inc. It was the greatest job ever.

The licensing and manufacturing of trading cards unfortunately comes with a never-ending revolving door, as countless people and companies have entered and exited the market over the last 150 years. There will always be new manufacturers of cards, and one thing is certain: people will always collect trading cards.

I know that passion well.

2000 Pacific Tom Brady Rookie Cards Checklist

2000 Pacific Football

#403 Base card silver foil
#403 Autographed by Brady, 200 cards signed and issued
#403 Pacific Authentic Autograph gold foil stamped card. Not signed, three cards made
#403 Copper Foil, Hobby, serial numbered 1 through 75
#403 Copper Foil, Hobby, serial number left blank, three cards made
#403 Gold Foil Retail-serial numbered 1 through 199
#403 Gold Foil Retail-serial number left blank, three cards made
#403 Sliver Foil, Hobby, numbered rookies, serial numbered 1 through 999
#403 Sliver Foil, Hobby, numbered rookies, serial number left blank, three cards made
#403 Platinum Blue Rookies, Hobby and Retail, serial numbered 1 through 399
#403 Platinum Blue Rookies, Hobby and Retail serial number left blank, three cards made
#403 Premiere Date gold foil May 24, 2000. Hobby, serial numbered 1 through 78
#403 Premiere Date gold foil May 24, 2000. Hobby, serial number left blank, 3 cards made
#15 Finest Hour insert card, 1483 cards made

2000 Pacific Revolution

#128 Base card, gold foil, serial numbered 1 through 300
#128 Base card, gold foil, serial number left blank, five cards made
#22 First Look Rookies insert card, 866 cards made

2000 Pacific Tom Brady Rookie Cards Checklist

2000 Pacific Vanguard

#139 serial numbered 1 through 762

2000 Pacific Aurora

#84 Base card
#84 Premiere Date, Hobby, gold foil, serial numbered 1 through 85
#84 Premiere Date, gold foil, serial number left blank, three cards made

2000 Pacific Paramount

#138 Base card Silver foil
#138 Holographic silver foil, Hobby, serial numbered 1 through 85
#138 Holographic silver foil, Hobby, serial number left blank, three cards made
#138 Rookie Variation Holographic Purple foil, Hobby, serial numbered 1 through 325
#138 Rookie Variation Holographic Purple foil, serial number left blank, three card made
#138 Premiere Date, July 19, 2000, Hobby, serial numbered 1 through 79
#138 Premiere Date, July 19, 2000, serial number left blank, three cards made
#138 Holographic Gold foil, Retail, serial numbered 1 through 130
#138 Holographic Gold foil, serial number left blank, three cards made
#138 Platinum Blue foil, Hobby and Retail, serial numbered 1 through 75
#138 Platinum Blue foil, Hobby and Retail, serial number left blank, three cards made

2000 Pacific Prism Prospects

#156 Base card, numbered 1 through 1000
#156 Base card, number left blank, three cards made

2000 Pacific Private Stock

#128 Base card rookies, Gold foil, Hobby, serial numbered 1 through 278
#128 Base card rookies, Gold foil, Hobby, serial number left blank, THREE cards made

#128 Base card rookies, Silver foil, Retail, serial numbered 1 through 650
#128 Base card rookies, Silver foil, Retail, serial number left blank, three cards made
#128 Gold Portraits, Hobby, serial numbered 1 through 181
#128 Gold Portraits, Hobby, serial number left blank, three cards made
#128 Silver Portraits, Retail, serial numbered 1 through 330
#128 Silver Portraits, Retail, serial number left blank, three cards made
#156 Premiere Date, September 19, 2000, serial numbered 1 through 95
#156 Premiere Date, September 19, 2000, serial number left blank, three cards made

2000 Pacific Omega

#192 Base card, Silver foil, serial numbered 1 through 500
#192 Base card, Silver foil, serial number left blank, three cards made
#13 NFL Generations, Drew Bledsoe/Tom Brady insert card

2000 Pacific Crown Royale

#110 Base card, Hobby, Silver crown, Gold inlay
#110 Base card, Hobby, numbered rookies, serial numbered 1 through 499
#110 Base card, Retail rookie, Silver crown/Burgundy, serial numbered 1 through 144
#110 Base card, Retail rookie, Silver crown/Burgundy, serial number left blank, three made
#110 Premiere Date, serial numbered 1 through 145
#110 Premiere Date, serial number left blank, three cards made
#110 Base card, numbered rookies, serial number left blank, 10 cards made
#110 Limited Series, Red bar, serial numbered 1 through 144
#110 Limited Series, Red bar, serial number left blank, three cards made
#2 Rookie Royalty, insert card
Note: The unnumbered serial cards were made as replacement cards. However, because they exist in the collecting world and are a variation, they are listed.

Index

Numbers in *bold italics* refer to pages with illustrations

Aaron, Hank: cards 43–45, 52; 2000 Pacific Baseball FanFest Hank Aaron card 184–*185*
Action, PS-206 card set 190
Adak Island 1972 king crab fishing season, on *Honey-B* 30–31
Advil: 1996 Pacific Nolan Ryan Advil cards 139; PTC national publicity campaign 3, 97
Alaskan king crab fisherman, becoming 3
Alexander, Shaun 173
ambition and drive 34
The American Card Catalog (Burdick) 13, 20
Anderson, Harold, Treat Hobby founder 115
The Andy Griffith Show card sets 94–95
Apple computers, introduction at PTC 106
Arctic Sea (crab boat): author with king crab *60*; Ballard Locks (1978) *58*; construction 56; crab pot rigging (1977–1978) 58–59
Arizona Sports Collectors Show (1977) 53–54
autographs: Hank Aaron 52–54; Ernie Banks 53; Tom Brady, 2000 deal 174; Drew Brees 191; Joe DiMaggio 78–80, *81*; getting first 9–11; Bob Griese 176; Charlie Grimm 53; Tony Gwynn 154, *186*; Steve Largent 104–5, 176; George Lindsay 102; through mail 10–11; at National Sports Collectors Convention (1991) 102; Nolan Ryan *96*, 176; Tom Seaver 176; Hal Smith 102; Rick Stelmaszek 52; LaDainian Tomlinson 191; Michael Vick 191; Kurt Warner 177; Jim Zorn 68

Babe Ruth see Ruth, Babe, card
Backyard Baseball (video game company) 184
Ball Card Collector, placing ads in 14
Banks, Ernie 9, 145
Baseball All-Star Game FanFest (2000), PTC sponsorship 184
baseball card plastic photo sheets, production and sale 52

baseball card trunks, moves: Detroit to Phoenix (1970) 23; to Dutch Harbor (1971) 26; to Phoenix (1973) 36–40, 213
baseball cards 118; all-Spanish-language card set, first production and sales 109–10; collections, acquisition of 7, 12–13; decision to collect 6; first love 3; first packs (1982) 70; growing business 52; Hank Aaron signature 43–45; "Home Run History: The Mark McGwire and Sammy Sosa Home Run Race of 1998," boxed set 155–57; industry reinvention, in 21st century 4; mail-order business, start of 14; making of first 46; for MLB kid's video game 184; 1910 T-206 baseball card back variations 181; 1910 T-206 cigarette baseball commons, purchase of 23; 1910 T-206 Tobacco baseball card set 45, 166–67; 1933 Goudy Gum Co. baseball cards 13; 1975 Phoenix Giants set 45; 1976 Motorola Baseball Old Timers set 49; 1976 Phoenix Giants set 49; 1978 Hawaii Islanders 60; 1978 Phoenix Giants Valley National Bank 60; 1980 Mickey Mantle Baseball Legends set *69*; 1991 Nolan Ryan no-hitter #7 card *95*; 1993 Nolan Ryan Pacific Pride *94*; 1993 Tom Seaver Pacific Pride *94*; 1994 Pacific Crown Collection 117; 1994 Pacific Invincible, creation 117; 1995 Pacific Baseball Prism brand 125; 1995 Seattle Mariners Memories Commemorative trading card set 126; 1996 Cramer's 10-card insert set 138; 1996 Pacific Nolan Ryan Advil 139; 1996 Pacific Prism Baseball cards 139; 1998 Cramer's Choice Awards insert 154–55; 1998 Pacific Aurora 150, 154; 1998 Ripken Gold Crown die-cut card 155; 1999 Pacific Prism baseball cards 168; 1999 Pacific Private Stock brand, release 166; 1999 Pacific Prizm baseball cards *168*; 1999 Pacific Revolution Icons *162*; Nolan Ryan Texas Express 95–96; Omega brand 155, 178, 186; Phoenix Suns

set 47; production 82; purchase from Frank Nagy 23; Topps baseball wax cases, purchase 40, 55; transport to Phoenix 36–39; 2000 brands 178; 2000 Pacific Aurora Tony Gwynn **186**; 2000 Pacific Baseball FanFest Hank Aaron **185**; 2000 Pacific Invincible, baseball card #16, bat cork problem 182–84; 2000 Pacific Prism Hank Aaron commemorative baseball 184; 2000 Pacific Private Stock release 184; 2001 Pacific Baseball set, last production 190; 2001 Pacific Private Stock Baseball release 190; 2001 PS-206 Pacific Private Stock 190; visit to Detroit show 21–23; *see also* Cramer's Choice Award cards
baseball, growing interest 7
Baseball Hall of Famers, featured on PTC cards: Cramer's Choice Award 122; Cramer's Choice 10-card insert set 138; 1990 Pacific Baseball Legends set 120; 1993 all-Spanish language set 110; 1994 Pacific Crown Collection Baseball players 117; 1994 Pacific Crown Collection, launch 113; 1995 Pacific Crown Collection players 125; 1995 Pacific Prism Baseball brand 125; 1996 Pacific Prism Baseball 139; 1998 Cramer's Choice Awards 155; 1998 Gold Crown die-cut 155; Pacific Aurora Baseball 154; players 11, 89, **105**, 110, 120, 138, 154–55, 167, 184, 190; 2001 Pacific Baseball set, last production 190
Baseball Legends: card sets 69–70; pack (1982) **73**; sepia set 21, 82
Baseball photos, acquisition (1969) 20–21
Baseball Players Alumni Association 82
Baseball World Series game, San Francisco Giants (1989) 89–90
basketball cards 118; Classic sub-license 116, 139, 155; 1993 Pacific Prism Basketball cards 116; 1994 Pacific Crown Collection, launch 113; 1996 Pacific Power Basketball 139; Pacific Crown Collection, launch 113; Pacific Prism Basketball 116; Phoenix Suns 47; Topps and Bowman, purchase 13; Topps cards, purchase 40, 51, 55
Basketball Hall of Famers, featured on PTC cards 116, 139
Bastion Capital Corp., Donruss sale, partner with PTC 137–38
Belair (crab boat): crab fishing 1974 33–35; meeting Kris Poulsen on 30
Bennett, Chuck, football card advisor 101-2
Berger, Sy (Topps) 135–36, **136**
Bergeron, Patrice, rookie cards 205
Bering Sea (crab boat) 42, **42**
Bering Sea, crab fishing, dangers 30
Berkley Publishing Co., and Pacific Trading Cards 82–83
Berra, Yogi: dinner with author 119–20
Bimbo Bakeries, PTC contracts 134–35

Blackaby, Ethan 45, 46, 51
bobbing head dolls 193–94, 199, 205
Boggs, Wade, candy bar 93
Bomarko, wax wrap printer 77
Boso, Cap, card 101
Bowman cards, purchase 13
Bradshaw, Terry 116
Brady, Tom (GOAT): cards 200; New England Patriots starter 175; PTC cards, 2021 market value 222; 2000 NFL draft pick 173–74; 2000 Pacific rookie card 4; 2000 Shrine Bowl 172–73; 2002 Super Bowl 198
Brastad, Adam (son-in-law) 209
Brastad, Ryder (grandson) 104
Bread, Remar 45
Brees, Drew 191
Broder, Ed 23
Brodeur, Martin 157, **200**, 205, 206
Brown & Bigelow 76
Brown and Williams Tobacco Company 33
Bryant, Kobe 139
Burdick, Jefferson 13
Burrows, Matt 4, 223–24
Bush, Homer 146

Caffey, Mike, meeting with author 120–22
California Angels, headshots by author 114
California Sports Investments 177
Canada: marketing 141–42, 168–69, 188; Pacific Atomic card set 206; PTC hockey cards, prominence in 170; red parallel cards 205; sales 51; *see also* McDonald's of Canada
Canadian Football Hall of Fame 204
Canadian Football League license 204
The Candy Wholesaler, advertisement in 69
canneries: at Dutch Harbor 18, 19, 25, 32; Kodiak 35; Pan Alaska 41; Wakefield Cannery, Captains Bay 29, 30; Whitney-Fidalgo, work at 27
card packs *see* baseball cards
Carey, Max 11
Chappelear, Bruce (PTC VP national sales manager) 114–15, 148, 164
Circle K Convenience stores, sponsor 45
C.J. McConnell (uncle) *see* Uncle C.J.
Classic Games company 116
Clemens, Roger 135, 136
Clouston, Robert 137
Coates, Ben, rookie card 108
Coca-Cola, sponsor of 1976 Phoenix Giants set 49
Comrie, Mike: NHL player doll 193; redemption card 194
Cook, Bill, predicting author's future 34
Cornish College of the Arts 117
Cottier, Chuck 7
crab boat playing cards: selling in Dutch Harbor (1978) 58

Index

crab fishing seasons: crab boat fleet catch 19; crab fishing, dangers of 215; end of fishing career 66; 1969 with Uncle C.J. 17–19; 1971 on *Honey-B* 26, 29, 30; 1972 and 1973 in Bering Sea 30–32; 1973 on *Belair* 33–35; 1973 on *Scotty* 32–33; 1974 king crabs, on *Bering Sea* 42; 1974 tanner crabs, on *Shellfish* with father 40, 41; 1975 king crabs, on *Judi B* 47–48; 1976 on *Bering Sea* 50–51; 1976 king crab season on *Scorpio* 49–50; 1977 king crabs, on *North Pacific* 57; 1979 king crabs, on *North Sea* 61–64, **63**; playing card set, crab fleet boat pictures on 50

crab fleet strike, 1976 season 50

crab pots 17–18, 33, 56, 58, **59**, 60, 220

Cramer, Angela Kathleen (daughter) 4, 68, 156, 209, **210**

Cramer, Anji (sister) 13, 25–26, 30

Cramer, Arnold (father) 7, 10–15, 19, 24, 215; death 69; Reynolds Aluminum, millwright (1965) 8; and Uncle C.J., forming partnership 25; Wakefield Cannery, chief engineer 30; and wife Dorothy, in Dutch Harbor **28**

Cramer, Cheryl (wife): 38–40, 45, 47, 49, 51, 56–58, 61, 76, 104, 112–13, 118, 120, 126, 128, 134, 153, 156, 158, 163, 208–9, 211–21, 224; in Billings (MT) 41; coming to Dutch Harbor 31–32; Europe trip 195–96; falling in love with author 31; golden wedding anniversary 36; marriage 35–37, **36**; second pregnancy 65; in Stelmaszek picture 52; Unalaska winter (1975) 48; Vern's Store employment 32, 33, 41–42

Cramer, Cory Michael (son) 4, 76, 209, **210**

Cramer, Dorothy (mother) 15, **28**, 32–33, 69, 195–96

Cramer, Kathi (sister) 13, 25, 33, 68

Cramer, Kristine (daughter-in-law) 4

Cramer, Marty (brother) 7, 25, 27, 30, 88, 105, 110, 115, 135, 215, 219; company vice president 102; leaving PTC 136–37

Cramer, Michael (Mike): antique militaria collection 213; antique military uniform collection 162–63; Bill Cook, predicting future 34; blogs 222; Bob Gibson, dinner with 119–20; Bob Uecker, dinner 119–20, **120**; bobbing head doll 194–95; California Angels, headshots 114; cancer 4, 219–24; card sales, first 14; card sales on eBay 223; caribou hunt 30–31; Cheryl Robinson, falling in love with 31; Cramer Sports Promotion; *Detroit News*, posing for photo 21; dreams come true 225, 227; "elephants off," post-PTC sale 211–12; Europe trip with Cheryl 212–13; fishing injury, and new life 51; football card collection 8; football cards, interest in 8; football cards wrapping factory **169**; golden wedding anniversary 36; golf at MLB Players Choice Awards (Miami, 1996) 135–36; golf, hole in one 216; headshots, MLB players 113–14; home chores 13–14; Joe Torre, dinner 119–20; with king crab **60**; Little League, glass shattering pitch 11–12; Little League, playing in **8**; marriage 35–37, **36**; and Matt Burrows meeting 223–24; meeting Cheryl's father 39; Mexico City sales trip (1996) 134–35; Mike Caffey meeting 120–21; MLB players, headshots 113–14; NFL game photos 3, 103–5; NFL Properties, annual licensing meeting (1994) 115–16; NHL photo shoots 158–60; 1960 Fleer All-Time Greats, first pack purchase of 5–6; 1995 NFL Season, Seahawks photos 127; 1998 sales trips 162; and Nolan Ryan **96**; Pacific Trading Cards, Inc. (PTC); painting historical miniatures 214; personal PTC card collection 213; playing in Little League **8**, 11–12; podcasts 224; PTC sole owner 167; PTC trading card factory, touring 186–88; retirement fun 212; sale of non-PTC cards at Sotheby's 213, 214; Seahawks 1995 season end game, attendance and reflection 127–34; Seattle Mariners, fan of 56, 85, 126; and Seattle Seahawks 127–34, 216; success, basis for 227–29; Sy Berger, meeting 135; Topps and Bowman cards purchase 13; Topps vending card purchase 51–53, 55; 2000 Baseball All-Star Game FanFest, baseball workout 184–86; 2000 Hawaii Trading Card Conference, attendance 175; 2000 Shrine Bowl, Tom Brady photoshoots 172–73; 2001 family trip to Europe and 9/11 195–97; 2002 dinner at Palm restaurant, Washington, D.C. 201; 2017 World Model Expo Show, gold medal 217–18; and Uncle C.J. 15, 17–19, **17**, **18**, 25–28, 30; "Vikings: Two Generations," gold medal winner 217–18, **217**; Yogi Berra, dinner 119–20; *see also* Cramer, Cheryl (wife)

Cramer, Michael Ross (son) 4, 78, 209, **210**, 213, 215–16, 221–22; New York Yankees, batboy 144, **145**, 146

Cramer, Michelle (sister-in-law) 88

Cramer, Rachael Elizabeth (daughter) 4, 57, **59**, 61, 104, 209, **210**

Cramer, Shiloh (granddaughter) 4

"Cramer Museum" 214

Cramer Sports Promotion 169–70; catalog 57; first card set 46; mail-order card business 14, 42–43, 57; mail-order catalog 42–43, 49; renaming to PTC 57–58; trading card promotions 169–70

Cramer's Choice Award cards 108, 121–22, **121**; creation of insert cards 121; Jumbo **121**, 122, 157–58, 166; 1996 MLB Players 135–36;

Index

1998 Baseball insert 154–55; 1999 Pacific Football set 166; 10-card insert set 138; top player picks (1998) 155; 2001 football insert set 192; 2002 football set 198; 2004–05 NHL insert cards 206; Wayne Gretzky inserts 142; *see also* Jumbo Cramer's Choice Award

Crown Royale Football cards, Tom Brady signature 174

Crystalline Collection (1994) 117

Dallas Cowboy cards 8
Davenport, Jimmy 9
Dayne, Ron 182
Deadliest Catch (TV series), *Patricia Lee* in 3, 215
Dean, Dizzy 5
Detroit baseball card show 21–24
DF-1 card wrapping machine: brass medal folding box *75*, 112; gravity card feeder (1992) *74*; scrapping 111–12; wax wrapping 71–76, *72*, *93*, 112
DiMaggio, Joe, guest at sports card show 78–80, *81*
Donruss Trading Card company 92, 137–38
Draft Picks Basketball cards 139
Dutch Harbor (AK) 16; back after graduation 29; Cheryl moving to 31–32; end of fishing (1979) 65–66; family migration to, reason 33; marriage 35–37, *36*; 1969 first crab fishing trip to 15–19; 1971 family move to 25–28; 1973 return to 31; 1974 return to 41–42; 1979 return to 65; parents in *28*; return to Phoenix (1969) 19–20; settling in 28; *see also* Phoenix (AZ)
Dynagon brand 139

earthquake, San Francisco (1989) 90
Eight Men Out (movie), card set 83

Favre, Brett, rookie card 101–2
Ferguson, Tommy 43–44
Fleer cards 3, 7, 201
Fleury, Marc-Andre, rookie card 205
"flow wrapper" 110
football cards 118; competition 102; Dallas Cowboy cards 8; NFL card brands 200; NFL Pro Bowl die-cut insert set 202; 1991 Pacific Crown Royale Football 166; 1991 "Pacific Picks the Pros," insert 101, *101*; 1991 Pacific Plus NFL Football card brand, launch 100–101; 1992 Pacific NFL Football Plus 111; 1992 Pacific Pro Plus Football, Prism card insert 108; 1993 Pacific Prism brand name launch 112; 1993 Pacific Prism NFL Football 112, 118; 1994 Crystalline Collection 117; 1994 Pacific Crown Collection, launch 113; 1994 Pacific Invincible, creation 117; 1996 NFL football card line 139; 1996 Pacific Crown Royale 123–24; 1996 Pacific Football, Vanove photos by author 132; 1996 Pacific Gold Crown Die-Cuts cards 122; 1996 Shannon Sharpe Pacific Crown Royale *123*; 1997 NFL Football brand 142; 1997 Pacific Philadelphia, Adam Vinatieri rookie card *143*; 1997 Pacific Philadelphia, release 142; 1997 Pacific Prism Invincible 143; 1998 NFL Football brands 157; 1998 Steve Largent set 89; 1998–99 Pacific Revolution Football brand 157; 1999 NFL Football card products 166; 1999 NFL Rookie of the Year Award 166; 1999 Pacific Football Cramer's Choice Awards set 166; 1999 Pacific Football, release 164–66; 1999 Pacific Revolution Icons *162*; Pacific Crown Collection 113, 122; Pacific Crown Royale Football 166; Pacific Football set 174–75; Pacific Gridiron Football 125; Pacific NFL Football card kit 155; Pacific Prism brand, announcement 112; Pacific Prism NFL Football cards, translation to hockey 141; Pacific Revolution brand 157; Pacific Revolution Football brand, translation to hockey 141; Tom Brady's 2000 Pacific rookie cards, auction price 4; Topps and Bowman 13; Topps cards, purchase 40, 51, 55; Topps 1964 cards, PTC sale 8; 2000 NFL Pacific Football Tom Brady rookie 174, 175, *176*; 2000 Pacific Paramount Tom Brady rookie card *223*; 2001 Cramer's Choice Awards insert set 192; 2001 Pacific Crown Royale Football 197; 2001 Pacific Football rookie card, Pork Chop Womack 191–92; 2001 Pacific Prism Atomic *192*; 2002 Cramer's Choice Awards 198; 2002 NFL Exclusive card brand 200; 2002 Pacific Private Stock Reserve 200; 2002 Pacific Cramer's Choice Tom Brady *199*; 2002 Pacific Heads Up NFL Football 198–99; 2002 Pacific NFL Football 198; 2002 Pacific Private Stock Reserve 200, *202*, 203; 2002 Private Stock Titanium 200, 203; 2003 end of production 203; 2003 Pacific NFL Football cards die-cut insert set 202; 2003 Pacific Private Stock Football 202; *see also* Cramer's Choice Award cards

Football Hall of Famers, featured on PTC cards: 1991 Pacific Football set 101; 1994 Crown collection Football 117; 1994 Pacific Triple Folder cards 117–18; 1997 Pacific Philadelphia *143*; 1998 NFL Football card brand 157; 1998 Pacific NFL Football 157; 1998 Pacific Revolution 157; 1999 Pacific Football 166; Pacific Pro Plus Football 108; players 68, 89, 101, 108, 122, 143, 157, 166, 175, 192; 2000 Pacific NFL Football card set 175;

Fowler, Jim 228
Frisch, Frankie ("*The Old Flash*") 11

Index

Galloway, Joey 132
Garfield: The Movie, card set 205, 207
Ghirardelli Chocolate Company 86
Gibson, Bob, dinner with author 119–20
Gold Crown Die-Cut set 122–23, 166
Goldberg, Brian 85, 86, 89
Goldfaden, Goodie 564
Goldin, Ken: "Home Run History" card set idea 155; owner of Classic Games 116
Grand, Paul 151
Gray Flannel, game-used baseball jerseys 177
Green Bay team 8
Gretzky, Wayne 142
Griffey, Ken, Jr. 108, 145, 190; candy bars 85–89; in Cramer's Choice 10-card insert set 138; on 1999 Pacific Prism baseball card **168**; on 2001 Pacific Baseball set 190
Grove, Wayne 57, 90–91
Gunsmoke card set 94
Gwynn, Tony 190; candy bar 93; PTC endorsement 154; 2000 Pacific Aurora card **186**; on 2001 Pacific Baseball set 190

Hawaii Trading Card Conference (2000), author attendance 175
Herbel, Ron 10
Hershey Candy Co., acquisition of DF-1 wrappers from 92
Hicks, Rob (PTC VP Head of Graphics Dept.) 106–7, 108, 121–22, 127, 178
hobby boxes 193, 194, 199
hockey cards: in Canada, prominence 170; Gold Crown Die Cuts 206; marketing 141; 1994 Pacific Invincible, creation 117; 1997–98 Pacific Crown Collection Hockey 142; 1997–98 Pacific Paramount Hockey set 142; 1998–99 Pacific Revolution Hockey set 157; 1999 Pacific Revolution Hockey **170**; 1999 Pacific Revolution Icons **162**; Pacific Hockey, inclusion of Lemieux card #66 193; prominence in Canada 170; Topps cards, purchase 51, 55; 2000 Pacific NHL Hockey cards, release 188; 2000–01 Pacific Prism hockey set and inserts, at McDonald's 170–71; 2001 NHL FanFest event, PTC-sponsored 193; 2001 Pacific Heads Up hockey cards 193–95; 2002 Limited Edition boxed red parallel sets 200; 2002 Pacific Atomic brand 199; 2002 Pacific Cramer's Choice Martin Brodeur card **200, 201**; 2002 Pacific Private Stock Game-Used Jersey Patch **201**; 2002 success of 199; 2002–03 NHL Pacific Calder brand 200; 2002–03 NHL Pacific Quest for the Cup brand 200; 2002–03 NHL Pacific Vanguard brand 200; 2003 Pacific Prism reissue 205; 2003–04 NHL Pacific Calder Collection 206; 2003–04 Pacific Exhibit brand 205; 2003–04 Pacific Heads Up hockey brand, with player mini sweater 205; 2003–04 Pacific Luxury Suite 205; 2003–04 Pacific NHL Hockey 204–5; 2004–05 Atomic brands 206; 2004–05 Pacific NHL Hockey, last sports trading card set 206; *see also* Cramer's Choice Award cards
Hockey Hall of Famers, featured on PTC cards: 1997–98 Pacific Crown Collection Hockey 142; 1997–98 Pacific Paramount Hockey 142; 1998 Pacific NHL Hockey cards 157; 1998–99 Pacific Revolution Hockey 157; players 142, 159, 193, 206
"Home Run History" card set, sale on QVC 155–57
"Home Run History: The Mark McGwire and Sammy Sosa Home Run Race of 1998," boxed set 155–57
Honey-B (crab boat) 26; 1971 crab fishing 29; 1972 crab fishing, Bering Sea 30–31; 1973 king crab fishing, Bering Sea 32; partnership, dissolution 30; Seattle to Dutch Harbor on (1971) 26–28
Hossa, Marian 142
Howard, Frank 22

I Love Lucy card sets 94–95
Irabu, Hideki 146

Jack's Wholesale, closeout cases at 55
Japanese Baseball Hall of Famers, features on PTC cards 154, 190
Jeter, Derek 144
John Hancock All-Star FanFest, 1999 PTC sponsor 167
Johnson, Shannon 108–9, 180, 183, 189, 209–10
Johnson, Walter, card 6
Judi B (crab boat), rigging crab pots (1975) 47–48
Jumbo Cramer's Choice Award: card holder **121**, 122; Kurt Warner 166; parallels 157–58; *see also* Cramer's Choice Awards cards

Ken Griffey Jr. Bar blue wrapper (1989) **87**
Ken Griffey Jr. candy bars 85–89
Kennedy, Cortez 129
Keyport 215–16
king crab fishing *see* crab fishing seasons
Kipling, Mike 99–100, 150–53, 228
Kodiak (AK) 27
Kodiak Island crab grounds, crab fishing (1973) 33–35; *see also* crab fishing seasons
Koufax, Sandy, cards 52
Kramer, Jerry 8
Kung Fu cards 40

Largent, Steve 68, 89, 104–5, **105**
Lea, Oliver 168–70
Leaf *Munsters* cards 40

Index

Leave It to Beaver cards 72, 81, 94
Lemieux, Mario 201, 205, 206; NHL player doll 193; 2001–02 Pacific Hockey #66 card 193–94
Leo's corner store 5, 6
Libby, Dr. Edward 220
Lindsay, George "Goober" 102
Litho-Cel brand 139
Little League *see* Cramer, Michael (Mike)
Lynch Package Machinery 75

M101-2 Sporting News Supplements 20
Major League Baseball (MLB): All-Star Game (1999) 167; Card Collectors Kit for Scholastic (1998) 155; game, first attendance 9, 21–22; player jerseys, addition to PTC line 175–76; player prototype cards, permission to print 100; 2000 All-Star Game 184; 2001 license, failure to renew 189–90
Major League Baseball Players Association (MLBPA): card license award 147–48; license application 80–81; license, failure to renew 189–90; Spanish-language baseball card license 109; World Baseball Organization in Barcelona, PTC invitation to 112–13
Major League Baseball Players Choice Awards, Miami 135–36
Major League Baseball Properties: law suit 150–53; license (1988) 82, 83; team logo license 149; team logos, card license 149
Major League Baseball Properties v. Pacific Trading Cards, Inc. 150–53
Major League Indoor Soccer cards, license 81
"Man on the Moon" cards (1968), purchase from Topps 40
Manning, Peyton 157
Mantle, Mickey, 1980 Baseball Legends set 52, **69**
Martinez, Edgar, card 190
Maryvale High School 15, 29
Mawae, Kevin 130
Mays, Willie 9
McConnell, Jim 23
McCormick & Company, PTC Nolan Ryan campaign 97
McCovey, Willie 9, 10
McDonald's of Canada: card promotion, award 167–69; Pacific Prism 205; PTC publicity campaign 3; 2000–05 NHL hockey card promotions 167–71, 191, 204, 206; 2001–02 NHL card promotion award 191; *see also* Canada
McGwire, Mark 114
Mendez, Felix 91–92, 186–87
Messier, Mark 159, 193
Mirer, Rick 129
MLB *see* Major League Baseball (MLB)

MLBPA *see* Major League Baseball Players Association (MLBPA)
Modano, Mike 141–42, 205
Mokihana (processing ship) 35, 36–37, 38, 213
Montana, Joe, 1991 Pacific Picks the Pros card **101**
Morris, Jeff (marketing director) 189, 193, 201, 205
Moss, Randy 157, **192**
Motorola Baseball Old Timers set (1976) 49
My Three Sons card set 94–95

Nagy, Frank 21, 23
Napoleonic Historical Society conference (2006) 214
National Sports Card Convention (2002), promo cards 200
National Sports Collectors Convention (1991), autographs at 102
New Wave, PS-206 card set 190
NFL (National Football League): bobbing head doll, first hobby box addition 199; game photographers, PTC employment 102–3; game-wear jerseys, acquisition 177; player jerseys, addition to PTC line 175–76; Rookie Card of the Year Award to PTC (1999) **165**, 166
NFL Players Association: failure to renew PTC 2003 license 202–4; 1991 license for 99; 2000 NFL draft prospects photo session 173
NFL Properties: annual licensing meeting (1994) 115–16; license grant 100; license law suit, effect on reputation 100; license law suit settlement 99–100
NHL Players Association, license award 139–40
NHL Properties, license award 140
NHL: All-Star Game (2001) 193; Atomic Authentic Game-Used Gear (2004–05) 206; bobbing head doll introduction 193; brand, memorabilia acquisition 176–77; card sales 157; draft (2000), first trading card show 193; hockey player mini sweaters 205; hockey sweaters, addition to PTC line 175–76; player cards, design and production 140–41; 2001–02 McDonald's of Canada NHL card promotion award 191; 2003–04 season hockey cards 204
Ninneman, Ann (Ann Hicks) 67, 86, 106
Nolan Ryan Texas Express baseball cards 95–96
Nomo, Hideo 154, 190
North Pacific (crab boat) 57
North Sea (crab boat) 60–61, **62**, 63, **63**

Oakland A's, headshots by author 114
Oakland Oaks team set 45
Omega Baseball cards 155

O'Neal, Don 219
O'Neill, Paul 144
Oroweat Bread 89
Ott, Mel 12
OXXO retail chain, bi-lingual cards on sale 134
Oyi, Huhtamaki 137

Pacific Aurora Baseball card set 150, 154
Pacific Baseball Legends: color set production 81; first mass retail wax box (1984) 77; wax pack (1985) **73**
Pacific Candy Company subsidiary 86
Pacific Coast League cards 45
Pacific Coast League teams, Trading Card Night at 51–52
Pacific Crown Collection: launch 113; 1995 baseball card sales 125; 1996 Cramer's Choice 10-card insert set 138; translation to hockey 141; *see also* baseball cards; basketball cards; football cards; hockey cards
Pacific Crown Royale: brand launch 123–24; die-cut 154; 1999 Football player cards 166; Tom Brady signature 174; transition to hockey 141; 2001 Football player cards 197; *see also* football cards; parallel cards
"Pacific Press Plate" 188–89
Pacific Prism cards 96–97, 108; Hank Aaron 184; new foil introduction 178–81; *see also* baseball cards; football cards; hockey cards
Pacific Trading Cards, Inc. (PTC): author's sales trip to Mexico City (1996) 134–35; baseball cards for MLB kid's video game 184; and Bastion Capital Corp., partners in Donruss purchase 137–38; and Berkley Publishing Co. 82–83; Bimbo Bakeries contract 134–35; Canadian sales team 141; card designs 117–18; card foils, introduction of new 178–81; classic TV card sets, production 94–95; collectible cards, major manufacturer of 46; from collector to 3–4, 6; condition grade #10 award 76; Cramer Sports Promotions renaming to 57–58; cut and collate machine 76–77; desktop graphics production, introduction 106–7; dinner at Rigazzi's, St. Louis 118–20; Donruss, attempt to buy 137–38; Donruss card factory equipment, purchase 138; European sales team 141; evolution to manufacturer 76; factory **107**; "flow wrapper," introduction 110–11; game-used baseball jerseys, acquisition 177; growth problems 110; at Hawaii Trading Card Conference 147; hockey products, sales performance 188; ideas, incorporation by Fleer 201; in-house graphics department 116–17; incorporation 3, 14; Ken Griffey candy bars 85–89; Kurt Warner game-used jersey and pants cards 177–78; laser- and die-cut cards, success 162; last product cards 207; licenses, acquisition of new 98; major manufacturer 167; manufacturing system 82; memorabilia (relic) Cards, addition 175; MLB Properties law suit 150–53; at National Sports Collectors Convention (1995) 118–21; new foil introduction 178–81; new headquarters 83–84, 91; newspaper promotions 68; NHL Players Association, license award 139–40; 9/11 effects 197; and Oroweat Bread (1989) 89; "Pacific Press Plate" 188–89; Pinnacle bankruptcy effect on 160–61, 181; plant expansion 149; profitable 163–64, 1998; range of player cards 108; retail store distribution 102; sale to Playoff 207–10; sales growth 77–78; and Seattle Seahawks 127; Seattle Seahawks Oroweat bread trading cards promotion 127; state-of-the-art trading card factory 200; store management 67–68; store opening (1980) 66, **67**; Topps card cases, purchase 40, 51, 55; trading card pioneer 223–24; trading card production process 186–87; trading card promotions 169–70; trading card sets, use by Panini 224–25; 2000 card sales 178; 2003 upcoming card series preparation 202; 2004 good bye to **210**; and Walmart sales 115; wax paper supply; *see also* Cramer, Michael (Mike); Cramer Sports Promotion; trading cards; *and specific trading cards*
Pacific Triple Folder cards (1994) 117–18
pack-off belts, computerized 92
Paine, Shep, militaria collector and miniature figure painter 214
Panini: Prizm, Prism trading cards renamed to 112, **168**, 224; purchase of PTC football brands 204; trading cards, use of PTC cards 224–25
parallel cards 101; blue foil 204; *I Love Lucy*, first 96; Jumbo Cramer's Choice Award cards 157–58; Limited Edition boxed red 200; new foil colors 162, 178–81; 1996 Pacific Power Basketball release 139; 1997 Pacific Crown Royale, purple foil set 143; Nolan Ryan insert 97; Pacific Aurora Baseball 154; Pacific Philadelphia 142; red foil 190, 204, 205; 2001 Cramer's Choice Award cards 190; 2001 PS-206 Pacific Private Stock 190; 2003–04 Pacific NHL Hockey 204
Patricia Lee (crab boat), in TV series 215
Pennington, Chad 173, 182
Peterson, Cap 9
Peterson, Todd 130
Phoenix (AZ): falling in love with Cheryl 31–32; finishing high school 29; 1965 move

Index

to 8–9, 10; 1969 first trip to Dutch Harbor 15–19; 1973 return to, as newlyweds 38–39; 1973 trip back to 31; 1974 card purchases 39–40; 1974 condominium purchase 42; 1974 return to 42; 1974 trip back to, with Cheryl 42; 1975 back to 48–49; 1975 trip to Seattle 47; 1976 return to 51; West Osborn Road, life at 10; *see also* Cramer Cheryl (wife); Dutch Harbor (AK)
Phoenix Giants AAA baseball team, "Trading Card Night" proposal 45
Phoenix Municipal Stadium 8, 9, 14, 45
Phoenix Suns, basketball card set for 47
Piersall, Jimmy, card 7
Pink Apartments 32, 37, 41
Pinnacle: bankruptcy 149, 160–61; Donruss acquisition 137–38
Piper, Roddy ("Rowdy") 206
Plank, Ed 23
Play Ball cards 14
Playoff, acquisition of PTC 207–8
pocket plastic sheet business 52
"Pork Chop Womack" card 191–92
Post Cereal cards 7
Poulsen, Edward (nephew), Patricia Lee, in TV series 215
Poulsen, Kris (brother-in-law) 30, 33–35, 50, 58; *Arctic Sea*, construction 56; *Bering Sea* owner 42; *North Sea*, construction 60–66
Presley, Elvis, meeting 22
Pro Set Press LTD 100
PS-206 card sets 167, 190
PS-206 Pacific Private Stock (2001), last card set 190

Ramirez, Manny, bat cork 182–84
Randall, Rae 67, 82, 103
Red Dog Saloon, visit 27
redemption cards 194
Reese, Pee Wee 5
Rhodes, Dusty 206
Rhome, Jerry 68
Rice, Jerry, card ***202***
Ripken, Cal, Jr. 108, 155
Robinson, Cheryl *see* Cramer, Cheryl (wife)
Robinson, Eugene 129
Robinson, Vern 35; *see also* Vern's Aleutian Mercantile Store
Rollem Company 76
Rookies, PS-206 card set 190
Roth, Phil (PTC VP and CFO) 68, 99, 138, 147–48, 164, 181, 197, 201, 204, 207, 209–10, 212, 219, 228
Roy, Patrick 194, 205
Ruth, Babe, card 5, ***6***
Ryan, Nolan 94–97, ***94***, ***96***, 108, 139

St. Louis, Martin 157, 206
Sakic, Joe 206
San Francisco Giants, headshots by author 114

San Manuel (AZ), move to (1969) 5, 8–9, 10
Santo, Ron 9
Sasaki, Kazuhiro, rookie card 190
Saskin, Ted 140, 168, 207
Saved by the Bell card set 116, 207
Scholastic program 155
Scorpio (crab boat) 50
Scotty (crab boat) 215; 1973 crab fishing 32, 33; sinking of 34
"Sea" boats ***62***
Seattle (WA): on *Judi B* with Cheryl back to 48–49; on *Judi B*, move to Dutch Harbor 48; on *Judi B*, rigging crab pots (1975) 47–48; move to Edmonds 56; settling in (1980) 66; trip to Dutch Harbor, on *Honey-B* 26–28
Seattle Mariners 56, 85, 126
Seattle Pilots (baseball team) 20
Seattle Post Intelligencer, Pacific Cards promotion 68
Seattle Seahawks and PTC, relationship: 1995 NFL season photos by author 127; 1995 season end game, author's attendance 127–34; Steve Largent football card set, license 89
Seattle Times, Pacific Cards promotion 68
Seaver, Tom ***94***
Senators (baseball team) 6
Senior League 92, 98
"The Shannon Books" 109, 180, 208, 224
Shaw, Bob 10
Shellfish (crab boat) 41
Sick's Stadium, visit 20
Sisler, George 11
Smalling, Jack 10
Smith, Emmitt 103, 104, ***105***
Smith, Hal "Otis" 102
soccer cards 81, 109
Sojo, Luis 144–45
Soriano, Alfonzo, rookie card 190
Spence, Will 4, 223
"Sporting News Supplement," baseball photos 20–21
sports collectors club Arizona, starting 46
Staal, Eric, rookie card 205
Stars, PS-206 card set 190
Steinbach, Terry 135, ***136***
Stelmaszek, Rick, taking photo of 52
Styles, A.J., Pacific TNA rookie card 206
Super Bowl 198, 201–2

Temkin, Victor, 98–99, 109, 118, 135, 137, 139, 201, 228
Theresa Lee (processing ship), trip to Bellingham on 19
Thomas, B.J. 189
Thornton, Joe, cards 200, 206
Thorpe, Lloyd 21
TNA Wrestling cards 205–6
Tomlinson, LaDainian 191, 192

Tony Gwynn Base Hit Candy Bar 93
Topps: Baseball Cloth Stickers (1977), purchase and sale of 54; baseball vending cases *53*; closeout cases, Dutch Harbor (1979) 65–66
Topps baseball cards 3, 7; cases, purchase of 40, 51, 55; minis (1975), purchase 47, 49; wax cases purchase 40; wax pack, first purchase (1967) 12; *see also* Cramer, Michael (Mike)
Topps cards: bulk closeout cases, purchase of 59; cases, PTC purchases 40, 51, 55; 1964 football cards 8; PTC ideas incorporation 201; refractor card 108; *see also* Cramer, Michael (Mike)
Topps-Pacific closeout sale 54–55
Torre, Frank: 91, 100, 118, 144; visit to PTC 98
Torre, Joe 119–20, 144
The Trader Speakes (hobby publication), placing ads in 14, 21, 65
"Trading Card Night": at Pacific Coast League teams 57; production of sets 51–52; proposal 45; success of 51
trading cards: collection 13; from collector to manufacturer 6–8; declining market 181–82; greatest purchase in history 55; Pacific sets, use by Panini 224–25; PTC pioneer of 223–24; PTC production process 186–87; PTC promotions 169–70; standard size 74; *see also* Cramer, Michael (Mike); Cramer Sports Promotion; *and specific cards*
Trueman, Jim 51
Tuten, Rick 130–31, 132

Uecker, Bob 4, dinner with author 119–20, *120*
Unalaska (AK): Cheryl's 1975 winter in 48; settling in 29, 32, 48; wedding 36
Uncle C.J. (mother's brother): and author 16–19, *17*, 26–28, 30; and father, forming partnership 25; visit to Phoenix (1968) 15
Upper Deck cards, PTC ideas incorporation 201
Upshaw, Gene 203, 204

Vanover, Tamarick, 1996 cards 132
Vern's Aleutian Mercantile Store 32, 33, 41–42
Viceroy (processing ship) 35
Vick, Michael 191
"Vikings: Two Generations," gold medal winner 217–18, *217*
Villanueva, Danny 137
Vinatieri, Adam, rookie card 143, *143*

Wade Boggs .352 Candy Bar 93
Wagner, Honus 23, 213
Wakefield Cannery 29, 30, 32
Waldenstrom's macroglobulinemia (WM) 220–21
Wallin, Jack 103, 113, 202
Warner, Kurt: card 164–66, *165*, 192; PTC game-used jersey and pants cards 177–78; 2002 Super Bowl 198
Warren, Chris 129
Warrick, Peter 182
Washington Senators 7
Washington State Sport Collectors Association, sports card show Seattle (1986) 78–80
Whitney-Fidalgo cannery, work at 27
The Wild Wild West card set 94–95
Wilke, Bob, 115
Williams, Bernie 144
Williams, Pete 67
Williams, Tom 55
Wills, Maury, card 7
Wings cigarette trading cards 33
World Model Expo Show (2017), gold medal 217–18
wrestling cards (TNA) 205–6
Wright, Gary 126–27

Yaquinto, Tom 77
Yaquinto Printing company 77–78
Yastrzemski, Carl, card 7, 167
Young, Kit 147, 175

Zetterberg, Henrik 205
Zorn, Jim 68

www.ingramcontent.com/pod-product-compliance
Ingram Content Group UK Ltd.
Pitfield, Milton Keynes, MK11 3LW, UK
UKHW041938140426
5217IPUK00014B/547